Globe

An International Travel Guide

David J. Forsythe, MD

Island Publishing
Jensen Beach, Florida

Globetrotting Pets
An International Travel Guide

By David J. Forsythe, MD

Published by:
Island Publishing
Jensen Beach, FL 34957
www.GlobetrottingPets.com

All rights reserved. No part of this book may be reproduced or transmitted in any form or by any means, electronic or mechanical, including photocopying, recording or by any information storage and retrieval system, without written permission from the author or publisher.

Cover design: Robert Mason
Website design: Jeff Forsythe

Copyright 2003
Printed in the United States of America

Publisher's Cataloging-in-Publication
(Provided by Quality Books, Inc.)

Forsythe, David J.
   Globetrotting pets : an international travel guide / David J. Forsythe. -- 1st ed.
   p. cm.
   LCCN 2002117347
   ISBN 0-9724156-0-2

   1. Pets and travel. I. Title.

SF415.45.F67 2003   636.088'7
                                    QBI03-200037

Contents

Preface
Acknowledgements

1	Pet Considerations	7
2	Owner Considerations	11
3	Making Plans	13
4	Planes, Trains, Automobiles, and Ships	19
5	Pet Supplies	29
6	Pet Identification	33
7	Returning Home	41
8	Help from the Internet	45
9	Traveling with Exotic Pets	49
10	Countries of the World	53

Appendix
   International Telephone Codes   403
   Airlines of the World   406
   Glossary   414
   Quick Order Form   415

Preface

I love to travel. My wife knows that during each vacation I often begin to plan and anticipate the next one. For us there has always been a problem associated with travel...what to do with the family pet. We have always had a dog and thus have had to make arrangements for the care of our pet during our absence, often for three weeks or more. Then, while we were away, we would wonder how our dog was doing. We frequently wished our dog were with us, particularly when our trips lasted two weeks or more. The solution finally occurred to me: take Izzy along!

I would admit that taking Izzy, our six-pound Maltese, presents a different scenario than taking our previous pet, a 140-pound Rottweiler. With such a small dog, we were optimistic that we would be able to travel and take Izzy along. When we started looking for destinations, we could not find the specific regulations for our proposed destinations. We also found that there was no single source for finding information on whether or not pets were allowed into a certain country. Realizing other travelers with pets might have similar questions about traveling internationally and thus appreciate a resource to help them explore the possibilities, I came up with the idea for this book.

I hope that you will consider traveling internationally with your pet and that this book will provide useful information as you pursue a new travel adventure. The information provided in this book was verified as much as possible before publication. I have included as many countries of the world as I could. Only two countries did not reply after repeated attempts to obtain information about importing pets. Most tourist offices flooded my mailbox with beautiful brochures and applications for visas. I strongly recommend contacting the tourist offices, airlines, hotels, and other sources listed in this book before leaving home. Your mailbox may suddenly have an influx of brochures.

The main thing to remember about traveling with your pet is to plan as much as you can while at home to have as much fun as you can while away. Whether you travel for business, education, pleasure, or a combination, have fun and enjoy.

Acknowledgements

The completion of a book never occurs without help and support. My wife was the most supportive person in this process. She often "encouraged" me when the process slowed down or too much time elapsed without writing a word. My friends, Janet Lein and Leigh Robinson, edited and offered grammatical and practical advice. The book would have been even more amateurish without their expert assistance.

Our Michigan veterinarian of almost 20 years, Dr. Dale Borders, assisted in some of the health related aspects of the book as well as in providing the veterinary forms. Our Florida veterinarian, Dr. Rodney Graves, also took the time to talk about my book and provided insights into pet identification as well as telling stories about travels with their Yorkie. Both acknowledged a need for this book because in their experience other pet owners had difficulty finding this information.

Many individuals in the various tourist offices and embassies deserve special mention. They submitted information, talked to me, E-mailed me, and provided pre-publishing corrections and advice, which was necessary to publish this book. Many encouraged me; acknowledging the need for this book to assist travelers. Many of these individuals have traveled with their pets to diplomatic and corporate positions in various countries. They are well aware of the many and often complicated procedures and practices that are necessary to travel with pets. Sharing this vital information is appreciated.

Special thanks go to my parents for instilling in me a strong desire to travel and learn from other places, cultures, and experiences. The many trips during summer vacations were a highlight of my childhood. We also took the family pet wherever we went. Now there is no excuse not to travel even more since we know how Izzy can go with us.

1
Pet Considerations

There are several important considerations when traveling with your pet. Not every pet is suitable for international travel. Long flights, long delays in airports and changes in climate, not to mention the loss of familiar surroundings are enough to make us humans question our sanity at times. Not every pet is adaptable to new surroundings and new people associated with travel. Not every pet is anxious to leave home and travel in an automobile, much less on airplanes, buses, ships, or trains. Deciding if your pet and your travel plans are compatible will depend on your pet and its particular characteristics and temperament. Not all pets are up to touring, sightseeing, eating out, staying in strange hotels, and walking for hours each day. In many countries, as in the United States, pets are not allowed in certain public places. There are, however, countries where dogs are allowed in stores, restaurants, and many other places. While dining in Turkey, we saw a small dog sitting on a chair next to its owner. We were flabbergasted. Restaurants in the U.S. would never allow such a thing.

Here are some considerations regarding your pet:
- Is your pet physically fit?
- Is your pet accustomed to being with you much of the time?
- Has your pet traveled much away from home and is it comfortable in unfamiliar surroundings?
- Is your pet well mannered? Is it socialized and capable of adjusting to change?
- Is the destination climate hotter or colder than your pet is accustomed to?
- Is your pet accustomed to being kenneled?
- Are there adequate sources of food and water?

If your pet has serious medical problems or is feeble, keep your pet at home. Perhaps a pet sitter would be advisable. Be sure to have your veterinarian determine if your pet is suitable for the type of travel and vacation plans you are making. Naturally, if your pet has medications, be sure to pack them and ensure an adequate supply. Having the prescription for the medicine may be advisable because most countries are very particular about drugs entering their country. The prudent traveler might consider finding a local veterinarian at the destination before departure.

Is your pet accustomed to spending hours each day with you or is it used to being a couch potato with only limited exercise and social interaction? Too much togetherness may alter your personalities and lead to conflict and malcontentment. Putting stress on yourselves and your pet is not part of the plan of extended international travel.

Not all pets are used to traveling. Izzy, our Maltese, travels with us a lot and does not seem to be overly concerned. Izzy goes to our children's homes and plays with the grandchildren. She goes to my parents' house and has stayed overnight with them on numerous occasions. She has traveled for days at a time in our car, content to sit on my wife's lap rather than in her carrier. She has truly become accustomed to travel and to new and unusual places. She has gone to flea markets on a leash and in a pet carrier that I strap on, carrying her like a small infant. Strangers often stop us to comment about her and ask about her breed or pose other questions. She takes travel in stride, but such may not be the case with your pet. Do not expect your pet to act any differently than at home just because you are on vacation in Europe or elsewhere.

Most international travel will require some type of containment. In some cases, your pet may be in a soft-sided carrier rather than a rigid kennel. Certainly, aboard aircraft and often on trains or even in a car your pet will need to be in a carrier. Be sure to familiarize your pet with the carrier beforehand. When we had our Rottweiler, Max, he spent a lot of time in his "house" which was placed in the laundry room. The door was kept open and he went in and out, as he pleased. The point is, he was used to the idea of being in a kennel and would have been a great international traveler. Let your pet get used to a kennel, and you may decide it has other benefits, too. Once accustomed to being in a kennel, dogs tend to feel safe and consider it their space. A sick or stressed pet may welcome the reprieve from all the commotion of travel. Kennels may keep your pet from certain situations, which may be harmful, or not in their best interest. Kennels also give owners some time free from worry about their pet and its safety or behavior. While in a car, kennels prevent your pet from jumping around and causing a distraction for the driver and other occupants. This is important as you sightsee and make frequent stops. Always leash your pet while it is still in the kennel so it does not bound out at the stop and become injured or lost.

The kennel should be large enough that your pet is able to stand and turn around comfortably. Transit time can be long and comfort is extremely important. Be sure the kennel has enough ventilation. The kennel should have adequate handles for the airline staff to move the animal on and off the aircraft and into the proper place in the terminal. Plenty of absorbent material on the bottom of the kennel will facilitate pet comfort and cleanup later. Don't forget comfort. Your pet may be confined for many hours so also make it comfortable with something soft. The airlines often dictate the type and size of the kennel. Check with them well in advance to avoid purchasing the wrong kennel. Some airlines actually sell them. See Chapter 4 for additional information about kennels and regulations.

One last word on kenneling. Do not make kenneling a form of punishment. This only leads to behavior problems and your pet will not associate the kennel with its primary purpose, safety, but rather with fear, isolation, and owner disapproval.

A well-trained dog is a remarkable sight. Have you ever seen a dog pulling on the leash, dragging its owner along? Or just the opposite, a dog balking and refusing to walk, as a well-behaved dog ought? It's not a pretty sight. Your dog may need some additional training if it is to be a well-behaved international traveler. The training will come in handy when walking in strange places where the people look and dress differently and even speak some unintelligible language. Leash training is only part of the training. Does your pet chew, bite, jump on people, bark incessantly, particularly when alone, mess at inopportune times, like in hotel rooms or cower at strangers? These behaviors are apt to worsen in unfamiliar places and around unfamiliar people, who may not be as familiar with pets. Obedience training ought to be a travel prerequisite for your pet.

Supplying your pet with suitable water and food for the duration of your travels is very important. Give your pet only water that you would drink yourself. Taking enough food for months at a time may be quite a chore for a larger breed of dog. With Izzy, it is quite simple. She eats about 10 pounds of food in six months. If your pet eats only a certain brand of canned food, that could cause considerable concern unless it is dealt with during the planning stage. Do not expect your pet to acclimate to all the environmental changes and to a change in diet, too. If your brand of pet food is unavailable abroad, you will want to know ahead of time and begin a dietary change in anticipation of the final destination. Planning will make the trip go much better for the owner and pet.

2
Owner Considerations

Just as every pet is not suitable for international travel, there are equally important considerations for people who may wish to travel with their pet. Once you are abroad, you do not want to discover that you cannot have a pet along and things are not going well. Sending your pet home is a costly and disruptive task. Here are just a few of the things to consider about yourself and your travel plans:

- Is your reason for travel conducive to having a pet along?
- Is the travel destination appropriate for a pet?
- How well do you tolerate the disruptions a pet generates?
- Are the accommodations pet friendly or at least pet tolerant?
- Will the chores associated with your pet be shared or the sole responsibility of one person?
- Is the added expense and possible exasperation worth the joy of having your pet accompany you on your vacation?

If your plans are for a short business trip of only a few days or a week, it may not be the time to go to all the aggravation and effort to take along a pet. On the other hand, if your plans are for an extended stay in a country for business or pleasure, that may be the perfect opportunity to take your pet along so that neither one of you has to be deprived of the other's company. It would be just like home, only a long way from home.

There are a few countries in the world I would not consider taking Izzy or any other pet. The red tape is not worth the trouble and the overall acceptance of pets may not be great anyway. Some countries consider Izzy appropriate dinner fare rather than a dinner companion.

The health risks associated with some countries are considerable for humans and, they are no different for your pet.

Not every country, hotel, resort, or tourist attraction welcomes pets. Not everyone feels the same as you do about your beloved pet and will welcome him or her with quite the same exuberance and open arms. Certain cultures are not familiar with pets and consider them only a nuisance or a possible food source.

Preparation for travel is extensive, particularly when traveling internationally. While researching and planning your trip, be sure to include questions regarding pet accommodations. Checking ahead of time about your accommodations is most important. A phone call, E-mail, or fax will save hours of time if you do it before you go rather than at your final destination with pet in hand. Researching your accommodations, mode of travel, and travel itinerary at home will greatly enhance your enjoyment while abroad. The national tourist offices and embassies listed in this book will be invaluable in preparing for your international travels.

Taking the time each day to care for your pet is another issue. Can you keep up with your travel plans or business commitments while caring for a pet? Will the chores be shared or be done by only one individual? Make these decisions before leaving home to diminish the last minute disruption this might cause. On the other hand, taking your pet along and just going with the flow can also be fun and part of the travel adventure. Can you be flexible enough to have a pet along and still have a good time?

Finally, yet importantly, consider the monetary cost of international travel with your pet. The extra veterinary expenses of examinations, documents, pictures, translation fees, importation fees, shipping fees and always the unforeseen expenses need to be taken into account. Of course, these expenses could easily be offset by the cost of boarding your pet in your hometown. Besides, which is more fun for you and your pet? Can you put a price on that?

3
Making Plans

Having chosen your destination, the next step is to obtain information regarding entry requirements (See Chapter 10- Countries of the World). The national tourist office is a great place to start because they can supply you with a lot of information regarding their country and give you a head start in your vacation planning. They may also be able to supply the necessary entry forms for your pet. They can assist you in document translation and other services that are helpful in planning your travels. Embassies and consulates can assist you with the proper documents for travel such as passport, visa, inoculation requirements, and other official papers that require advance preparation. A special import permit may be required. I have attempted to indicate, whenever possible, what countries require a pet permit. Some countries require the approval of the pet documents by the consulate before your leaving home. Usually this process entails a fee. These importation documents are in addition to the usual rabies vaccination certificate (See figure 3-1) and International Health Certificate (See Figure 3-2). Some countries require proof of ownership (See figure 6-1). It may be advisable to inquire what type of document would suffice. Bills of sale, AKC registrations, and microchip documentation (See figure 6-2) may all be acceptable methods of documentation.

Allow extra time for documents to be properly authorized before your travel. This may include translation of certain certificates into foreign languages. Always inquire if there are special considerations for your particular destination. Some countries charge fees not only for visas but for the pet documents as well. Always inquire how these are to be paid. Most countries need to have these documents dated within a certain number of days before travel. Some countries require the documents to be sent to their consulate or the country's veterinary officer for verification and final approval. This may take some time, so plan ahead. The time frame for the health certificate varies from country to country. Some are as short as 2-3 days and some are 7-10 days. Be sure to follow these instructions to the letter. The last thing you want to happen is for your pet to be forced to take the next plane back home, alone. Consider all the red tape to be part of the process and try not to let it get you down or dissuade you from taking your pet on a trip to far-away places. Red tape, long forms, and more official stamps than you can imagine are the status quo for international travel.

Always keep the original vaccination certificate (or any other certificates) in your possession. Have your veterinarian certify copies, or, if they are being sent to the state veterinarian or the USDA, send the copies so they may be certified as well. Do the same for vaccinations certificates for distemper, hepatitis, leptospirosis, parvovirus, parainfluenza (DHLPP), Lyme disease, feline enteritis, and respiratory virus complex. Some countries require dogs and cats to be dewormed for Echinococcus tapeworms. Check with the embassy or consulate of your destination country.

OWNER'S COPY **RABIES VACCINATION CERTIFICATE**

NASPHV Form #51

Owner's Name and Address **Print - use ball point pen or type**

PRINT - Last	First	M.I.	Rabies Tag Number
			Telephone
No. Street	City	State	Zip

Species:	Sex:	Age:	Size:	Predominant Breed:	Colors:
Dog ☐	Male ☐	3 mo to 12 mo ☐	Under 20 lbs. ☐		
Cat ☐	Female ☐	12 mo or older ☐	20 - 50 lbs. ☐		
Other: ☐ (Specify)	Neutered ☐		Over 50 lbs. ☐	Name:	

DATE VACCINATED: ________, 19__ Month Day	Producer: ☐☐☐ (First 3 letters)	Veterinarian's: # ________ (License No.)
VACCINATION EXPIRED: ________, 19__ Month Day	☐ 1 yr. Lic./Vacc. ☐ 3 yr. Lic./Vacc. ________ Other ________ Vacc. Serial (lot) no.	________ (Signature) Address:

Figure 3-1 Rabies Vaccination Certificate

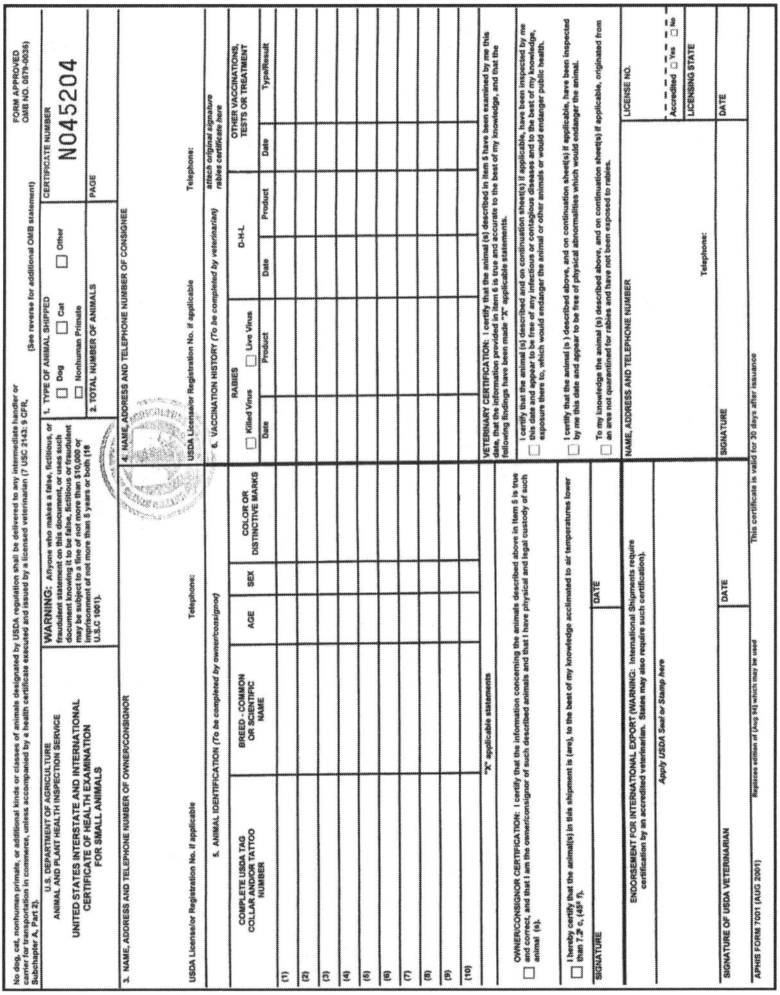

No dog, cat, nonhuman primate, or additional kinds or classes of animals designated by USDA regulation shall be delivered to any intermediate handler or carrier for transportation in commerce, unless accompanied by a health certificate executed and issued by a licensed veterinarian (7 USC 2143: 9 CFR, Subchapter A, Part 2). (See reverse for additional OMB statement)

FORM APPROVED
OMB NO. 0579-0036

U.S. DEPARTMENT OF AGRICULTURE
ANIMAL AND PLANT HEALTH INSPECTION SERVICE

UNITED STATES INTERSTATE AND INTERNATIONAL CERTIFICATE OF HEALTH EXAMINATION FOR SMALL ANIMALS

WARNING: Anyone who makes a false, fictitious, or fraudulent statement on this document, or uses such document knowing it to be false, fictitious or fraudulent may be subject to a fine of not more than $10,000 or imprisonment of not more than 5 years or both (18 U.S.C 1001).

1. TYPE OF ANIMAL SHIPPED ☐ Dog ☐ Cat ☐ Other ☐ Nonhuman Primate

CERTIFICATE NUMBER N045204

2. TOTAL NUMBER OF ANIMALS

PAGE

3. NAME, ADDRESS AND TELEPHONE NUMBER OF OWNER/CONSIGNOR

USDA License/or Registration No. if applicable Telephone:

4. NAME, ADDRESS AND TELEPHONE NUMBER OF CONSIGNEE

USDA License/or Registration No. if applicable Telephone:

5. ANIMAL IDENTIFICATION *(To be completed by owner/consignor)*

6. VACCINATION HISTORY *(To be completed by veterinarian)* *attach original signature rabies certificate here*

	COMPLETE USDA TAG COLLAR AND/OR TATTOO NUMBER	BREED - COMMON OR SCIENTIFIC NAME	AGE	SEX	COLOR OR DISTINCTIVE MARKS	RABIES ☐ Killed Virus ☐ Live Virus Date	RABIES Product	D-H-L Date	D-H-L Product	OTHER VACCINATIONS, TESTS OR TREATMENT Date	OTHER VACCINATIONS, TESTS OR TREATMENT Type/Result
(1)											
(2)											
(3)											
(4)											
(5)											
(6)											
(7)											
(8)											
(9)											
(10)											

"X" applicable statements

☐ OWNER/CONSIGNOR CERTIFICATION: I certify that the information concerning the animals described above in Item 5 is true and correct, and that I am the owner/consignor of such described animals and that I have physical and legal custody of such animal (s).

☐ I hereby certify that the animal(s) in this shipment is (are), to the best of my knowledge acclimated to air temperatures lower than 7.2º c, (45º f).

SIGNATURE DATE

VETERINARY CERTIFICATION: I certify that the animal (s) described in item 5 have been examined by me this date, that the information provided in item 6 is true and accurate to the best of my knowledge, and that the following findings have been made "X" applicable statements.

☐ I certify that the animal (s) described and on continuation sheet(s) if applicable, have been inspected by me this date and appear to be free of any infectious or contagious diseases and to the best of my knowledge, exposure there to, which would endanger the animal or other animals or would endanger public health.

☐ I certify that the animal (s) described above, and on continuation sheet(s) if applicable, have been inspected by me this date and appear to be free of physical abnormalities which would endanger the animal.

☐ To my knowledge the animal (s) described above, and on continuation sheet(s) if applicable, originated from an area not quarantined for rabies and have not been exposed to rabies.

ENDORSEMENT FOR INTERNATIONAL EXPORT (WARNING: International Shipments require certification by an accredited veterinarian. States may also require such certification).

Apply USDA Seal or Stamp here

NAME, ADDRESS AND TELEPHONE NUMBER

Telephone:

LICENSE NO.

Accredited ☐ Yes ☐ No

LICENSING STATE

SIGNATURE OF USDA VETERINARIAN DATE

SIGNATURE DATE

APHIS FORM 7001 (AUG 2001) Replaces edition of (Aug 94) which may be used

This certificate is valid for 30 days after issuance

Figure 3-2 International Health Certificate

Generally, an International Health Certificate generated by your pet's veterinarian and a rabies vaccination certificate are sufficient to enter most countries. Some countries want documentation regarding a multitude of inoculations, not just rabies. After looking at the regulations for some countries, you will see that some countries want to know the specific batch of serum used and other particulars. The best way for accurate information on the certificate is to attach the label from the vaccine vial directly to the vaccination certificate. Most countries require the rabies vaccination to be given at least 30 days before travel. Some other countries allow a shorter length of time. This length of time insures that the animal has adequate immunization. Have your pet inoculated early in the planning stage to avoid the "no travel" interval. Consult with your veterinarian early in the planning stage so their office can assist with the forms and comply with all the regulations regarding inoculations and inspection.

After your veterinarian completes the International Health Certificate, all copies are forwarded to the USDA-APHIS office for the official "stamp," then it is returned to the veterinarian and owner. A fee of $22.00 is required for this process (except if the pet is going to Canada, in which case the stamp is not necessary). If the departure time is quite short, send an additional fee for the Federal Express (or insert a pre-paid return Fed-Ex envelope). Each state has a single office and your veterinarian will know how to accomplish this step of the process. Although not all countries require the International Health Certificate to be "stamped," it is always a good idea to have this step done. It might prevent the unaccompanied return of your pet back home.

Many countries require the certificates and translations to be "legalized." This process may also be referred to as "authorized" or "certified." This process requires the following steps:
1. Obtain notarization of the document.
2. Obtain authentification of the Notary Signature (In most states this may be done directly by the State's Secretary of State; if not, the County Clerk authenticates the Notary signature.)
3. Obtain the State's Secretary of State Certification (In states where the Notary Signature may be authenticated directly by the State's Secretary of State, steps 2 and 3 are combined.)
4. Obtain U.S. Secretary of State Certification of the document.
5. The notarized, authenticated, and certified documents are sent to the consular office or embassy of the country to be legalized.

The above process may differ slightly from country to country. Once the pet owner has determined that legalization is necessary, the proper steps, in the proper sequence are accomplished. Make multiple

Making Plans 17

photocopies of each document before mailing in case the mail system fails. Always make multiple copies of documents at each stage and especially after the process is completed.

At the time of printing this book, the British "Pet Travel Scheme" (PETS) was revised. The new changes include the U.S. and Canada in the long-haul countries and make it possible for pets to enter the UK without quarantine after meeting certain requirements. Other countries will most likely change their rules on quarantine after the procedure becomes more commonplace. Meanwhile, quarantines may still be utilized. The length of quarantine varies considerably. The quarantine for the Turkish Republic of North Cyprus is one month, whereas it was six months for the United Kingdom. This may discourage many travelers from taking pets to destinations that require quarantine. Be aware that some island destinations do not have quarantine facilities although they require quarantines. This usually necessitates a stay in an approved quarantine elsewhere, such as the UK or Hawaii, if you are going to a Pacific island. Not all islands have quarantines, however, so don't be discouraged from your island fantasies.

If you need a passport, visa or other travel documents and do not wish to tend to the red tape yourself, consider consulting with Travel Document Services. TDS is a visa agency that has been helping international travelers since 1985. They work closely with the U.S. Passport Agency and embassies representing many governments, so that international travelers can depart on very short notice, for many worldwide destinations. TDS provides visa services for U.S. citizens for most countries for which an entry visa is required, and they can assist with visa requirements for U.S. permanent residents for many countries. They also expedite U.S. passports (new issues, renewals, amendments, and additional pages). Very urgent passports are available the same day. They also have a lot of general information about each country including the custom regulations.

Travel Document Systems
925 Fifteenth Street, NW
3rd Floor
Washington, DC 20005
Telephone: (800) 874-5100 toll-free in USA
Telephone: (202) 638-3800

Fax: (202) 638-4674
E-mail: info@traveldocs.com
Website: www.traveldocs.com

The U.S. Department of State issues passports for U.S. citizens to travel abroad. Consular offices overseas issue visas for foreign citizens to enter the United States. Contact passport agencies located in Boston, Chicago, Honolulu, Houston, Los Angeles, Miami, New Orleans, New York, Philadelphia, San Francisco, Seattle, Stamford, and Washington, DC, listed in local phone books or a U.S. Embassy or consulate abroad. For emergency assistance for U.S. citizens traveling overseas, call (202) 647-5226. For recorded travel information, call (202) 647-5225. Also, check the State Department's Website at www.travel.state.gov.

Accurate identification for your pet is very important (See Chapter 6- Pet Identification). Take extra photographs of your pet for customs officials and in case, the pet becomes lost. Placing a photograph of the pet on the carrier along with other identification may also be advisable. Consider having your pet tattooed or better yet, a microchip implanted for identification purposes. This is a permanent and humane means of identification. If you plan to travel with your pet a lot, it may be worth the expense and prevent the loss of your beloved pet and companion. Check with your veterinarian regarding these methods of identification. Always have photocopies of all documents in case of loss or in case some official insists on keeping them. Replacing these documents at your destination will be considerably more difficult than at home.

4

Planes, Trains, Automobiles, and Ships

Traveling by plane is the usual mode of international travel today. Not all airlines treat pets the same. Some do not allow them at all. Always check with your airline early in the planning stage. Your travel agent may be of invaluable assistance with this portion of your planning. I have included a listing of the major world airlines (over 250), their Websites, and telephone numbers for additional assistance (see the Appendix). They will dictate to some degree the type of kennel, and the number of animals allowed in the cabin and in the cargo compartment at any one time. There are limits, so plan and book your flights early. Last minute changes in your plans may occur, so have a "Plan B" if Fido cannot go.

The Animal Welfare Act (AWA) protects dogs, cats, and most other warm-blooded animals transported in commerce. The U.S. Department of Agriculture's (USDA) Animal and Plant Health Inspection Service (APHIS) enforces this law. APHIS shipping regulations help ensure that people who transport and handle animals covered under the AWA treat them humanely. Airlines and other shippers are affected by these regulations established to protect the well-being of animals in transit. The International Air Transport Association (IATA) also regulates the transportation of animals during international travel. Remember, the pet owner is still responsible to ensure that all the proper paperwork is in order.

When you make your airline reservations, advise the airline directly that your pet will be with you. Be sure to reconfirm your pet reservations with the airline 24-48 hours before departure. Advance arrangements are not a guarantee that your pet will travel on a specific flight.

Use non-stop flights whenever possible to avoid accidental transfers (you would not like your pet to arrive in a different destination than you) or delays. Travel on the same flight as your pet whenever possible. In the summer, choose early morning or late evening flights to avoid temperature extremes that may affect your pet or negate travel for the pet. Avoid holiday traveling whenever possible. These details will lessen the stress on both owner and pet.

Arrive at the airport with plenty of time to spare. If your pet is traveling as a carry-on pet, check-in will usually be at the passenger terminal. If you are sending your pet through the cargo system, inquire if your pet can be accepted at check-in as baggage or if it must go to the airline cargo terminal, which is usually located in a separate part of the airport. Be sure to check with your airline for the acceptance cutoff time for your flight. Note that by regulation an animal may be presented for transport no more than 4 hours before flight time (6 hours by special arrangement).

No airline will guarantee acceptance of a pet it has not seen. Important considerations for acceptance of pets include the health and disposition of the pet, proper health certificates, and kennel markings and sizing. Airlines also require that wheels installed as part of a kennel be removed or rendered inoperable before transport. This prevents kennels from rolling, protecting both the pet and airline employees. USDA assigns airlines the final responsibility for determining the safety and compliance of the kennels they accept.

Some airlines allow passengers to carry their pets in the cabin of a plane if the carrier is capable of fitting under the passenger's seat. Carry-on pets are not protected under the AWA. Airline policy governs the rules for in cabin pets. For the specific requirements pertaining to your pet, make advance inquires and arrangements with your airline.

Airlines must ensure that they have facilities to handle animals at the airports of transfer and final destination. Airlines must comply with USDA-APHIS (or IATA) guidelines on allowable temperature limits for animal-holding areas. Finally, airlines are not required to carry live animals, and they reserve the right to refuse to carry an animal for any reason.

Health Requirements and Documentation for Airline Travel:
- Your pet must have a health certificate from your veterinarian dated within 10 days of travel stating that the animal is fit to travel. Please have at least one extra copy.
- The health certificate and vaccination certificates must be attached to the kennel.
- If your pet will be tranquilized, your veterinarian must supply the name of the drug, the dosage and how the drug was administered. This information must be on the kennel.
- USDA requires that your pet be at least eight (8) weeks old and weaned before traveling by air.
- Most airlines will not transport an ill animal or one of a violent nature.
- If forecasted temperatures are below 45 degrees Fahrenheit (6 C), a Certificate of Acclimation must be issued by your veterinarian stating that the animal can travel in that temperature. The statement reads, "This animal appears healthy for transport but needs to be maintained at a temperature within the animals thermoneutral zone."
- No animal may travel by air (except as a carry-on) if the temperatures enroute are below 10 degrees Fahrenheit (-12 C).
- High temperatures may also hinder animal transportation by air. If the planned itinerary is above 85 degrees Fahrenheit (29.5 C), animals may not be accepted.
- Instructions for feeding and watering the animal over a 24-hour period must be attached to the kennel. The 24-hour schedule will assist the airline in providing care for your animal in case it is diverted from its original destination. The pet owner is required to document that the animal was offered food and water within 4 hours of transport, and the documentation must include the time and date of feeding.
- If the pet does not require food or water for the duration of the flight, a signed statement from your veterinarian will be required.

- Food and water dishes must be securely attached and be accessible to caretakers without opening the kennel. Food and water must be provided to puppies and kittens every 12 hours if they are 8 to 16 weeks old. Mature animals must be fed every 24 hours and given water every 12 hours.

Most veterinarians recommend shipping dogs and cats on an empty stomach, bladder, and colon. A healthy dog or cat can easily go 12-18 hours without food or water. They can eat and drink on arrival. Water invariably is spilled in the crate. Urinating in the crate or stool in the crate is a mess and vomiting during turbulence can be dangerous or even life threatening.

Remember that short faced dogs, such as the boxer, bulldog, Shih Tzu, or certain breeds of cats, such as Himalayans, are more likely to experience breathing problems during transport. This is due to the restricted airway. Although the cabin and cargo areas are pressurized, it is equivalent to an altitude of approximately 8,000 feet. This reduction in oxygen may significantly affect their breathing.

The kennels utilized on airplanes are constructed of heavier material than some of the plastic models used in automobiles and in homes. All-wire kennels are not allowed. Do not have a lock on the kennel door. Federal regulations require that the pet be evacuated in an emergency. Check with your air carrier to ensure the proper kennel is selected. You may be able to purchase the kennel directly from the airline. All kennels require the label "Live Animal" on the top and at least two sides. This must be in one-inch letters. The kennel should be labeled "This Way Up" or with directional arrows on two sides. Do not count on the airlines to have these labels. Bring your own and avoid last minute hassles.

The kennel for air travel needs to be comfortable and the bottom covered with some absorbent material, especially for long flights, when accidents are apt to happen. The kennel needs to have complete identification of the pet along with the owner's name, stateside address, and final destination address. The name and phone number of the veterinarian familiar with the pet might come in handy in a time of medical emergency. Do not forget to label the kennel with the pet's name. Handling personnel may reduce your pet's stress by

Planes, Trains, Automobiles, and Ships

addressing it by name. Be sure the pet is wearing a proper ID tag. Something familiar to the pet in the kennel, such as a toy, blanket, or chewie can reduce stress. Water should be available for extended flights only. Label the kennel with food and water instructions so that handling personnel can assist with this important item of travel.

Kennels must be well ventilated with openings that make up at least 14 percent of the total wall space. At least one-third of the openings must be located in the top half of the kennel. Kennels also must have rims to prevent ventilation openings from being blocked by other cargo. These rims usually placed on the sides of the kennel must provide at least three-quarters of an inch clearance. Kennels must have grips or handles for lifting to prevent cargo personnel from having to place their fingers inside the kennel and risk bites.

Be sure to walk your pet away from the terminal just before boarding to reduce the possibility of a messy kennel. Try not to feed your pet for several hours before takeoff. Try also to keep the time in the airport terminal to a minimum. This is difficult in today's travel environment, but it is quite stressful on pets as well as humans to contend with crowds, security checks and all the other hubbub of air travel. Do not take your pet out of its kennel inside the airport (unless requested by security personnel). This is an airport regulation and a courtesy for other passengers, let your pet out only after you leave the terminal building.

Generally, only one pet may occupy a kennel. The exception is with kittens or puppies between eight (8) weeks and six (6) months. There is a 20-pound weight limit per pet if they are traveling as a pair.

Always notify the flight crew that you have a pet on board before takeoff to insure that it gets the proper attention during boarding, in flight, and at the final destination. A reminder to the flight crew at your destination may expedite the transfer of the pet to the proper area in the terminal.

In many countries, a veterinarian will examine the pet on arrival when the documents are submitted for approval. Find out in advance what the procedure at the final destination airport will be.

If your pet requires inspection by a veterinarian or other official, at the time of arrival, they may need advance notice. Be sure to walk and water your pet as soon after arrival as possible.

If your pet should turn up missing during transport, immediately speak to airline personnel. Many airlines have computer-tracking systems that can trace a pet transferred to an incorrect flight. Should there be no report of your animal, proceed with the following steps:
- Contact animal control agencies and humane societies in the local and surrounding areas. Check with them daily.
- Contact the APHIS Animal Care regional office closest to where your pet was lost. Outside the U.S., contact the local animal authorities.
- Provide descriptions and photographs to the airline, local animal control agencies, and humane societies. Help may be available from radio stations. Leave telephone numbers and addresses with all these people or businesses should you have to return home.

If you need to file a complaint regarding the care of your pet during transport, contact USDA-APHIS. You may call (800) 545-USDA, visit Website, www.aphis.usda.gov/ac, or write to:
Deputy Administrator
USDA-APHIS Animal Care
4700 River Road, Unit 84
Riverdale, MD 20737-1234

The International Air Transport Association (IATA) Website: www.iata.org may be helpful for additional information.

When traveling with your pet in a terminal, remember that not all people appreciate pets. Be considerate of other people by not bringing attention to your pet. This also puts less stress on the animal. Exercising your pet before entering the terminal may help quiet it down and reduce the likelihood of its becoming rambunctious. Keeping the bag zipped and sitting in the quietest area you can find may help lessen the stress. Taking your pet on an airplane is a privilege and how you and your pet behave will determine the future of pet travel for others.

Planes, Trains, Automobiles, and Ships 25

Since September 11, 2001, many individuals have begun traveling by private aircraft. These planes vary from single engine planes, twin-engine aircraft, and jets. Most metropolitan and even not so large cities have charter services available. There are many benefits to private aircraft travel. You are not at the mercy of the airline schedules, crowds, multiple security checks (although some check is usually undertaken), and poor (or non-existent) food. The possibility exists to take your pet on a privately chartered aircraft to an international destination. The arrangements must be made ahead of time and the documents must still be available for the customs officials at your destination. Because the expense is primarily for the aircraft and not necessarily for the number of occupants, there may not be additional charges for a pet (a clean up charge may apply in some cases). This method of travel may be appealing to some, and certainly to those with the monetary means to choose this option.

Train Travel
If your plans for travel include trains, check with the countries' train carriers to learn the official stance on pets aboard. If your plans are for Europe, the following countries are part of the Eurail system: Austria, Belgium, Bulgaria, Denmark, Finland, France, Germany, Greece, Hungary, Ireland, Italy, Luxemburg, Netherlands, Norway, Poland, Portugal, Slovenia, Spain, Sweden and Switzerland. In Europe, generally, except in Spain, dogs are permitted on trains. Sometimes they may need to be contained in a pet carrier, or they may have to wear a muzzle or leash. Dogs normally travel at half the fare of a second-class ticket; this charge is payable directly to the conductor. Eurailpass also includes certain ferries, buses, and steamer in the cost of the pass. Check with these other modes of travel to ensure the passage of your pet.

Great Britain does not participate in the Eurail system. The BritRail Pass does not allow pets. Eurostar, the high-speed system connecting London, Paris, and Brussels does not allow pets. Unfortunately, Amtrak does not allow pets other than dogs for disabled individuals. The Orient Express does not allow pets other than "Guide Dogs." If traveling by train, contact these Websites for more information.
- Eurail: www.eurail.com (800) 274-8724
- Rail Europe: www.raileurope.com (877) 456-7245

- Amtrak: www.amtrak.com (800) USA-RAIL
- Japan Rail Pass: www.jreast.co.jp/jrp/index.htm
- Orient Express: www.luxury-trains.co.uk

Auto Travel

Traveling by car at your destination should not be significantly different from at home (unless of course, you must drive on the "wrong" side of the road). The same precautions apply. Always think of the pet's safety and comfort. They cannot do much themselves for their safety and comfort. Keep your pet's documents handy just as you would your own passport.

One of the most serious problems with automobile travel is the threat of heatstroke. The temperatures inside a car can often reach temperatures in excess of 125 degrees Fahrenheit very quickly. Even lowered windows may not provide sufficient safety for your pet. Putting your car in the shade may help for a while, but remember that shade is transient and the car can become engulfed in sun very quickly. The best remedy is to take your pet with you on the hot days. Try going into stores, museums, restaurants (the ones with outdoor areas) and anywhere else, you go. Always carry two or three gallons of water to soak and cool your pet in case of overheating.

Pets need some type of restraint during automobile travel for their own protection as well as the safety and sanity of the human occupants. All occupants of the car should be seat belted in. This includes all pets. Harnesses are available to provide restraint. A kennel may be a better solution for some pets. A restrained pet will decrease the chance of driver distraction and pet injury in the case of and accident or violent car movement. When stopping to exercise your pet, be sure to attach the leash before it exits the kennel or car so it does not get lost, injured, or become a pest to others in the area. This is not a good time to deal with pet emergencies.

Some pets become carsick. The onset of symptoms is usually rapid (unlike humans) and is usually accompanied by increased salivation and lip licking. Your pet may also look uncomfortable. The cure may be as easy as cracking a window for fresh air and restraining the pet to prevent excessive movement. Fortunately, pets often become accustomed to car travel and the symptoms lessen over time and with prolonged travel. Over-the-counter anti-motion sickness tablets may be the only solution. Call your veterinarian for the precise dosage.

Travel by bus may be quite an adventure with a pet. Most likely, you will get considerable attention. Keep in mind that not all individuals are pet lovers. Some countries don't give much thought to seeing pets (or other animals) on board a bus. Some countries have pets and their owner's sit in the back of the bus. Other countries may not allow them at all. If someone on board has pet allergies, you may be asked to exit the bus, in some countries. Always ask and do not assume they can go wherever you wish.

Ship Travel
Cruise lines generally do not allow pets. The only exception I was able to confirm was transatlantic travel on the Cunard Line, which allows pets in an on-board kennel. However, if you do a lot of checking, you might come up with some obscure line that does. If your idea of travel is a slow boat to China, then maybe you have a chance with some shipping lines that take a few passengers along with the freight. Be sure that you consider all the ports of call in your planning, and things might work out just fine. Being on board a freighter for a few days would probably be less stressful than an extended flight. The same may be said for humans, too. Jet lag would not be a problem with this method of travel.

The Easy Way
Fortunately, there is a simpler method of getting your pet to your destination. Hire someone else to do all the work. Several companies specialize in transporting pets around the world. They transport pets, livestock, zoo animals, and any other type of animal. It does not come cheap but the results are a bit more certain. They typically do all the necessary shipping arrangements and have the connections with the major airlines to do the job efficiently and quickly. They can take a lot of the stress out of the trip by doing this part of the work for you. I have listed several of the companies so you can contact them and make your choice. Some travelers are the do-it-yourself type and some are not.

Here are just a few of the advantages of utilizing a pet moving company.
- These companies are experts at moving pets. They handle the complexities of shipping animals every day.
- Multiple flights may necessitate different airlines and different countries, therefore different regulations.
- These companies can arrange the veterinarian visit to ensure the proper paperwork without complications.
- They can arrange the "difficult" countries much easier than the individual traveler who will only do the process one time.
- They can arrange the quarantine procedures that are necessary with some countries.

Pet Moving Companies

Animal Land, Inc.
Telephone: (877) 379-8625
Website: www.animalland.com

Air Animal Pet Movers
Telephone: (813) 879-3210 ext. 130
Website: www.airanimal.com

Airborne Animals
Website: www.airborneanimals.com

Global Animal Transport
Website: www.globalanimaltransport.com

Companion Air
Website: www.companionair.com

5
Pet Supplies

The supplies needed for an international vacation are quite similar to those everyday items needed for a trip across the country: food, water, dishes, toys, leash, blanket, "pooper scooper," disposable plastic bags, brush, comb, first-aid kit and medications. Other things that might come in handy are moist towelettes, deodorizers, paper towels, or regular washable towels. An extra collar and leash might come in handy too.

If a full supply of food from home is impractical, you might consider mixing the food available at your destination (presuming you know ahead of time what brand is available) with the home food to acclimate your pet to the new supply. Taking even a limited supply of your pet's usual food might help with the transition. Plan a complete change to a different food over two weeks. This will decrease the possibility of digestive problems as well as promoting general pet acclimation.

Water for your pet needs to be of the quality you would drink. Do not give your pet water from a questionable source. Bottled water is the best choice. You may drink other beverages, but your pet needs clean and safe water rather than sodas, alcohol or other human drinks.

Purchase emergency medical supplies needed from home, where you speak the language, rather than at your foreign destination. An emergency kit may be purchased or made up at home. Consider starting with some of the items that are in your own emergency supply and adding pet-specific items. These include scissors, gauze, Telfa pads, tape, elastic bandage, a syringe, hydrogen peroxide, antibiotic ointment, latex gloves, tourniquet, tranquilizers (pet and human), and suture kit if you are medically inclined. Be sure to check with your pet's veterinarian about pain medications and tranquilizers before leaving. Not all pets tolerate tranquilizers or sedation. Many problems develop because pet are sedated. Avoid them if possible and use them only with the specific recommendation of your veterinarian. Human pain medications and pets may not be compatible, so do not assume that your medications can be given to your pet. It is not a bad idea to have an emergency kit in your car at all times if you travel with your pet a lot at home. Commercially prepared emergency kits are available at pet stores and numerous online sources (See Chapter 8-Help from the Internet). The average price range is $25-$40.

Before leaving home, consider getting the advise of your veterinarian regarding simple ailments and medications/treatments that you may be capable of doing yourself. You may also consider a book about pet emergency first aid. It may come in handy when you are in a country and find it difficult to communicate with the local veterinarians.

Izzy with her Sherpa Bag®, ready to go.

Small pets fit in a carrier similar to those for newborns and infant children. There are papoose, shoulder bags, and backpack styles. Izzy often travels around in public places by this method and doesn't

Pet Supplies

seem to mind. Carriers eliminate tangled leashes, bumped legs, and stepped-on paws when in public. These are available at pet stores although we had to check ten places before we found one. We recently acquired a Sherpa Back Pack® that straps on my back and is very comfortable, for both Izzy and me. She also has the Sherpa Tote Around Town® shoulder bag that is quite stylish and looks like a fine leather handbag.

There are several commercial soft-sided carry-on bags specifically designed for pet travel. The best way of determining which type or brand suits your pet is to go to one of the large pet stores and try them. Your veterinarian may sell them as well. Sherpa® and Samsonite® are two of the most popular brands. Sherpa® offers many styles of bags with various features and are very stylish. These bags have an appropriate amount of ventilation along with other features that enhance their use. These bags need to be airline approved so not just any bag will do when you transport your pet on an aircraft. Ticket agents have unzipped Izzy's bag to ensure there was adequate ventilation and space for her. Be sure your bag will pass inspection before you head to the airport.

It is especially important to allow your pet to acclimate to the bag/carrier before leaving home. Our Florida veterinarian's Yorkie gets all excited when she sees the Sherpa Bag® coming out of the closet. She is quiet, composed, comfortable, and content. Their dog is so accustomed to traveling; fellow travelers don't even knows she is in the bag. Heading off for an extended trip is not the time for your previously well-trained pet to act up.

Use the same line of reasoning if your pet must go as cargo. The experience of being loaded into a plane by strangers is not the opportune time to introduce the kennel.

Kennels were discussed in some detail in Chapter 4. Individuals who travel extensively may wish to purchase a kennel for their pet. Others may wish to borrow one or rent one if that is an option. Always be certain that the kennel is airline approved. Purchasing one from the airline will ensure that it is adequate. They are available in several sizes and the airlines are quite specific about how the animal must be able to move about, etc. Make the decision early in the planning if your pet will accompany you in the cabin or the cargo hold. This will help determine the type of carrier.

Stylette makes many sizes to fit even the biggest of dogs. Their newest style fits under an airliner seat.

Sherpa® carriers are available in several styles, colors, and sizes.

6
Pet Identification

Hopefully you will not have to deal with a missing or distressed pet during your travels. However, with all the various steps involved in transporting and lodging, it could happen, so it is very important to have adequate identification for your pet. Several methods are available. In fact, it may be necessary to use two or three of these methods to increase the likelihood of locating your pet should you become separated.

If you and your pet are separated while traveling, notify the officials immediately, whoever they may be. If this occurs in an airport, then security personnel and airline personnel should be notified as soon as possible to facilitate relocating your pet. If this happens within a resort or hotel, the security and desk staff need to be notified. If the loss occurs in public places, then the proper animal-control authorities, humane societies, veterinarians, and police agencies need to be notified. Being able to provide these individuals with a photograph and an accurate description of your pet will be most helpful. Carry several extra photographs of your pet for such purposes. Other means of locating your pet may include posting notices in public places or notifying businesses and others within the area where your pet was last seen. It may even be necessary to advertise or place notices in local papers and perhaps to contact radio stations and other media to assist. This "all-out" endeavor may be necessary to locate your pet, especially if it is lost in a foreign country where language difficulties and cultural differences may impede its rapid recovery. If you must return home without your pet, you will want to maintain contact with those involved in the search once you return.

Before leaving home, investigate and adopt various means of pet identification. The most obvious and easily obtained form of identification is a tag and collar. Be sure the collar is sturdy and adequate so that it does not easily become dislodged, thereby removing the identification tag. The tag itself should have the pet's name, owner's name, address, and contact phone numbers. An additional tag that indicates whether the pet has some other means of identification, such as a tattoo or microchip, may also be important so that the tattoo or microchip is not overlooked as a means of identifying the pet. These tags may also indicate a certain pet registry to contact in case of loss or emergency.

The two major means of permanent identification for pets are tattoos and microchips. Tattooing has been available for many years. There are various systems of pet tattooing. Veterinarian offices, humane societies, and individually owned tattooing businesses all do them. Because organizations use numerous letters and numerical combinations, finding the appropriate registry for any given tattoo on your pet can be confusing and difficult. In order to facilitate identification in an emergency, the tattoo needs to be registered with an organization. There are several such organizations, some of which are listed later in this chapter.

Once a particular tattoo has been identified in a database, somebody must find the owner by telephone or other means. Obviously, if you are going out of the country, you want to give the database company your address and phone number abroad to enable contact. Oftentimes, owners fail to update their addresses and other pertinent information when they move about, thereby making it nearly impossible to reunite the owner and the pet. This may also occur when a new owner purchases a pet and this individual has neglected to re-register the animal under the new ownership.

Several problems exist with a tattoo. Fur often hides tattoos placed on the inner thigh. Pet thieves can cut off an ear tattoo. Fights might make the ear tattoo illegible. Confusion between numbers and letters may be impossible to decipher. Tattoos may be illegible for various reasons (it could be altered by pet thieves). Tattoos also fade with time. Today, there is increasing support for multiple means of

Pet Identification

identification, and this approach may in fact be most beneficial if used in conjunction with a microchip.

Microchip identification, the most accurate method of identification, has been available for the past 15 years and widely used outside the United States. It has become more popular in the United States over the last several years. This means of identification uses a tiny microchip (about the size of a grain of rice), which is implanted between the animal shoulder blades by means of a hypodermic needle and becomes an "electronic identification tag." There are two major manufacturers of chips and scanners. Avid® developed the FriendChip®, and Destron® developed a microchip that sells under various names depending on the country. In the United States, HomeAgain™ is the major brand. The cost of microchipping is about $30-$40. Microchip identification is mandatory before importing your pet into some countries.

A certificate of ownership (See figure 6-1) is provided with the Avid® microchip. This is required in some countries for proof of ownership and a positive means of connecting the pet with a certain owner. This certificate is also helpful if the owner wishes to sell the pet because it positively transfers ownership in the Avid® database.

Figure 6-1 Avid® Certificate of Ownership

Another certificate (See figure 6-2) is obtained when using the Avid® microchip. This particular document has a scannable sticker that matches the chip in the pet. This certificate with additional copies is important to have on hand when traveling to international destinations.

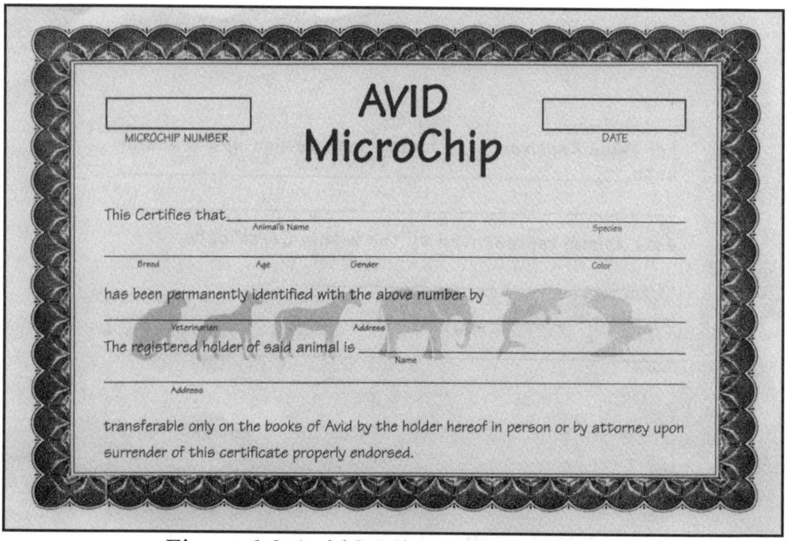

AVID MicroChip

MICROCHIP NUMBER

DATE

This Certifies that____

Animal's Name Species

____

Breed Age Gender Color

has been permanently identified with the above number by

____

Veterinarian Address

The registered holder of said animal is ______________________________

Name

____

Address

transferable only on the books of Avid by the holder hereof in person or by attorney upon surrender of this certificate properly endorsed.

Figure 6-2 Avid® Microchip Certificate

The topic of microchipping becomes quite complicated once you leave the U.S. Most of Europe uses an ISO chip, which is not compatible with the scanners used for the Avid® or HomeAgain™ brands. After talking to several individuals about this confusing topic, I have concluded that having your own scanner may simplify the identification process in some countries of the world (the Avid® scanner costs about $199.) Fortunately, the UK is able to read these two brands of microchips but elsewhere there may be compatibility problems.

Our Michigan veterinarian's dog was recovered three times because of its microchip. He considers this method the best. This method of pet identification will most likely become the industry standard as technology progresses and databases increase.

Izzy was microchipped just before completion of this book. Her teeth needed cleaning and that was a great opportunity to do it while she was anesthetized. Our veterinarian recommends this so the process is more tolerable to the pet. She had no problems following the procedure other than the usual post anesthesia cough and sedation.

Pet Identification 37

The American Kennel Club-Companion Animal Recovery program recommends the HomeAgain® brand of microchip. It has an anti-migration cap, which helps prevent movement of the microchip once placed in the animal. Many different scanners, including the universal scanner also read the HomeAgain® microchip. The universal scanner, developed in 1996, reads several major brands of microchips. A yellow collar tag, included with this microchip package, has a unique microchip number and the toll-free number for AKC-CAR imprinted on it. This alone can aid in the return of your lost pet.

Avid® FriendChip™ uses the PETtrac™ database to locate your lost pet. Veterinarians, pet shelters, and other sources have the appropriate scanner to determine the identity of the pet in order to facilitate pet retrieval. Veterinary Medical Associations across the United States back PETtrac's database. They have toll-free numbers to assist in the location of lost pets.

Occasionally, dislodged microchips migrate elsewhere from the original place of implantation. This necessitates careful scanning by personnel when they scan for a chip.

If you travel a great deal with your pet, you might want to provide more than one permanent means of identification in addition to a collar tag. Having a tag that provides the tattoo characters and the tattoo location increases the chances of proper identification of your pet. Having a tattoo that indicates that the animal is microchipped alerts recovery personnel that a microchip is implanted, even though it may have migrated from the original implant site.

Identification tags alone are inadequate for positive identification and recovery of your pet. They have benefit primarily when used in combination with a permanent form of identification, but they do have one major advantage. Anyone can read it and can respond to the information on them.

Here is a list of registries and organizations that assist pet owners who have lost their pets. Several registries only deal with tags. I included only registries that require a microchip or tattoo. International travel is not the place to rely solely on a tag to help retrieve your lost pet.

The American Kennel Club is a major source of assistance. They charge a one-time fee of $12.50 to enroll your pet in their recovery program. All microchipped or tattooed animals are eligible for enrollment in AKC-CAR, regardless of species, age, or size. Contact:
American Kennel Club
Companion Animal Recovery
5580 Centerview Drive, Suite 250
Raleigh, NC 27606-3394
Telephone: (800) 252-7894
Fax: (919) 233-1290
E-mail: Found@akc.org
Website: www.akccar.org

The American Pet Association has a number of membership benefits including the finding of lost pets. "The Guardian™" is a unique pet collar tag that increases the chance of locating your pet. In 1999, the recovery rate was 98.6%. For more information, contact:
American Pet Association
P.O. Box 725065
Atlanta, GA 31169
Telephone: (888) APA-FOUND
Website: www.apapets.com

FasTrac™ is an easy and affordable pet tracking system that provides a tag with a unique number and a national toll-free hotline number to locate lost pets. The pet owner creates a free PetProfile™ at the host site, www.PetDex.com, to register the pet's ID number and its tattoo or microchip number, too. The ID tag costs $8.95 with free lifetime registration. This is an Internet company requiring pet owners to maintain pet registration online. Contact: www.PetDex.com.

The National Dog Registry is America's oldest and largest pet recovery system. They register dogs, cats, horses, goats, and ferrets-- all species of animals. They have been finding lost and stolen pets for more than 30 years. The system uses a unique tattoo that is registered with their registry. They have Internet capability in addition to their toll-free telephone number. The fee to register the tattoo is $38.00.

Pet Identification

Contact:
 National Dog Registry
 P.O. Box 116
 Woodstock, NY 12498
 Telephone: (800) 637-3647 (NDR-DOGS)
 E-Mail: info@natldogregistry.com
 Website: www.natldogregistry.com

National Pet Network, LLC provides an identification tag with a unique number and a recovery Website address. You can upload a photo of your pet and update the information in your on-line profile as often as needed. The National Pet Network will also record your pet's microchip, tattoo, rabies tag, and your local pet license numbers. This information is cross-referenced for positive pet identification and recovery. This service costs $9.95. Contact:
 National Pet Network, LLC
 P.O. Box 258
 Cloverdale, MI 49035
 Telephone: (616) 623-7250
 Fax: (866) 851-7540 toll-free
 E-mail: customerservice@nationalpetnetwork.com
 Website: www.nationalpetnetwork.com

The Pet Club of America provides a service called "Petfinders." They provide an ID tag with a serial number and a toll-free telephone number to link your pet to their database. They also offer additional services and a newsletter. The annual fee is $15.00. On-line and mail registration are available. Contact:
 Pet Club of America (Petfinders)
 661 High Street
 Athol, NY 12810
 Telephone: (800) 666-LOST
 Website: www.petclub.org

PETtrac™ is associated with Avid®. Avid® manufactures the microchip and scanner and provides the global recovery network. This company can also provide a Certificate of Ownership when the microchip is implanted. A few foreign countries require a Certificate of Ownership before importation. The cost of PETtrac™ varies

according to how many pets are registered at one time. One pet costs $15, while $40 will pay for up to eight pets. Contact:
PETtrac™
3179 Hamner Avenue
Norco, CA 92860-9972
Telephone: (800) 336-AVID
Fax: (909) 737-8967
E-mail: Pettrac@aol.com
Website: www.avidmicrochip.com

Tattoo-A-Pet, established in 1972, is the world's largest network of pet protection registration and recovery using a permanent and painless pet tattoo. The cost is $35.00 for a tattoo and registry. If your pet is already tattooed, the cost is $25.00. This is a lifetime fee. Contact:
Tattoo-A-Pet
6571 S.W. 20th Court
Ft. Lauderdale, FL 33317
Telephone: (800) TATTOOS (828-8667) toll-free in USA
Fax: (954) 581-0056
E-mail: info@tattoo-a-pet.com
Website: www.tattoo-a-pet.com

During my research, I came across several references to an "International Pet Passport." This is a commercially available document used to give pertinent information regarding your pet. It is an excellent idea because it enables the owner to assemble a lot of information in one document and have it available at all times.
Contact:
MESID International, Inc.
5 Cowichan Way
Nepean, ON, Canada, K2H 7E6
Telephone: (613) 828-5435
Fax: (613) 828-3830
E-mail: jjr@internationalpetpasssport.com
Website: www.internationalpetpassport.com

7
Returning Home

Before leaving home, be sure that you can return to the U.S. without difficulty after visiting a particular destination. Here are some caveats from U.S. Customs. If you have other questions, consult with U.S. Customs' Website or the local U.S. Customs office.

Live animals and birds can enter the United States subject to certification, permits, inspection, and quarantine rules that vary with the animal and its origin. Dogs that have been in Central and South America pose a special health hazard if they have wounds infested with screwworms. If your dog has even a small wound, be sure to have it treated before you return to the United States.

Pet birds obtained overseas may be imported into the United States if quarantined in a USDA Animal Import Center for a minimum of 30 days. You must make quarantine arrangements in advance because facilities are limited and are available only at certain ports of entry (Honolulu, HI; Los Angeles, CA; McAllen, TX; Miami, FL; New York, NY; and San Ysidro, CA).

Personally owned pet birds returning to the United States that have been out of the country for more than 60 days, must be quarantined for 30 days in the owner's home. The original U.S. International Health Certificate that was issued before leaving the United States must accompany these birds. This certificate must identify each bird individually by a leg band, tattoo, or microchip identification number. There is no Federal quarantine required for pet birds originating in Canada. However, a USDA veterinarian must inspect all pet birds entering the United States.

All animal importations are subject to health, agriculture, wildlife, and customs requirements. Pets (including cats and dogs) taken out of the United States are subject, upon return, to the same requirements as those entering for the first time. Importation of certain species requires a permit from the Center of Disease Control and Prevention (CDC.) Young puppies may be imported without proof of rabies vaccination but must be confined at a place of the owner's choice until they are 3 months of age and then vaccinated. Confinement must then continue for 30 days. Monkeys and other nonhuman primates may not be imported for use as pets under any circumstances; importation for scientific or exhibition purposes is strictly controlled through a registration process. U.S. Customs Service Publication 509, "Pets and Wildlife," contains information that is more detailed.

Turtles with shells less than 4 inches long may not be imported for commercial purposes. You may import as many as six turtles with shells at least 4 inches long (or a combination of turtles and viable eggs not exceeding six) for your personal use as pets. A permit issued by CDC must accompany live bats and certain snails.

If you are unsure of the regulations, call for help. Look in your phone book for the nearest office of USDA, APHIS, or PPQ (Plant Protection Quarantine); or call PPQ's central office in Maryland at (301) 734-8645. If your question is specific to animals or animal products, contact National Center for Import and Export (NCIE.) U.S. consulates abroad may also be able to answer many of your questions. In addition, APHIS' Internet site at www.aphis.usda.gov provides information on this and other related topics.

Other Federal agencies have regulations pertaining to items that are allowed or prohibited entry into the United States as well. The U.S. Customs Service publishes the brochure "Know Before You Go (Customs Hints for Returning Residents)," and the U.S. State Department publishes the brochure "Your Trip Abroad" with general information for travelers.

USDA-APHIS Veterinary Services' National Center for Import and Export provides information about importing live animals and animal products.

Returning Home

Contact:
    USDA, APHIS, Veterinary Services
    Attn.: National Center for Import and Export
    4700 River Road, Unit 40
    Riverdale, MD 20737-1231
As an alternative, you may call NCIE's automated phone line at (301) 734-7830 or check their Website at www.aphis.usda.gov/ncie.

The U.S. Customs Service collects import duties (taxes) and assists the U.S. Public Health Service in regulating the importation of dogs, cats, monkeys, and birds. Contact:
    Customs Service
    P.O. Box 7407
    Washington, DC 20044
You may also check their Internet homepage for up-to-date information at www.customs.ustreas.gov.

The U.S. Fish and Wildlife Service regulate the import and export of wild and endangered plants and animals and their products. Contact:
    U.S. Fish and Wildlife Service
    Office of Management Authority
    4401 North Fairfax Drive
    Arlington, VA 22203
    Website: www.fws.gov

The Centers for Disease Control and Prevention regulate importation of certain animal species and have specific regulations regarding pets (including cats and dogs) and nonhuman primates. For more information, contact:
    Centers for Disease Control and Prevention
    Division of Quarantine
    1600 Clifton Road
    Mail Stop E-03
    Atlanta, GA 30333
    Telephone: (404) 639-8107
    Fax: (404) 639-2599
    Website: www.cdc.gov/ncidod/dq

The U.S. Public Health Service requires that domestic cats and dogs brought into this country be examined at the port of entry for evidence of infectious diseases that can be transmitted to humans. If the animal appears sick, further examination by a licensed veterinarian may be required. In addition, dogs must be vaccinated against rabies at least 30 days before entry into the United States, except for puppies less than 3 months of age and for dogs originating or located for 6 months or more in areas designated by the U.S. Public Health Service as being rabies free.

For cats and dogs, returning to Canada, the only requirement is a valid rabies vaccination certificate. It does not matter where the animal originates from, or where the vaccination was given, as long as the vaccine was given by a licensed veterinarian, the vaccine is valid, and the certificate is provided in English or French.

8
Help from the Internet

The Internet has revolutionized the way people locate and retrieve information. Without the Internet, I would still be researching this book. It was invaluable to locate tourist offices, embassies, send E-mails, download documents, and accomplish other writing tasks. I found it preferable and certainly cheaper to send a brief E-mail than write, stamp, and mail a letter or short note. The slowness of mail alone caused several delays in gathering information for this project.

E-mail enabled me to send messages during non-business hours and to read responses any time of the day or night. I spent many hours in the evenings working on this project and would not have been able to make all the calls during the daytime. It also kept me from getting placed on hold (and listening to Musak) during long-distance phone calls, which helped in keeping this project within a tight budget. Of course, I also had the capability to print out the responses so that the information was accurate and not prone to the problems of trying to interpret accents from all over the world and getting thoroughly confused as to content. The ability to research, communicate, decide and make reservations 24 hours a day, 7 days a week, is a very positive reason to use the Internet. When communicating with other time zones, I found it to be almost a necessity.

When searching for the names and addresses of all the tourist offices worldwide, I searched and found a Website that had much of this information. The information that was not readily available, took a very long time to find. This book will save readers the effort and time of repeating this task. Likewise, with embassies, they, too, were listed (many but not all) on a Website. Embassies without Websites required a great deal of effort to research. I hope that the sources in this book help shorten the planning for your next international trip.

Many commercial (non-governmental) Websites may be helpful in planning your travels. Here is but a brief summary of the possibilities. Websites come and go regularly. They also change their content regularly. Readers familiar with the Internet can use their own ingenuity to surf the Web for their own needs.

Health (Human)
- U.S. Center for Disease Control (www.cdc.gov) is the best resource for travelers' health information and individual country conditions and requirements.
- Travel Health Online (www.tripprep.com) features country-by-country profiles with detailed health information.
- The World Health Organization (WHO) (www.who.int) provides current vaccination requirements and other health advice.

Health (Pet)
- The American Veterinary Medical Association (www.avma.org/care4pets) has a very useful Website for pet owners interested in pet health.
- Pet diseases (www.vetinfo.com)
- On-line veterinarian (www.familypetservices.com)
- First Aid kits and information (www.petfirstaid.org), (www.oesl.com), (www.healthypet.com/firstaid.html) (www.interpetexplorer.com/html/firstaid.html), (www.medipet.com)

Maps
- The PCL Map Collection at the University of Texas (www.lib.utexas.edu/maps/index.html) has online maps.

Miscellaneous Topics
- The Universal Currency Converter (www.xe.net) converts most of the world's currencies.

Help from the Internet

- Currency Calculator (www.x-rate.com) is another excellent converter of world currencies.
- Ethnologue (www.ethnologue.com) specializes in information about languages and cultures.

Pet Supplies
- PetSmart (www.petsmart.com)
- Pets Warehouse (www.petswarehouse.com)
- Pets Prefer Us (www.petspreferus.com)
- Pet Street Mall (www.petstreetmall.com)
- Sherpa's Pet Trading Company (www.sherpapet.com)
- Dog beds/crates/carriers (www.dogbedsworks.com)
- Pet carriers, etc. (www.meowser.com)

Travel Advisories and U.S. Government Websites
- Travel Warnings and Bureau of Consular Affairs (www.travel.state.gov/travel_warnings)
- CIA World Factbook (www.portal.research.bell-labs.com/cgi-wald/dbaccess/411) contains information about the people, geography, and more about almost every country.
- U.S. Customs Service (www.customs.ustreas.gov)
- World Travel Watch (www.ora.com/ttales/editorial/wtw)
- The U.S. Department of State (travel.state.gov) travel resource site is a "must see" for American citizens.
- USDA-APHIS (www.aphis.usda.gov)
- The U.S. Fish and Wildlife Service (www.fws.gov)

Travel Planning
- Pet Travel (www.PetTravel.com) is your source for worldwide pet friendly accommodations and services.
- Travelocity (www.travelocity.com) is primarily a Web-based reservations system with worldwide information
- Orbitz (www.orbitz.com) obtains the flight and fares directly from the airlines (450).
- Lowestfare.com (www.lowestfare.com), an airline consolidator, offers fares below retail.
- Qixo (www.qixo.com) searches all travel sites on the Web and may find flights and fares not available on the other sites.

- TravelCOM (www.travelcom) provides information on the countries of the world.
- World Travel Guide (www.travel-guide.com) provides maps, history, and information about world regions and countries.
- CNN Travel (www.cnn.com/TRAVEL) provides news (what else?) from around the world.
- Lonely Planet (www.lonelyplanet.com/dest/) publishes online guides, including some unique departments.
- Fielding Guides (www.fieldingtravel.con) has a great Website in addition to their great travel books.
- Fodor (www.fodors.com) is worth a look.
- Airlines of the Web (www.itn.net/airlines) is the best resource for general and specific information about air travel.

Weather
- The Weather Channel (www.weather.com)
- Intellicast (www.intellicast.com)
- Accuweather (www.accuweather.com)
- Travelocity (www.travelocity.com)
  Click "Weather" on the menu bar.

For me, the most helpful Websites in researching this book were the tourism office and embassy Websites. These were the sites I searched in order to find the country specific regulations to import pets. Not every country of the world is represented on these Websites (which made for very extensive research to find the most complete and up-to-date information.) The addresses change, as do E-mails and other information. If the information from a specific country in the next section is no longer up to date, I would suggest you go to one of these sources online and check for changes. The third Website listed is another comprehensive source for country information. It takes navigating but it can be helpful.
- Embassies in Washington, DC (www.embassy.org)
- Tourism Office Worldwide Directory (www.mbnet.mb.ca/lucas/travel)
- World Travel Guide (www.travel-guide.com)

9
Traveling with Exotic Pets

Prior information in this book assumes that pet owners will be traveling primarily with cats and dogs. The reality of the situation, however, is many pet owners would like to take pets other than dogs and cats. Owners of birds, reptiles, ferrets and other small pets are just as interested in taking their pets along with them on vacation, or relocation, as dog and cat owners. Taking these more exotic pets might entail considerably more paperwork and prior research, but it is entirely possible. Some of these pets have peculiar habits and needs that require special consideration especially while traveling long distances and for a protracted time.

There is certainly less information available from various countries regarding their regulations on these types of pets. Do not assume that taking an iguana to Germany is quite the same as taking your poodle or Persian. Some countries may not allow them outright, but others may require specific forms or other procedures.

Most countries listed in Chapter 10 make a generic reference to "pets." While making initial inquiries regarding traveling with pets, it would be prudent to ask specifically about your type of pet. If written policies sent do not mention your type of pet specifically, get opinions regarding your pet in writing to avert possible problems at the time of importation.

Regulations for bringing some of these pets back into the United States might differ from cats and dogs. U.S. Customs, U.S. Fish and Wildlife, and USDA will be able to assist pet owners in determining the specific requirements for re-entry depending on the species of pets.

Birds

Most birds are small enough to travel as carry-on baggage and bypass the cargo hold. This is the safest way for them to travel because it allows owners continuous control over their care. The bird container may be a small wire cage similar home cages or a soft-sided bag similar to those used by dog and cat owners. You may also find a rigid plastic carrier suitable for the bird. The best way for you to decide which to use is to see how your bird adjusts to the different styles of cages. The cage must fit completely under an airliner seat.

Here are some tips to consider:
- Have your bird banded, tattooed or microchipped before leaving home. This is mandatory for return into the U.S.
- Provide dry food and leafy, succulent foods instead of water during travel.
- Take a toy for the bird to enjoy but not a sharp, heavy toy that could become a dangerous missile during turbulence.
- Take a cover for the cage to reduce stimulation and reduce passengers' curiosity.
- Take water from home for the initial period of transition.

The transition of pet birds form state to state (within the U.S.) may complicate international travel. The owner must comply with each state's regulations for birds. Do not overlook this important fact. You do not want your pet bird confiscated or a needless return trip home because the chosen route of travel was not bird friendly.

Bird owners who take their pets with them while abroad are generally exempted from some of the USDA quarantine and foreign certification requirements for imported birds. This exception applies only to U.S.-origin birds and is permissible as long as the owner makes special arrangements in advance. If you wish to take your bird abroad, you must obtain all necessary documents from the USDA and the Department of the Interior's U.S. Fish and Wildlife Service **before departing** the United States. Such preparation is especially critical for birds covered by the treaty known as the Convention on

Traveling with Exotic Pets 51

International Trade in Endangered Species (CITES). Get a health certificate endorsed by a USDA-APHIS veterinarian. This endorsement is subject to a user fee. U.S.-origin birds may reenter the United States through any international airport that is serviced by a USDA veterinary official.

For more information on traveling abroad with your bird, contact:
USDA-APHIS Veterinary Services
4700 River Road, Unit 39
Riverdale, MD 20737-1231
Telephone: (301) 734-5097
Website: www.aphis.usda.gov/ncie

Pet birds have specific requirements to reenter the U.S. See Chapter 7-Returning Home for more details.

Reptiles, Amphibians and Turtles

A carry-on bag suitable for the animal works well for transporting these pets. Be aware that not every airline allows these pets in the cabin. Large snakes (or others) weighing more than 15 pounds (the limit for many airlines) must travel as cargo. Keeping the animal out of sight limits responses from fellow travelers. Not everyone wants to travel with a snake or lizard nearby.

Here are a few tips to consider:
- Mark the container "DO NOT TOUCH." This discourages fellow travelers from approaching and wanting to see, touch, or handle.
- Never leave your pet unattended.
- Consider a lock on the travel container (some of these critters are real Houdinis). Federal regulations do not allow locks on containers in the cargo hold of aircraft.
- Consider all regulations at each city (state) in transit to ensure the legal transportation of your pet.
- Check with your airline to ensure that your pet can travel in the cabin.

Sending your pet via special means such as Fed-Ex, UPS, or USPS may also be less of a hassle and work out just as effectively as taking them as carry-on or excess baggage (cargo). This entails special packaging so check on the specifics according to your pet species.

The regulations regarding reptiles, amphibians, and turtles vary from country to country. When making your initial inquiries, be sure that you understand all the regulations.

Monkeys and other Primates

Monkeys and other primates may be brought into the United States for scientific, educational or exhibition purposes by importers who are registered with the CDC. However, under no circumstances may they be imported as pets. Registered importers wishing to import or export primates for a permitted purpose in accordance with CDC requirements are also required to obtain clearance from the U.S. Fish and Wildlife Service. The Convention on International Trade in Endangered Species (CITES) requires that all primates have permits.

Other Furry Friends

These pets include ferrets, rabbits, gerbils, hamsters, mice, rats, guinea pigs, chinchillas, hedgehogs and possibly other small animals. Fortunately, most of these pets are small enough to travel in carry-on baggage. Inquire with your airline if these pets are allowed in the cabin prior to showing up at check-in with pet in hand. If your pet is a "chewer," do not expect to put it into a soft-sided bag. Your fellow passengers might find your cuddly, furry pet an unwelcome seatmate.

Observe all state and local regulations if your departure is from a location other than your home state. Your itinerary may need revision if there are "no ferret zones" or other local prohibitions. California and Hawaii do not allow ferrets as pets. Consider contacting the Fish and Game Department, Department of Conservation or Wildlife Department (or whatever other official name the agency may be called) for the specific regulations for areas that may be destinations or waypoints in your itinerary. Other places to obtain useful information are the Humane Society and local ferret clubs or shelters.

10
Countries of the World

As I researched each of these countries and its current regulations regarding importing pets, I attempted to obtain complete and accurate information. Some countries provided complete information, and others suggested that individuals contact someone in the country for the appropriate information or forms. If you find inaccurate information, I apologize in advance for the error. Please contact me if you find errors. I contacted every country of the world, however, a few did not respond (or gave abbreviated information) despite numerous attempts. Most countries (tourist offices and embassies) were quite helpful and prompt. I am sure you will also find that to be the case as you plan for your travels with your pet. Information came from brochures, Websites, phone calls, and repeated letters and E-mails. I have attempted to use the original language as much as possible from the different sources. Some required modification to be more understandable, but most entries are in their original wording.

Under each country's heading, I have put its pet policy followed by the most useful Websites. I have included the in-country tourist office information when available, so the reader can make direct contact if desired even though I realize that this is not always convenient due to distance and language differences. In addition, I have included other tourist office information by country. I included Canada and the UK as often as I could so that readers in those countries could contact someone in their own country and someone who speaks their language. Those offices may serve as alternates in case the U.S. offices do not respond for some reason or another.

Tourist offices are the most likely places to supply information needed to prepare for a trip abroad. Consulates and high commissions may be helpful, too, and are included here if they were identified as providing tourist information.

Embassies are usually helpful and are included for each country. Some countries have official representation only at the United Nations, so the Mission to the UN information may be from these offices in some instances. An example is the country of Andorra. There is no embassy, but there is a Mission to the UN in New York.

A special note regarding phone numbers is in order. As each country responded to my requests, it provided the phone numbers in a certain format, and generally, they are printed in this book in that format. This may be confusing at times because some countries included the country code and some did not. For the reader's convenience, there is a listing of the world's international telephone codes in the appendix. Before calling any of the international numbers, consider whether the number printed here already includes the international code.

Afghanistan

A rabies inoculation certificate issued at the point of origin must accompany all dogs. Pets may enter as cargo only.

Afghanistan
    Afghan Tourist Organisation (ATO)
    Ansari Wat, Shar-i-Nau
    Kabul, Afghanistan
    Telephone: (93) 30512
    Website: micro.ifas.ufl.edu/~mmujtaba/afghan.html

Albania

A current International Health Certificate issued at the point of origin must accompany cats and dogs. Pets may enter as passenger's checked baggage, in the cabin or as cargo.

Website: www.albanian.com

Albania office
   Tourism Development Committee of Albania
   Bulevardi Dëshmorët e Kombit 8Tirana, Albania
   Telephone: (42) 58323
   Fax: (42) 58322
   E-mail: tdc@interalb.net

Albania office
   Albturist
   Bulevardi Zhan D'Ark 2
   Tirana, Albania
   Telephone: (42) 51051, 51046, or 51849
   Fax: (42) 51051 or 34359
   E-mail: none

Embassy of Albania
2100 S Street NW
Washington, DC 20008
Telephone: (202) 223-4942
Fax: (202) 628-7342
E-mail: albaniaemb@aol.com
Website: none

Algeria

A veterinarian rabies inoculation certificate, issued at the point of origin, must accompany cats and dogs. A health certificate, certificate of origin and statement by a veterinary surgeon that the bird is free from psittacosis must accompany psittacine birds.

Website: www.algerie-infotourisme.dz
Website: www.algeria-tourism.org

Algeria office
   Office Algérien National du Tourisme
   126A bis rue Didouche Mourad
   Algiers, Algeria
   Telephone: (21) 742 985
   Fax: (21) 747 049
   E-mail: none

Algeria office
    Office Algérien du Tourisme
    2, rue Ismaï Kerrar
    Algiers, Algeria
    Telephone: (21321) 71 30 60, 71 30 62
    Fax: (21321) 71 30 59
    E-mail: ont@wissal.dz

Embassy of Algeria
2118 Kalorama Road, NW
Washington, DC 20008
Telephone: (202) 265-2800
Fax: (202) 667-2174
E-mail: embalgus@cais.com
Website: www.algeria-us.org/

American Samoa

Cats and dogs need a certificate from Veterinary Officer stating that the animal has been given a prophylactic dose of anti-rabies vaccine not later than 120 days before entry and have been kept in quarantine for that same period. An Import Permit must be requested from the Department of Agriculture. Only a Certificate of Health must accompany animals from New Zealand, Australia, and U.K. from a salaried Veterinarian, attesting freedom from ecto and endoparasites.

Website: www.samoanet.com/americasamoa
Website: www.amsamoa.com

American Samoa office
American Samoa Office of Tourism
    P.O. Box 1147
    Pago Pago, American Samoa 96799
    Telephone: (684) 633-1092
    Fax: (684) 633-2092
    E-mail: samoa@samoatelco.com

American Samoa is an External Territory of the United States of America and is represented abroad by U.S. Embassies.

Andorra

Andorra states the requirements are the same as for France and Spain. Both a vaccination certificate and an International Health Certificate are required for your pet.

Website: www.sindicatinitiativa.ad

Andorra office
    Sindicat d'Initiativa Oficina de Turisme (Tourist Office)
    Carrer Dr Vilanova
    Andorra la Vella, Andorra
    Telephone: 820 214
    Fax: 825 823
    E-mail: none

UK office
    Andorra Tourism
    63, Westover Road
    London SW 2RF, UK
    Telephone: 171 874 48 06
    E-mail: none

USA office
    Andorra Tourism
    6800 N. Knox Avenue
    Lincolnwood, IL 60646
    Telephone: (708) 674-3091
    Fax: none
    E-mail: none

Permanent Mission of the Principality of Andorra to the United Nations
2 United Nations Plaza
25th Floor
New York, NY 10017
Telephone: (212) 750-8064
Fax: (212) 750-6630
E-mail: andorra@un.int
Website: www.andorra.ad

Angola

Dogs and cats must have a current International Health Certificate and a rabies inoculation certificate issued within four months preceding arrival.

For more information contact:
    Ministry of Health
    Rua Diogo Co 3, Caixa Postal 1201
    Luanda, Angola
    Telephone: 244-2-392787, 244-2-337994
    Telex: 3085, 1369 COMEX AN

Or
    State Import Agency
    Calcada do Municpio 10
    CP 1003
    Luanda, Angola
    Telephone: 244-2-392787, 244-2-337994
    Telex: 3085, 3169 COMEX AN

Website: www.angola.org/

Angola office
    Ministry of Trade and Tourism
    Ministerio do Comercio e Turismo
    Largo 4 de Fevereiro
    Luanda, Angola
    Telephone: 338-741
    Fax: 339-7833
    E-mail: none

Embassy of Angola to the United States
2100-2108 16th Street, NW
Washington, DC 20009
Telephone: (202) 785-1156
Fax: (202) 785-1258
E-mail: angola@angola.org
Website: www.angola.org

Anguilla

Animals must be accompanied by a health certificate issued by a veterinarian in the country of origin stating that the animal is free of any infections or contagious diseases and has not been in contact with any animals suffering from the same for the past 60 days. The animal must be vaccinated against rabies more than one month but less than one year before the date of importation.

The importation permit fee is U.S. $4.00 per animal. The inspection fee is U.S. $10.00 per animal. For more information contact the Department of Agriculture at Telephone: (264) 497-2615, Fax: (264) 497-0040.

Website: www.net.ai
Website: www.anguilla-vacation.com
Website: www.gov.ai

Anguilla office
    Anguilla Tourist Board
    P.O. Box 1388
    The Old Cotton Gin, Factory Plaza
    The Valley, Anguilla
    Telephone: 497-2759
    Telephone: (800) 553-4939 toll-free in USA
    Fax: 497-2710
    E-mail: atbtour@anguillanet.com

USA office
    Anguilla Public Relations & Marketing
    c/o The Wescott Group
    39 Monaton Drive
    Huntington Station, NY 11746
    Telephone: (516) 425-0900
    Telephone: (800) 553-4939 toll-free in USA
    Fax: (516) 425-0903
    E-mail: info@wescott-group.com
    Website: www.anguilla-vacation.com

Antigua and Barbuda

The Ministry has the following requirements for dogs entering Antigua and Barbuda:

- Pets must be in an acceptable quarantine facility in the United Kingdom for not less than six (6) months.
- Documentary evidence must be sent to the:
  Chief Veterinary officer
  Veterinary and Livestock Division
  Ministry of Agriculture
  P.O. Box 1284
  St John's
  Antigua and Barbuda
- The documents must contain:
  1. Flight and date of departure from USA.
  2. Name of kennel in United Kingdom.
  3. Flight Number and date of arrival into Antigua and Barbuda (Flight must be direct to Antigua and Barbuda).

The age of the dog is not important for entry into Antigua and Barbuda. No Pit Bulls or Ban dogs are allowed entry into Antigua and Barbuda. A fee of EC$150.00 is charged for services on arrival in Antigua and Barbuda.

Cats and dogs from Barbados, Dominica, Jamaica, Ireland, St Kitts &Nevis, St Lucia, St Vincent and the Grenadines, and United Kingdom may enter without the quarantine. They require a veterinarian good health certificate and a rabies inoculation certificate along with the import permit as mentioned above.

Website: www.antigua-barbuda.org
Website: www.interknowledge.com/antigua-barbuda

Antigua and Barbuda office
  Antigua Department of Tourism
  P.O. Box 363
  St John's, Antigua
  Telephone: 462 0480 or 463 0125

Fax: 462 2483
E-mail: info@antigua-barbuda.org

Canada office
Antigua and Barbuda Department of Tourism
60 St Clair Avenue East, Suite 304
Toronto, ON M4T 1N5, Canada
Telephone: (416) 961-3085
Fax: (416) 961-7218
E-mail: info@antigua-barbuda-ca.com

UK office
Antigua and Barbuda Department of Tourism
Antigua House
15 Thayer Street
London, WIM 5LD, UK
Telephone: 011 44 171 486 7073
Fax: 011 44 171 486 9970
E-mail: antbar@msn.com

USA: New York office
Antigua and Barbuda Department of Tourism
610 Fifth Avenue, Suite 311
New York, NY 10020
Telephone: (212) 541-4117
Telephone: (888) 268-4227 toll-free in USA
Fax: (212) 541-4789
E-mail: info@antigua-barbuda.org

Embassy of Antigua
3216 New Mexico Avenue, NW
Washington, DC 20016
Telephone: (202) 362-5122
E-mail: info@interknowledge.com
Website: none

Argentina

There is no quarantine in Argentina. A certificate stating that the animal is in good health and has been inoculated against rabies (for dogs and cats) is required. This document must be issued by a veterinarian and certified at the nearest Consulate of Argentina. These certificates must be submitted to the consulate for legalization. Be advised that all the documentation must be obtained within 10 days prior the departure of the animal or otherwise it will be void.

The airline must notify the station manager, at least 24 hours prior to arrival, at the point of entry giving notice of pets on board in order to ensure attendance of veterinary surgeon at the arrival airport.

RESTRICTIONS: All animals (including cats and dogs) coming from Africa or Asia (except Japan) must obtain prior telex authorization from quarantine department (Senasa) in Argentina.

An official International Health Certificate stating fowl plaque and psittacosis have not been diagnosed must accompany psittacine birds.

Website: www.sectur.gov.ar
Website: www.turismo.gov.ar
Website: www.wam.com.ar/tourism

Argentina office
    Secretaría de Turismo de la Nación (National Tourist Board)
    Calle Suipacha 1111, 20°
    1368 Buenos Aires, Argentina
    Telephone: (11) 4312 5621
    Fax: (11) 4313 6834
    E-mail: info@turismo.gov.ar

USA: California office
    Argentina Government Tourist Office
    5055 Wilshire Boulevard, Room 210
    Los Angeles, CA 90036
    Telephone: (213) 930-0681
    Fax: (213) 934-9076
    E-mail: none

USA: Florida office
    Argentina Government Tourist Office
    2655 Le Jeune Road, Penthouse Suite F
    Coral Gables, FL 33134

Telephone: (305) 442-1366
Fax: (305) 441-7029
E-mail: none

USA: New York office
    Argentina Government Tourist Office
    12 West 56th Street
    New York, NY 10019
    Telephone: (212) 603-0443
    Fax: (212) 315-5545
    E-mail: none

Embassy of Argentina
1600 New Hampshire Avenue, NW
Washington, DC 20009
Telephone: (202) 238-6400
Fax: (202) 332-3171
E-mail: argentina@veriomail.com
Website: www.embassyofargentina-usa.org

Armenia

Armenia requires a current International Health Certificate and a certificate of vaccination.

Website: www.cilicia.org
Website: www.armeniainfo.am
Website: www.arminco.com/tourarmenia/
Website: www.tourismarmenia.com

Armenia office
    Tourist Information Centre
    11, I Koryuni Lane
    Apartment 17
    Yerevan 375025, Armenia
    Telephone/Fax: (1) 524 158
    E-mail: info@tourismarmenia.com
    E-mail: tic@arminco.com

UK office
    Armenian Tourist Office
    Sunvil House
    Upper Square, Old Isleworth
    Middlesex, TW7 7BJ, UK
    Telephone: (020) 8758 4735
    Fax: (020) 8560 9889
    E-mail: none

Embassy of The Republic of Armenia
2225 R Street, NW
Washington, DC 20008
Telephone: (202) 319-1976
Fax: (202) 319-2982
E-mail: amembusadm@msn.com
Website: www.armeniaemb.org
The embassy also deals with inquires from Canada.

Aruba

Pets from South and Central America are not allowed. Otherwise, dogs, cats, parrots, and parakeets are permitted entry to the island when accompanied by a valid rabies and health certificate issued by a recognized veterinarian. The rabies vaccination should be issued 30 days prior to arrival. The International Health Certificate should be issued less than 14 days prior to arrival. Pets are not allowed at most hotels, however, so please check-in advance with your hotel to ask about its policy.

Website: www.aruba.com

Aruba office
    Aruba Tourism Authority
    P.O. Box 1019
    Oranjestad, Aruba
    Telephone: 297 (8) 23777
    Fax: 297 (8) 34702
    E-mail: ata.aruba@aruba.com

Canada office
Aruba Tourism Authority
5875 Highway No. 7, Suite 201
Woodbridge, ON L4L 1T9, Canada
Telephone: (905) 264-3434
Telephone: (800) 268-3042 toll-free in Ontario and Quebec
Fax: (905) 264-3437
E-mail: lourdes@aruba.com

UK office
Aruba Tourism Authority
25 Copperfield Street
London SE1 0EN, UK
Telephone: (020) 7928 1600
Fax: (020) 7928 1700
E-mail: aruba@saltmarshpr.co.uk

USA: Georgia office
Aruba Tourism Authority
1101 Juniper Street, NE
Suite 1101
Atlanta, GA 30309-7627
Telephone: (404) 89-ARUBA
Telephone: (800) TO-ARUBA toll-free in USA
Fax: (404) 873-2193
E-mail: ata.atlanta@toaruba.com
E-mail: ata.aruba@toaruba.com

Aruba is a dependency of the Netherlands and represented abroad by Royal Netherlands Embassies. See The Netherlands section for embassy contact details.

Australia

Australia has a very extensive and somewhat complicated system for importing pets. They categorize countries and have different quarantine requirements accordingly. Canada and the USA are in category 4 and there is a minimum of 30 days of quarantine. The UK is a category 2 country and they have 30-day quarantine for their pets.

All animals entering Australia require a permit to import, issued by AQIS (Australian Quarantine and Inspection Service). To obtain a permit to import, an application must be completed and returned to the quarantine station of your choice. Your application must include your pet's microchip number. Section 7 of your application form must be completed, signed, and stamped by an Official Veterinarian. The permit to import that will be returned to you defines additional import requirements. These additional requirements include tests, treatments, and inspections that must be completed before export. AQIS accepts that these requirements have been completed satisfactorily when certified on Veterinary Certificates A and B provided with the Import Permit. The original Import Permit, original Veterinary Certificates A and B, and the required laboratory reports and vaccination certificates must accompany your pet to Australia. Your pet and all accompanying documents must be linked unequivocally by means of your pet's microchip number, which must also be included on Veterinary Certificate A, and B and the laboratory reports.

There are 20 steps involved in the process. These are outlined on an information sheet for each category. These instructions may be obtained from the Website: www.affa.gov.au. Select "Quarantine" then select "Animals" and go from there.

Please note: a microchip is required, not optional.

Website: www.australia.com
Website: www.atc.net.au

Australian office
    Australian Tourist Commission
    P.O. Box 2721
    Sydney, NSW 2001, Australia
    Telephone: (2) 9360 1111
    Fax: (2) 9331 6469
    E-mail: none

UK office
    Australian Tourist Commission
    10-18 Putney Hill
    Putney, London SW15 6AA, UK

Telephone: 0990 022-000
Fax: 0181- 940-5221
E-mail: none

USA office
Australian Tourist Commission
2049 Century Park East
19th Floor
Los Angeles, CA 90067
Telephone: (310) 229-4870
Telephone: (800) 369-6863 toll-free in USA
Fax: (310) 552-1215
E-mail: none

Embassy of Australia
1601 Massachusetts Avenue, NW
Washington, DC 20036
Telephone: (202) 797-3000
Fax: (202) 797-3168
E-mail: public.affairs@austemb.org
Website: www.austemb.org

Austria

The importation into or transit through Austria of domestic dogs and/or cats is prohibited, unless a certificate issued by a licensed veterinarian in the state of residence of the owner is produced at the border station indicating in German (or in a certified German translation):
1. The name and address of the owner of the animal
2. The description of the animal (breed, sex, age, color)
3. The date of vaccination against rabies and lyssa (hydrophobia)
4. The brand of the authorized vaccine, the name of the producer, and the code of production.
5. The vaccination must be made at least 30 days and not more than one year before entry into Austria.

There is no quarantine in Austria. Pets may enter as passenger's checked baggage, in the cabin or as cargo.

For your convenience, the Austrian Embassy has a bilingual health and vaccination certificate, which can be used by a licensed veterinarian. Additional information may be obtained from the Austrian Embassy.

Website: www.austria-tourism.at
Website: www.anto.com

Austria office
Österreich Werbung (Austrian National Tourist Office - ANTO)
Margaretenstrasse 1
1040 Vienna, Austria
Telephone: (1) 587 2000
Fax: (1) 588 6620 or 588 6648 (information)
E-mail: oeinfo@oewwien.via.at

Canada: British Columbia office
Austrian National Tourist Office
200 Granville Street, Suite 1380
Vancouver, BC V6C 1S4, Canada
Telephone: (604) 683-5808
Fax: (604) 662-8528
E-mail: atradebc@uniserve.com

Canada: Montreal office
Austrian National Tourist Office
1010 Sherbrooke Street West, Suite 1410
Montreal, QC H3A 2R7, Canada
Telephone: (514) 849-3709
Fax: (514) 849-9577
E-mail: atc_mtr@istar.ca

Canada: Toronto office
Austrian National Tourist Office
2 Bloor Street East, Suite 3330
Toronto, ON M4W 1A8, Canada
Telephone: (416) 967-3381
Fax: (416) 967-4101
E-mail: anto-tor@sympatico.ca

UK office
    Austrian National Tourist Office (ANTO)
    P.O. Box 2363
    London W1A 2QB, UK
    Telephone: (020) 7629 0461
    Fax: (020) 7499 6038
    E-mail: info@anto.co.uk

USA: New York office
    Austrian National Tourist Office
    500 Fifth Avenue, Suite 800
    New York, NY 10110
    Telephone: (212) 575-7723
    Telephone: (800) 474-9696 toll-free in USA
    Fax: (212) 730-4568
    E-mail: info@oewnyc.com

Embassy of Austria
2343 Massachusetts Avenue, NW
Washington, DC 20008
Telephone: (202) 483-4474
Fax: (202) 895-6750
E-mail: usis@usia.co.at
Website: www.usembassy-vienna.at

Azerbaijan

Cats, dogs, other animals, birds (except pigeons), and fish may enter Azerbaijan. A health certificate and documentation of inoculations is required. Pets may enter as passenger's checked baggage, in the cabin or as cargo. Pets are not generally allowed in hotels.

Please be advised on the following procedure, which must be complied with in order to legalize different kinds of documents by the Consular Section.

All documents must be:
1. Acknowledged by a Notary Public;
2. Certified by the Secretary of your state;
3. Certified by the U.S. Department of State.

Consular fee for legalization is $20, except Power of Attorney, which is $35 for Azerbaijani citizens and $70 for non-citizens. All documents must be accompanied by a professional translation into the Azerbaijani language. Documents and translation must be printed. For information about translation, please call Consular Section at (202) 337-5912 from 10 a.m. to 1 p.m. Eastern Time.

Embassy of The Republic of Azerbaijan
2741 34th Street, NW
Washington, DC 20008
Telephone: (202) 337-3500
Fax: (202) 337-5911
E-mail: azerbaijan@azembassy.com
Website: www.azembassy.com/

Consular section:
Telephone: (202) 337-5912
Fax: (202) 337-5913
E-mail: consul@azembassy.com

Bahamas

An import permit is required to bring any animal into the Bahamas. This permit is available on line, www.Bahamas.com or by mail. There is a $10 processing fee.
 Director, Department of Agriculture
 P.O. Box N - 3704
 Nassau, Bahamas
 Telephone: (242) 325-7502 for more information
 Fax: (242) 325-3960
 E-mail: none

Dogs and cats less than six (6) months old from countries with rabies, such as the United States of America and Canada are prohibited entry into the Bahamas.

For the U.S. and Canada, the following are the main provisions of the import permit as it applies to dogs and cats:
 1. The animal must be 6 months of age or older.

Countries of the World

2. The animal must be accompanied by a valid certificate, which substantiates that it has been vaccinated against rabies within not less than 1 month and not more than 10 months before importation.
3. The animal must be accompanied by a Veterinary Health Certificate presented within 48 hours of arrival in the Commonwealth of The Bahamas to a licensed veterinarian for an examination.

All requirements listed on the import permit must be followed unless specifically authorized otherwise by the veterinary division of the department of agriculture in writing. No exceptions for sailing vessels, day visitors or otherwise.

Animals traveling without proper documentation may be denied entry or destroyed. Unless otherwise specified, an import permit is a single use document, which may be used at anytime up to the date of expiry (90 days).

Regulations for all other types of animals and relating to countries not mentioned above may be obtained from the Director of Agriculture (See address above).

Website: www.bahamas.com

Canada office
  Bahamas Tourist Office
  121 Bloor Street East, Suite 1101
  Toronto, ON M4W 3M5 Canada
  Telephone: (416) 968-2999
  Fax: (416) 968-6711
  E-mail: btoyyz@bahamas.com

UK office
  Bahamas Tourist Office
  3 The Billings
  Walnut Tree Close
  Guildford, Surrey GU1 4UL, UK
  Telephone: (01483) 448 900
  Fax: (01483) 571 846

E-mail: btogfd@bahamas.com
Website: www.bahamas.org.uk

USA: California office
Bahamas Ministry of Tourism
3450 Wilshire Boulevard, Suite 208
Los Angeles, CA 90010
Telephone: (213) 385-0033
Fax: (213) 383-3966
E-mail: none

USA: Miami office
Bahamas Tourist Office
19495 Biscayne Blvd.
Suite 809
Aventura, FL 33180
Telephone: (305) 932-0051
Telephone: (800) 823-3136 toll-free in USA
Fax: (305) 682-8758

USA: New York office
Bahamas Tourist Office
150 East 52nd Street, 28th Floor North
New York, NY 10022
Telephone: (212) 758-2777
Telephone: (800) 4-BAHAMAS toll-free in USA
Fax: (212) 753-6531
E-mail: none

Embassy of the Bahamas
2220 Massachusetts Avenue, NW
Washington, DC 20008
Telephone: (202) 319-2660
Fax: (202) 319-2668
E-mail: bahemb@aol.com
Website: none

Bahrain

All airlines and shipping agencies require a valid certificate issued by a competent Veterinary Authority in the country of origin for all domestic pets, birds, and animals, going to Bahrain. The certificate should state that the bird or animal is healthy and free from any infection or contagious disease.

For dogs, an additional valid certificate of vaccination against rabies and distemper is also required.

The Bahraini Health Authority has the right to refuse admission of birds and animals that are not accompanied by the required certificates or order their extermination if already entered in Bahrain. Under certain conditions, the owner may be asked to take his or her pet back to the country of departure.

The health certificate is valid for one month from date of issue, and the vaccination certificate is valid for six months. The U.S. Arab Chamber of Commerce must legalize all shipping documents.

Documentation for Pets:
Website: www.bahrainembassy.org/pets.html

Website: www.bahraintourism.com
Website: www.bahrainembassy.org/tourism.html

Bahrain office
    Bahrain Tourism Company (BTC)
    P.O. Box 5831
    Manama, Bahrain
    Telephone: 530 530
    Fax: 530 867
    E-mail: bahtours@batelco.com.bh

Embassy of The State of Bahrain
3502 International Drive, NW
Washington, DC 20008
Telephone: (202) 342-0741
Fax: (202) 362-2192
E-mail: info@bahrainembassy.org
E-mail: bahrain@consulate.org
E-mail: consular@bahrainembassy.org
Website: www.bahrainembassy.org

Bangladesh

All that is required to take a pet into Bangladesh is a certificate of vaccination from a registered veterinarian of the country of origin. An import permit is not required. The document should be in English.

Bangladesh office
National Tourism Organization
233 Airport Road
Tejgaon, Dhaka 1215
Telephone: 880 2 8119192
Fax: 880 2 8117235
E-mail: bpcho@bangla.net

Embassy of The People's Republic of Bangladesh
3510 International Drive, NW
Washington, DC 20007
Telephone: (202) 244-0183
Fax: (202) 244-5366
E-mail: BanglaEmb@aol.com
E-mail: bdenq@bangladoot.org
Website: www.bangladoot.org

Barbados

The following guidelines must be followed when importing any animal into Barbados:
- An import permit must be obtained from the Chief Veterinary Officer before the importation of all animals, reptiles, and birds.
- A Veterinary Officer must examine the animal before it is allowed to leave the customs area.
- Dogs and cats must be free of any communicable disease. These animals may be imported by permit directly from the UK, Ireland, Jamaica, St Kitts & Nevis, Antigua, St Lucia, and St Vincent. Cats and dogs originating from all other countries must undergo 6 months quarantine in Britain after which time an import permit can be secured.

For further inquiries, contact Veterinary Services at Telephone: (246) 427-5073 or Fax: (246) 420-8444.

Countries of the World

Website: www.barbados.org

Barbados office
 Barbados Tourism Authority
 P.O. Box 242
 Harbour Road
 Bridgetown, Barbados
 Telephone: 427 2623
 Fax: 426 4080
 E-mail: btainfo@barbados.org

Canada office
 Barbados Tourism Authority
 105 Adelaide Street West, Suite 1010
 Toronto, ON M5H 1P9, Canada
 Telephone: (888) BARBADOS toll-free in Canada
 Telephone: (416) 214-9880
 Fax: (416) 214-9882
 E-mail: btapublic@globalserve.net

UK office
 Barbados Tourism Authority
 263 Tottenham Court Road
 London W1T 7LA, UK
 Telephone: (020) 7636 9448
 Fax: (020) 7637 1496
 E-mail: btauk@barbados.org

USA: California office
 Barbados Tourism Authority
 3440 Wiltshire Boulevard, Suite 1215
 Los Angeles, CA 90010
 Telephone: (213) 380-2198 or 380-2199
 Telephone: (800) 221-9831 toll-free in USA
 Fax: (213) 384-2763
 Email: btala@barbados.org

USA: Florida office
 Barbados Tourism Authority
 150 Alhambra Circle, Suite 1270

Coral Gables, FL 33132
Telephone: (305) 442-7471
Telephone: (800) 221-9831 toll-free in USA
Fax: (305) 567-2844
Email: btamiami@barbados.org

USA: New York office
Barbados Tourism Authority
800 Second Avenue
New York, NY 10017
Telephone: (212) 986-6516
Telephone: (800) 221-9831 toll-free in USA
Fax: (212) 573-9850
E-mail: btany@barbados.org

Embassy of Barbados
2144 Wyoming Avenue, NW
Washington, DC 20008
Telephone: (202) 939-9200
Fax: (202) 332-7467
E-mail: BARBADOS@oas.org
Website: none

Belarus

Belarus does not have any Government-supported National Tourist Offices in the USA, Canada, or U.K. The information about travel should be obtained at the respective embassies.

Certification of Veterinarian's Examination Statement confirmed by a local office of USDA (or equivalent) is required. The documents are also needed that show that the pet has received all the vaccinations necessary for international travel (the list of vaccines is available through most local veterinarians). The vaccination should be made not earlier than 2 weeks before travel (i.e. 5 days before travel is not OK, and this is strictly enforced). The customs will charge the traveler a customs-processing fee for every pet, which is quite nominal and currently is about 7 US dollars.

Pets need to be registered with a local veterinary service in Belarus within one month of arrival. Normally it is possible to transport pets but it is possible that some transportation will not allow pets. General custom is that in a bus a pet should travel in the back of the bus (Back rows of seats, though it should stay on the floor, not on a seat) and if a bus has a rear door - to enter through the rear door.

Technically translations (to Russian/Belarussian) are required but this is normally not enforced. If a person arrives with a pet and documents are in English and not translated, most of the time there will be no problems. Certainly, a translation of the pet's documents will make travel more calm and easy.

Pigeons are prohibited entry. Pets may enter as passenger's checked baggage either in the cabin or as cargo.

Website: www.belintourist.by

Belarus office
    Belintourist
    Prospect Masherova 19
    220004 Minsk, Belarus
    Telephone: (17) 226 9840
    Fax: (17) 223 1143 or 226 9352
    E-mail: office@belintourist.by

Canada office
    Embassy of Belarus
    600-130 Albert Street
    Ottawa, ON 1P 5G4, Canada
    Telephone: (613) 233-9994
    Fax: (613) 233-8500
    E-mail: belamb@igs.net

UK office
    Embassy of Belarus
    6, Kensington Court
    London W8 5DL, UK
    Telephone: (44 207) 937 32 88
    Fax: (44 207) 361 00 05
    E-mail: Belarus@elemb.freeserve.co.uk

Embassy of Belarus
1619 New Hampshire Avenue, NW
Washington, DC 20009
Telephone: (202) 986-1606
Fax: (202) 986-1805
E-mail: usa@belarusembassy.org
E-mail: consul@belarusembassy.org
Website: www.belarusembassy.org

Belgium

There is no quarantine to bring a pet cat or dog to Belgium as long as you respect the following procedures, which vary depending on whether you are traveling with your pet, or you are sending the animal alone.

Traveling from the U.S. to Belgium with your pets (dog-cat):

The procedure is simple. A U.S. certified veterinarian surgeon must issue a rabies certificate and an International Health Certificate. The Belgian authorities do not require these certificates to be USDA stamped.

1. The Rabies Certificate:
   The Belgian form must be used. This includes the following pieces of information:
   - Statement in English that the animal has been inoculated with a U.S. official, inspected and approved rabies vaccine,
   - Date of vaccination,
   - Type of vaccine used and expiration date, the name of the manufacturer and the manufacturer's batch number
   - Description of the animal (sex, age, breed, hair color and markings),
   - Name and address of owner of the animal (in the U.S. and in Belgium).
   - The rabies vaccination has to be administered at least 30 days before the travel and not more than one year before.

   Remarks:
   - The 3-year vaccine commonly used in the U.S. will not be taken into account when traveling to Belgium. You

must comply with the 30 days to 1-year rule described above.
- For animals vaccinated before the age of 3 months, the validity of the vaccination is limited to 3 months.
- For animals revaccinated within the year after a previous vaccination (booster), the validity is immediate (date of the vaccination).

2. The International Health Certificate:
- A U.S. certified veterinarian surgeon must also issue this certificate. Your veterinarian will be able to provide you with a copy of the International Health Certificate. The health certificate must be issued within 10 days before entry into Belgium.

Sending pets unaccompanied from the U.S. to Belgium

You still have to ask your veterinarian to fill out a rabies certificate and a health certificate; and you must get an import permit. The importer can obtain the import permit by contacting:

The Ministry of Agriculture-Veterinary Services
WTC 3 –5th Floor
Boulevard Simon Bolivar 30
B- 1000 Brussels, Belgium
Telephone: 32.2.208.3655 or 3630
Fax: 32.2.208.3612

In order to get this permit, you must submit the following pieces of information:
- The form "Going to Belgium with a pet - Information Form" properly filled out,
- A copy of the rabies certificate issued by a certified veterinary surgeon,
- The Form "Application for Import or Transit Authorization for Live Animals."

After the Belgian Veterinarian Services in Brussels examine your request, they will send you back the Import Authorization. You will have to attach this authorization to the International Health Certificate and the rabies certificate and make sure that your animal will travel with this paperwork. The original documents must accompany the animal. Copies can be used to obtain the permit.

Special regulations for "dangerous breeds":
Please contact the Washington D.C. Agricultural Office if your dog belongs to the following breeds, as they fall under different regulations: Pit Bull Terrier, Bull Terrier, Fila Brasileiro, Mastiff (all origins), Tosa Inu, Band dog, Akita Inu, Rhodesian Ridgeback, Dogo Argentino, Dogue de Bordeaux, American Staffordshire Terrier, Rottweiler, English Terrier (Staffordshire bull-terrier).

Information about Identification and Registration of Dogs in Belgium:
All dogs must be identified in one of two ways:
1. Either a tattoo; or,
2. An electronic chip.

This regulation is also mandatory for the dogs of foreigners planning to stay in Belgium more than 6 months. This regulation will not apply to dogs of owners staying less than 6 months in Belgium; in this case, the owner will not have to do anything, regarding either the identification or the registration of his animal.

Dogs coming from foreign countries and which were already identified in their country of origin will not have to follow the identification procedure in Belgium as long as the identification system used conforms to the ISO standard. The owner of the animal will just have to register his dog at ABIEC (Belgian Association for Identification and Registration of Dogs).

If the dog coming from abroad does not have any tattoo and if its owner intends to stay more than 6 months on Belgian territory, the owner will have to go to a veterinarian in Belgium in order to identify the animal (by a tattoo or a chip) and ask the veterinarian to do the necessary in order to register the dog at ABIEC.

The registration cost for the owner is between 200 and 500 Belgian Francs and the identification cost is between 300 (for a tattoo) and 1500 Belgian Francs (for a chip); prices may vary.

If you need any further information on this subject, you may contact the Washington, DC office (Telephone: (202) 625-5839 or Fax: (202)

342-2683) or your veterinarian in Belgium or ABIEC, the Belgian association in charge of identification and registration.

Association Belge d'Identification et d'Enregistrement Canins (ABIEC)
Boîte postale 168
B-1060 Bruxelles
Belgium
Telephone: 070/22.24.45
Fax: 070/22.24.46

- You can obtain a copy of the required forms (Health Certificate, Rabies certificate, and "Going to Belgium with a pet - Information Form") by downloading them directly from www.diplobel.fgov.be/usa/GoingtoBelgium.
- There will be no derogation granted for a kitten or puppy. Kittens and puppies, as older animals must be vaccinated against rabies. If they are too young to get a rabies shot, the owner has to wait until the animal can be vaccinated and then wait 30 days after the vaccination to be able to travel.
- The importation of young animals, less than 7 weeks old is forbidden (for their welfare), except when a mother travels with her unweaned offspring.
- We highly recommend that you check with your airline company for additional requirements.
- IATA regulations applying to air transport must be respected.
- Some airline carriers, for good reason, do not accept gestating animals.

Parrots, parakeets, and other birds of the family psittacidae (limit of 2 per family) may enter with an International Health Certificate less than 2 months old stating that the birds are free of fowl plague, Newcastle disease, cholera, psittacosis, pullorum disease, and Pacheco's disease.

For any additional questions, you may contact:
The Agricultural Office
At the Embassy of Belgium
3330 Garfield Street, NW
Washington, DC 20008
Tel (202) 625-5839

Fax (202) 342-2683
Email: Ldba3@cais.com

Website: www.visitbelgium.com
Website: www.visitflanders.com
Website: www.belgique-tourisme.net (Brussels & Ardennes Information)
Website: www.belgium-tourism.com (Brussels & Flanders Information)
Website: www.tib.be (Brussels Information)

Belgium office
    Belgian Tourist Office - Brussels & Ardennes
    63 rue du Marché-aux-Herbes
    B-1000 Brussels, Belgium
    Telephone: (2) 504 0390
    Fax: (2) 504 0270
    E-mail: info@opt.be

Belgium office
    TIB - Tourist and Information Office of Brussels
    Town Hall
    Grand'Place
    B-1000 Brussels, Belgium
    Telephone: (02) 513 8940
    Fax: (02) 513 8320
    E-mail: tourism.brussels@tib.be

Belgium office
    Belgian Tourist Office - Brussels & Flanders
    Grasmarkt 63
    B-1000 Brussels, Belgium
    Telephone: (02) 513 0390
    Fax: (02) 504 0270
    E-mail: info@toerismevlaanderen.be

Canada office
    Belgian Tourist Office - Brussels & Ardennes
    43 rue de Buade, Bureau 525

Québec City, QC G1R 4A2, Canada
Telephone: (418) 692-4939
Fax: (418) 692-4974
E-mail: opt.walbru.quebec@videotron.net

UK office
Belgian Tourist Office Brussels & Wallonia
217 Marsh Wall
London E14 9FW, UK
Telephone: 0800/9545 245 free brochure line (UK only)
Telephone: 0906/3020 245 live operator (50p/minute)
Fax: 20 7531 0393
E-mail: info@belgiumtheplaceto.be
E-mail: info@belgium-tourism.org

UK office
Tourism Flanders - Brussels
31 Pepper Street
London E14 9RW, UK
Telephone: 20 7867 0311 (public information line)
Fax: 20 7458 0045
E-mail: office@flanders-tourism.org

USA: New York office
Belgium Tourist Office
780 Third Avenue, Suite 1501
New York, NY 10017
Telephone: (212) 758-8130
Fax: (212) 355-7675
E-mail: info@visitbelgium.com

Embassy of Belgium
3330 Garfield Street, NW
Washington, DC 20008
Telephone: (202) 333-6900
Fax: (202) 333-3079
E-mail: washington@diplobel.org
Website: www.diplobel.org/usa/default.htm

Belize

Pets require a health certificate from a certified veterinary clinic from the country of origin. An import permit needs to be issued by the Veterinary Clinic in Belize. You can contact them at Telephone/Fax: 501-2-45230 or E-mail: deshield@btl.net.

Your pet will not be quarantined as long as you follow the procedures and the animal is healthy. Documents do not require translation. English is the official language.

The Belize Agricultural Health Authority (BAHA) is considering removing the requirement of an import permit for pets visiting Belize. This will probably be dealt with sometime this coming year. For now, however, an import permit can be obtained from any of the official BAHA offices. Belize City: 501 2 44794, Fax: 501 2 45230. Belmopan: 501 8 20197, Fax: 501 23084. Orange Walk: 501 3 22301 (Fax/Phone).

The permit outlines the conditions of importation, which usually states that the animal has proof of current vaccinations (especially rabies), and a recent (within 72hrs) health certificate from an accredited (registered) veterinarian of the country of origin. The Animal Health Authority of Belize (BAHA) can also be reached by E-mail: baha@btl.net.

The Animal Medical Centre of Belize is a private veterinary clinic in Belize that provides the service of getting the permit for those people who may not be able to access BAHA offices. Contact Michael DeShield, BVSc, MSc, Senior Veterinary Surgeon at 011 501 2 33781(Telephone/Fax) or E-mail: deshield@btl.net.

Website: www.travelbelize.org
Website: www.belize.com
Website: www.belizenet.com

There is no longer a Belize tourist office in the USA. The toll-free number for the USA is (800) 624-0698.

Belize office
    Belize Tourist Board
    New Central Bank Building, Level 2
    Cabourel Lane
    P.O. Box 325
    Belize City, Belize
    Telephone: 011-501-2-31913
    Fax: 011-501-2-31943
    E-mail: info@travelbelize.org

Embassy of Belize
2535 Massachusetts Drive, NW
Washington, DC 20008
Telephone: (202) 332-9635
Fax: (202) 332-6888
E-mail: bcci@btl.net
Website: www.embassyofbelize.org

Benin

Pets are welcome in Benin with a recent International Health Certificate and a vaccination certificate that indicates that the pet has been properly vaccinated within 15 days of arrival. No translation or certification of documents is required.

Benin office
    Ministère du Commerce et du Tourisme
    BP 2037
    Cotonou, Benin
    Telephone: 397 010 or 397 014 or 315 426
    Fax: 301 970
    E-mail: none

Benin office
    Benin-Societe Beninoise Pour La Promo du Tourism
    BP 1508
    Cotonou, Benin
    Telephone: 229-30-05-84, 31-54-02, 30-19-84
    Fax: none
    E-mail: none

Embassy of Benin
2124 Kalorama Road, NW
Washington, DC 20008
Telephone: (202) 232-6656
Fax: (202) 265-1996
E-mail: none
Website: none

Bermuda

Pet owners should apply for an Import Permit as far as possible in advance of arrival, by letter or application form, to:

Director
Department of Agriculture & Fisheries P.O. Box HM 834
Hamilton HM CX
Bermuda
Telephone: (441) 236-4201
Fax: (441) 236-7582
Telex: 3246 CWAGY-BA

Application must specify particulars of the animal(s) involved and origin of shipment. In order to simplify this process, application forms (not permits) are available from any of the Bermuda Department of Tourism offices abroad (New York, Atlanta, Boston, Chicago, Toronto, and London, England).

Upon receipt of the application, the Department of Agriculture & Fisheries will reply requesting the specific health documentation necessary for the animal in question. This information may be sent by mail, courier, or by FAX. If satisfied with the information supplied, the Department of Agriculture & Fisheries will issue an import permit for the animal. This Import Permit, (original or FAX copy), together with the original health document must accompany the animal and be available for inspection upon arrival.

Website: www.bermudatourism.com

Bermuda office
Department of Tourism
P.O. Box HM465

Hamilton HM BX, Bermuda
Telephone: 292 0023
Fax: 292 7537
E-mail: travel@bermudatourism.com

Canada office
Bermuda Department of Tourism
Suite 1004, 1200 Bay Street
Toronto, ON M5R 2A5, Canada
Telephone: (416) 923-9600
Fax: (416) 923-4840
E-mail: gfairhurst@bermudatourism.com

UK office
Bermuda Tourism
1 Battersea Church Road
London SW11 3LY, UK
Telephone: (020) 7771 7001
Fax: (020) 7771 7037
E-mail: bermudatourism@cibgroup.co.uk

USA: Georgia office
Bermuda Department of Tourism
245 Peachtree Center Avenue, NE
Suite 803
Atlanta, GA 30303
Telephone: (404) 524-1541
Telephone: (800) 223-6106 toll-free in USA
Fax: (404) 586-9933
E-mail: none

USA: Massachusetts office
Bermuda Department of Tourism
44 School Street, Suite 1010
Boston, MA 02108
Telephone: (617) 742-0405
Telephone: (800) 223-6106 toll-free in USA
Fax: (617) 723-7786
E-mail: none

USA: New York office
    Bermuda Department of Tourism
    205 East 42nd Street, 16th Floor
    New York, NY 10017
    Telephone: (212) 818-9800
    Telephone: (800) 223-6106 toll-free in USA
    Fax: (212) 983-5289
    E-mail: frontdesk@bermudatourism.com

Bermuda is a British Overseas Territory and is represented abroad by British Embassies. See also: United Kingdom.

Bhutan

There is no quarantine of pets upon arrival to Bhutan. Pets need to have an International Health Certificate and a vaccination certificate. No translation or certification of the documents is required.

Travel to Bhutan is highly regulated. All visitors must be on a pre-paid, pre-planned guided tour. Independent travel is not permitted.

Website: www.kindomofbhutan.com
Website: www.btb.com.bt
Website: www.farfungplaces.com

Bhutan office
    Tourism Authority of Bhutan
    P.O. Box 126
    Thimphu, Bhutan
    Telephone: (2) 323 251/2 or 325 121/2
    Fax: (2) 323 695
    E-mail: tab@druknet.net.bt
    E-mail: btb@druknet.net.bt

Bhutan office
    Bhutan Tourism Corporation Limited (BTCL)
    P.O. Box 159
    Thimphu, Bhutan
    Telephone: (2) 324 045 or 322 045 or 322 647 or 322 854
    Fax: (2) 323 392 or 322 479
    E-mail: btcl@druknet.net.bt

USA office
  Bhutan Tourism Corporation Limited (BTCL)
  c/o Far Fung Places
  1914 Fell Street
  San Francisco, CA 94117
  Telephone: (415) 386-8306
  Fax: (415) 386-8104
  E-mail: info@farfungplaces.com

Consulate-General of Bhutan
2 UN Plaza, 27th Floor
New York, NY 10017
Telephone: (212) 826-1919
Fax: (212) 826-2998
E-mail: pmbnewyork@aol.com

Bolivia

Pets may be imported into Bolivia with a vaccination certificate and an International Health Certificate (form APHIS-7001) issued by a veterinarian. These must be dated no more than 3 months before arrival. A Bolivian Consulate must legalize the documents. No translation is necessary.

Website: www.mcei.gov.bo

Bolivia office
  Viceministerio de Turismo
  Avenida Mariscal Santa Cruz, Palacio de Comunicaciones
  Piso 16
  La Paz, Bolivia
  Telephone: (22) 367 464
  Fax: (22) 374 630
  E-mail: vturismo@mcei.gov.bo

Embassy of Bolivia
3014 Massachusetts Avenue, NW
Washington, DC 20008
Telephone: (202) 483-4410
Fax: (202) 328-3712

E-mail: bolembus@erols.com
Website: www.bolivia-usa.org

Bonaire

Bringing dogs and cats to Bonaire presents no problem. You must have a current International Health Certificate and a rabies certificate. Air Jamaica does not allow pets. Other airlines may also have similar restrictions.

Website: www.infobonaire.com
Website: www.bonaire.org
Website: www.interknowledge.com/bonaire

Bonaire office
    Tourism Corporation Bonaire
    Kaya Grandi 2
    Kralendijk, Bonaire, NA
    Telephone: (717) 8322 or 8649
    Fax: (717) 8408
    E-mail: info@tourismbonaire.com or tcb@infobonaire.com

Canada office
    Bonaire Government Tourist Office
    Telephone: (800) 826-6247 toll-free in Canada

USA: New York office
    Bonaire Government Tourist Office
    Adams Unlimited
    10 Rockefeller Plaza, Suite 900
    New York, NY 10020
    Telephone: (800) BONAIRE toll-free in USA
    Telephone: (212) 956-5912
    Fax: (212) 956-5913
    E-mail: usa@tourismbonaire.com

Bosnia and Herzegovina

Birds, cats, and dogs require a veterinarian Good Health Certificate issued at the point of origin. Additionally cats and dogs require a rabies inoculation certificate.

Website: www.mvp.gov.ba
Website: www.geog.gmu.edu/gess/jwc/bosnia/bosnia.html

Bosnia and Herzegovina office
   Ministry of Foreign Affairs
   Musala 2
   71000 Sarajevo, Bosnia and Herzegovina
   Telephone: (33) 281 100
   Fax: (33) 472 188
   E-mail: info@mvp.gov.ba

Embassy of Bosnia and Herzegovina
2109 E Street, NW
Washington, DC 20037
Telephone: (202) 337-1500
Fax: (202) 337-1502
E-mail: info@bosnianembassy.org
Website: www.bosnianembassy.org
The embassy also deals with inquires from Canada.

Botswana

Cats and dogs need an import permit from the Director of Veterinary Services (See below) Moreover, a health certificate stating that the animal was vaccinated against rabies:
- Dogs: at least 30 days and not more than 3 years before importation with the Flury or Kelev strain of vaccine;
- Cats: at least one month and not more than one year before importation.

Translations may be required.

An import permit for pets may be obtained from:
   Director of Animal Health and Production
   Private Bag 0032
   Gaborone, Botswana
   Telephone: (+267) 350
   Fax: (+267) 303-744

Website: www.botswanatourism.org
Website: www.gov.bw/tourism

Botswana office
    Department of Tourism
    Ministry of Commerce and Industry
    Private Bag 0047
    Gaborone, Botswana
    Telephone: (+267) 353 024
    Fax: (+267) 308 675
    E-mail: botswanatourism@gov.bw

UK office
    Department of Tourism UK Representation Office
    Southern Skies Marketing
    Index House
    St George's Lane
    Ascot
    Berkshire SL5 7EU, UK
    Telephone: (0) 1344 636430
    Fax: (0) 1344 873737
    E-mail: botswanatourism@aol.com

USA office
    Botswana Department of Tourism
    Kartengener Associates, Inc.
    631 Commack Road
    Suite 1A
    Commack, NY 11725
    Telephone: (631) 858-1270
    Fax: (631) 858-1279
    E-mail: kainyc@att.net

Embassy of Botswana
1531-3 New Hampshire Avenue, NW
Washington, DC 20036
Telephone: (202) 244-4990
Fax: (202) 244-4164
E-mail: none
Website: www.gov.bw

Brazil

To import a domestic pet into Brazil, please follow these instructions:
- International Health Certificate issued by a local veterinarian. This must be dated within one week before departure.
- Take this document to the USDA to be endorsed.
- Legalization by the Brazilian Consulate – Fee U.S. $20.00 (Twenty Dollars) in cash or U.S. Postal Money Order.

Legalization is valid for 30 days from the stamped date of the USDA.

Website: www.rioconventionbureau.com.br
Website: www.embratur.gov.br

Brazil office
 EMBRATUR - Instituto Brasileiro do Turismo (Brazilian Tourist Board)
 SCN, Quadra 02, Bloco 'G'
 CEP 70712-907 Brasília, DF, Brazil
 Telephone: (61) 429 7777
 Fax: (61) 429 7910
 E-mail: webm@embratur.gov.br
 Also in Rio de Janeiro: Telephone: (21) 2509 6017, E-mail: rio@embratur.gov.br).

UK office
 Brazilian Tourist Office
 32 Green Street
 London W1K 7AT, UK
 Telephone: (020) 7629 6909
 Fax: (020) 7399 9102
 E-mail: tourism@brazil.org.uk
 Website: www.brazil.org.uk

USA: Florida office
 Brazilian Tourism Office
 2828 SW 22nd Street
 Miami, FL 33145
 Telephone: (800) 544-5503 toll-free in USA
 E-mail: none

USA: New York office
Brazilian Tourism Office
551 5th Avenue, Suite 590
New York, NY 10176
Telephone: (212) 286-9600
Fax: (212) 490-9294
E-mail: none

Brazilian Consulate in Miami
2601 South Bayshore Drive, Suite 800
Miami, FL 33133
Telephone: (305) 285-6200/6209
Fax: (305) 285-6229
E-mail: consbras@brazilmiami.org
Website: www.brazilmiami.org

Embassy of Brazil
3006 Massachusetts Avenue, NW
Washington, DC 20008
Telephone: (202) 238-2700
Fax: (202) 238-2827
E-mail: webmaster@brasilemb.org
Website: www.brasilemb.org

British Virgin Islands

The following information has been provided by the British Virgin Islands Department of Agriculture, Veterinary Division. The BVI is a rabies free territory and in order to protect against the spread of this disease, the following regulations are strictly adhered to and enforced. Please note that there are two sets of regulations regarding the importation of pets to the BVI. The first deals with pets from countries, which are known to have outbreaks of rabies, such as mainland USA & Canada. The second set of regulations is for countries, which are believed to be rabies free.

Importation of Dogs & Cats from Nonscheduled (Rabies Endemic) Countries
Your dog or cat will only be permitted entry into the British Virgin Islands accompanied by an Animal Health Certificate issued by the Veterinary Authority (Government) in the country of origin stating:

- Proper identification of the animal.
- That the dog or cat is healthy and free from symptoms of infectious or contagious disease.
- That the dog or cat has been treated against internal and external parasites.
- That the dog has been vaccinated against canine parvovirus, distemper, hepatitis/adenovirus, parainfluenza, leptospirosis, and lyme disease.
- That the cat has been vaccinated against panleukopenia, feline rhinotracheitis, feline calicivirus & feline leukemia.
- That the area of origin is not currently under Rabies quarantine.
- That the dog or cat has had at least two Rabies INACTIVATED vaccines; the first not earlier than three months of age and another at least six months later. That four months after the first inoculation and at least on month after the second or subsequent vaccines, serological test has been carried out to determine the presence of adequate virus neutralizing antibody titers, prior to departure.
- Animals will be permitted to enter the BVI up to twelve months after the last booster shot, subject to positive blood tests.

1. Original vaccination certificate and laboratory test reports must accompany the animal.
2. The Dog or Cat must be found clinically healthy upon arrival in the BVI.
3. Young animals not subjected to vaccination and serology are allowed entry under special quarantine arrangements.
4. The veterinary division must be given at least 24 hours notice of confirmed arrival date, time, airline or vessel and port of entry. This will facilitate unnecessary delays and avoid detention of animal for veterinary clearance at port of entry.
5. The animal will be taken at port of entry directly to a place of quarantine and will be held there for a period of three to six months. This will be determined upon arrival.
6. All cost associated with quarantine are to be borne by the owner.

7. All required conditions must be met and all documents including; Import Permit, Veterinary Health Certificate, Vaccination Certificate & Lab Test Reports must be presented at the port of disembarkation in order to facilitate clearance and to avoid the otherwise unpleasant but necessary options such as animals being kept in a quarantine facility, deportation or euthanasia.

Importation of Dogs & Cats from Scheduled Countries
Conditions of entry from the following countries: Antigua, Australia, Barbados, Dominica, Jamaica, Montserrat, New Zealand, Republic of Ireland, St. Kitts, Anguilla, St. Lucia, St. Vincent, United States Virgin Islands, & the United Kingdom

Your dog or cat will only be permitted entry into the British Virgin Islands accompanied by an Animal Health Certificate issued by the Veterinary Authority (Government) in the country of origin stating:
- Proper identification of the animal.
- That the dog or cat is healthy and free from symptoms of infectious or contagious disease.
- That the dog or cat has been treated against internal and external parasites.
- That the dog has been vaccinated against canine parvovirus, distemper, hepatitis/adenovirus, parainfluenza, leptospirosis, and lyme disease.
- That the cat has been vaccinated against panleukopenia, feline rhinotracheitis, feline calicivirus & feline leukemia.
- That the animal has been in the country of origin for at least 6 months immediately preceding importation to the British Virgin Islands.
- That there has been no rabies among unquarantined animals in country of origin/export for the past 24 months.

1. The dog or cat must be found clinically healthy on arrival.
2. The veterinary division must be given at least 24 hours notice of confirmed arrival date, time, airline or vessel and port of entry. This will facilitate unnecessary delays and avoid detention of animal for veterinary clearance at port of entry.

3. All required conditions must be met and all documents including; Import Permit, Veterinary Health Certificate, Vaccination Certificate & Lab Test Reports must be presented at the port of disembarkation in order to facilitate clearance and to avoid the otherwise unpleasant but necessary options such as animals being kept in a quarantine facility, deportation or euthanasia.

For more information and advice, please contact the Chief Agricultural Officer, Dr. Arthur Peterson at: (284) 495-2532/2451 or E-mail: bvigovvet@hotmail.com.

Website: www.bviwelcome.com
Website: www.bvitouristboard.com

BVI office
British Virgin Islands Tourist Board
P.O. Box 134
Road Town
Tortola, British Virgin Islands
Telephone: 43134
Fax: 43866
E-mail: bvitourb@surfbvi.com

Canada office
British Virgin Islands Tourist Board
801 York Mills Road, Suite 210
Don Mills, ON M3B 1X7, Canada
Telephone: (416) 283-2235
Telephone: (800) 835-8530 toll-free in Canada
Fax: none
E-mail: none

UK office
British Virgin Islands Tourist Board
55 Newman Street
London W1T 3EB, UK
Telephone: (020) 7947 8200
Fax: (020) 7947 8279
E-mail: bvi@bho.fcb.com

USA: California office
 British Virgin Islands Tourist Board
 1804 Union St
 San Francisco, CA 94123
 Telephone: (415) 775-0344
 Telephone: (800) 835-8530 toll-free in USA
 Fax: (415) 775-2554
 E-mail: none

USA: New York office
 British Virgin Islands Tourist Board
 370 Lexington Avenue, Suite 1605
 New York, NY 10017
 Telephone: (212) 696-0400
 Telephone: (800) 835-8530 toll-free in USA
 Fax: (212) 949-8254
 E-mail: bvitouristboard@worldnet.att.net

The British Virgin Islands are a British Overseas Territory represented abroad by British Embassies. See also: United Kingdom.

Brunei Darussalam

The following regulations are presently in force under the Quarantine and prevention of Disease Enactment (Cap. 47 of the Laws of Brunei) and subsequent enabling regulations duly promulgated.

1. Dogs, cats, and related species imported shall be accompanied by an International Health Certificate and a certificate from the Veterinary authority of the exporting country that the country has been free from rabies for the period of six-months before date of export of the animal or animals. The certificate shall also state that the animal or animals exported have been kept in that country for the previous six months or from birth, provided that the animal or animals have not been in quarantine during the six months period before export.
2. Dogs, cats, and related species vaccinated against rabies may be permitted entry if such vaccination has taken place not less than 60 days before export.
3. All dogs, cats, and related species shall be subject to veterinary inspection at the port of entry.

4. The captain of the carriers involved in the shipment of the animals shall certify that the animal(s) were carried separately form other animals on board and if landed in transit the captain of the carrier shall also certify that the animal(s) were kept in isolation in an approved quarantine during transshipment, which shall be by the first available carrier from any intermediate port.
5. All dogs, cats, and related species, except those from United Kingdom, New Zealand, Sabah, Australia, Ireland, Sarawak, and Singapore shall be kept in quarantine in an approved station for a period of six months from the time of arrival. Such quarantine shall also apply to dogs, cats, and related species from the above countries if they have not fully observed the regulations as to certification and transshipment. The Veterinary Authority in Brunei will consider each application from other countries on its own merits.
6. Intending importers are required to obtain a written import permit specifying the precise regulation, which will apply to each particular importation. This permit should be obtained before export commences from the:
   Veterinary Department
   Agriculture Department
   Bandar Seri Begawan, 2069
   Brunei Darussalam

Website: www.brunei.gov.bn
Website: www.visitbrunei.com

Brunei Darussalam office
   Brunei Tourism
   Ministry of Industry and Primary Resources
   Jalan Menteri Besar
   Bandar Seri Bagawan BB3910, Brunei Darussalam
   Telephone: (2) 382 822
   Fax: (2) 382 824
   E-mail: bruneitourism@brunet.bn

Canada office
>High Commission of Brunei Darussalam
>395 Laurier Avenue East
>Ottawa, ON K1N 6R4, Canada
>Telephone: (613) 234-5656
>Fax: (613) 234-4397
>E-mail: bhco@cyberus.ca
>Website: www.brudirect.com

UK office
>High Commission of Brunei Darussalam
>19-20 Belgrave Square
>London SW1X 8PG, UK
>Telephone: (020) 7581 0521
>Fax: (020) 7590 7817
>E-mail: bruhighcomlondon@hotmail.com
>*This office also provides tourist information.*

Embassy of Brunei Darussalam
3520 International Court, NW
Washington, DC 20008
Telephone: (202) 237-1838
Fax: (202) 885-0560
E-mail: info@bruneiembassy.org
Website: www.bruneiembassy.org/

Bulgaria

If you are traveling with pets, you should have a certificate of veterinarian examination carried out within one week before departure as well as certificate of rabies shot made during the last six months. The Bulgarian Embassy also indicated that a special "apostille" certificate and in most cases a translation of the documents are required.

Website: www.bulgariatravel.org
Website: www.bulgaria.com

Bulgaria office
  National Information and Advertising Centre to the Ministry of Economy
  1 St Sophia Street
  Sofia 1040, Bulgaria
  Telephone: (2) 987 9778 or 987 1152
  Fax: (2) 989 6939
  E-mail: info@bulgariatravel.org

USA office
  Sofia Travel
  545 West 59th Street
  New York, NY 10019
  Telephone: (212) 247-8091
  Fax: none
  E-mail: none

USA office
  Balkantourist
  161 East 86th Street
  New York, NY 10028
  Telephone: (212) 722-1110
  E-mail: none

Embassy of The Republic of Bulgaria
1621 22nd Street, NW
Washington, DC 20008
Telephone: (202) 387-0174
Fax: (202) 234-7973
E-mail: office@Bulgaria-embassy.org
E-mail: consulate@bulgaria-embassy.org (consulate)
Website: www.bulgaria-embassy.org

Burkina Faso

The ambassador responded personally from the Burkina Faso Embassy. Here are the pet regulations.
1. Pets must be accompanied by a health certificate issued by an official veterinarian in the country of origin attesting that the animal is from a region declared unaffected for more than six weeks with any transmissible disease. Dogs and cats must

additionally be accompanied by an international rabies vaccination certificate dated more than two weeks and less than six months before arrival. These documents must be translated into French.
2. Upon arrival in Burkina Faso, all animals are subject to a veterinary health examination by an official veterinarian.

There are no specific regulations on time limits for travel, nor for travel on rail, bus, or airline system within Burkina Faso. The traveler would need to contact the particular transport company to inquire about individual restrictions. Pets are not permitted in restaurants for health reasons. For stays in hotel, the owner should contact the particular hotel to check for restrictions.

Website: www.primature.gov.bf

Burkina Faso office
  Burkina National Tourist Office
  BP 1310
  Ouagadougou 01
  Burkina Faso
  Telephone: 31.19.59
  Fax: 31.44.34
  E-mail: none

Canada office
  Ambassade du Burkina Faso
  48, Range Road
  Ottawa, ON K1N 8J4, Canada
  Telephone: (613) 238-4796
  Fax: (613) 238-3812
  E-mail: none

UK office (located in Brussels)
  Ambassade du Burkina Faso
  16, Place Guy d'Aresso
  1060 Bruxelles, Belgique
  Telephone: (32) 23 45 66 09
  Fax: (32) 23 45 06 12
  E-mail: none

Embassy of Burkina Faso
2340 Massachusetts Avenue, NW
Washington, DC 20008
Telephone: (202) 332-5577/8956
Fax: (202) 667-1882
E-mail: Ambawdc@primanet.com
Website: www.burkinaembassy-usa.org

Burundi

Pets may enter Burundi with a certificate of vaccination and an International Health Certificate. The certificate of vaccination must be issued not more than 15 days prior to departure. A veterinary inspection will take place upon arrival.

Website: www.burundi.gov.bi (in French)
Website: www.burunditoday.org

Burundi office
    Office National du Tourisme
    BP 902
    2 avenue des Euphorbe
    Bujumbura, Burundi
    Telephone: 222 023 or 222 202 or 229 390
    Fax: 229 390
    E-mail: ontbur@cbinf.com
    Website: www.burundi.gov.bi/tour.htm

Embassy of The Republic of Burundi
2233 Wisconsin Avenue, NW
Suite 212
Washington, DC 20007
Telephone: (202) 342-2574
Fax: (202) 342-2578
E-mail: burundiembassy@erols.com
Website: none

Cambodia

The only requirement to bring your pet into Cambodia is an International Health Certificate. Bring along a current rabies vaccination certificate just in case it is requested.

Website: www.camtour.org
Website: www.cambodia-web.net

Cambodia office
    Ministry of Tourism
    3 Boulevard Monivong
    Phnom Penh, Cambodia
    Telephone: (23) 213 911
    Fax: (23) 426 364 or 426 107
    E-mail: info@cambodia-web.net
    E-mail: mot@camtour.org

Cambodia office
    Diethelm Travel (Cambodia) Ltd
    N.65, Street 240
    P.O. Box 99
    Phnom Penh, Cambodia
    Telephone: (23) 219 151
    Fax: (23) 219 150
    E-mail: dtc@dtc.com.kh
    Website: www.diethelm-travel.com/cambodia

The Royal Cambodian Embassy
4500 16th Street, NW
Washington, DC 20011
Telephone: (202) 726-7742
Fax: (202) 726-8381
E-mail: cambodia@embassy.org
Website: www.embassy.org/cambodia

Cameroon

The individual contacted at the Embassy had a very difficult time understanding why anyone would want to bring a pet into Cameroon. The requirements to bring in your pet are simply the International

Health Certificate and a certificate of vaccination. The International Health Certificate must be issued less than 48 hours prior to departure. Owners may be subject to a tax of XAF 5,000 per pet. Only dogs and cats are permitted.

Website: www.camnet.cm/mintour/tourisme

Cameroon office
  Ministère du Tourisme
  BP 266
  Yaoundé, Cameroon
  Telephone: 224 411
  Fax: 221 295
  E-mail: mintour@camnet.cm

Embassy of The Republic of Cameroon
2349 Massachusetts Avenue, NW
Washington, DC 20008
Telephone: (202) 265-8790
Fax: (202) 387-3826
E-mail: cdm@embcam-usa.org
Website: none

Canada

The National Animal Health Program is responsible for establishing import requirements for animals and animal products coming into Canada, including pets.

The Canadian Food Inspection Agency has prepared basic guidelines for frequently imported pets. Before importing any animal, clients should verify the conditions with a local CFIA Office or Headquarters contact.

Importation of Cats

The following outlines the current conditions applicable to the import of cats into Canada. The conditions are different depending on the origin of the cats, i.e. rabies-free countries vs. non-rabies-free countries. Please note that current policy does not impose quarantine in Canada on the import of pet cats from any country.

Cats from a Rabies-Free Country (officially recognized as such by Canada)

Cats may enter Canada if accompanied by a certificate of an official government veterinarian.

The certificate must clearly identify the animals and show that:
1. Rabies has not existed in that country for the six (6) month period immediately preceding the shipment of the animals; and,
2. The animals have been in that country for the six (6) month period referred to in above paragraph, or since birth.

The same applies to cats that originated from Canada and are being returned directly from a country designated by the Minister as having been free from rabies for not less than six (6) months. This would include cats coming out of a quarantine imposed by the exporting country before that quarantine period is completed.

As an alternative to the conditions above, the animals could enter Canada, subject to rabies vaccination upon arrival in Canada at the owner's expense.

Cats from countries where rabies is present (or not recognized officially rabies-free by Canada)

Cats may enter Canada if accompanied by a valid rabies vaccination certificate issued, in either English or French, by a licensed veterinarian from the country of origin, which clearly identifies the cats and shows that they are currently vaccinated against rabies. This certificate should identify the animal, as in breed, color, weight, etc., plus indicate the name of the licensed rabies vaccine used (trade name), serial number and duration of validity (up to 3 years). Please note that if a validity date does not appear on the certificate, then it will be considered a one-year vaccine.

As an alternative, the animals could be vaccinated for rabies upon entry into Canada at the owner's expense.

Vaccination is not required if the animal is less than three (3) months of age.

Fees
Fees are payable for inspection of cats being imported into Canada from countries other than the United States. In certain cases, cats imported from the United States will require inspection; inspection fees will apply. Upon arrival at the first port of entry in Canada, the cat and the accompanying paperwork will be inspected. The fee must be paid at the time of inspection.

The current fees are:
- $30.00 + tax for the first animal in the shipment,
- In addition $5.00 + tax for each additional animal in the shipment.

If the option is taken to have a cat vaccinated upon arrival in Canada, the following fees apply:
- $55 + tax for the first animal in the shipment,
- In addition $30.00 + tax for each additional animal in the shipment.

If you are importing cats and the above conditions do not apply, please refer to www.airs-sari.agr.ca/airs-sari.asp.

Importation of Pet Dogs

The following outlines the current conditions that apply to the import of pet dogs into Canada

Note 1: Current policy does not impose quarantine in Canada on the import of pet dogs from any country.

Note 2: These conditions apply only to pet dogs. If you have many dogs, you may be asked to provide certification that they are your personal pets and are not for resale.

Pet dogs eight (8) months of age or over from a rabies free country (officially recognized as such by Canada)
Dogs may enter Canada if accompanied by a certificate, in either English or French, of an official government veterinarian. The certificate must clearly identify the animals and show that:
1. Rabies has not existed in that country for the six (6) month period immediately preceding the shipment of the animals; and,

2. The animals have been in that country for the six (6) month period or since birth.

Pet dogs eight (8) months of age or over from countries where rabies is present (or not recognized officially rabies-free by Canada)
Dogs may enter Canada if accompanied by a valid rabies vaccination certificate issued, in either English or French, by a licensed veterinarian from the country of origin, which clearly identifies the dogs and shows that they are currently vaccinated against rabies. This certificate should identify the animal, as in breed, color, weight, etc., plus indicate the name of the licensed rabies vaccine used (trade name), serial number and duration of validity (up to 3 years). Please note that if a validity date does not appear on the certificate, then it will be considered a one-year vaccine.

If the above provisions are not met, an inspector will order the owner to have the animals vaccinated for rabies within a period specified in the order and to provide the vaccination certificate to an inspector, all at the owner's expense.

Pet dogs eight (8) months of age or younger from any country
Pet dogs accompanied by the owner between the ages of three (3) and eight (8) months require certification for rabies if from a rabies-free country or if from a country that is not designated as Rabies-free. No additional certification is required. *Rabies vaccination or certification that the dog comes from a rabies-free country is not required if the animals is less than three (3) months of age.*

Pet dogs not accompanied by the owner require, in addition to the certificate requirements:
1. A detailed health certificate, in English or French, of a veterinarian that bears the signature of the licensed veterinarian and the name of the veterinarian recorded legibly in the veterinarian's handwriting, and that clearly identifies the dogs and states:
    - That the veterinarian has examined the dogs and is satisfied that the dogs
    - Are not less than eight (8) weeks of age at the time of examination,

- Are free of any clinical evidence of disease,
- Were vaccinated not earlier than at six (6) weeks of age for distemper, hepatitis, parvovirus and parainfluenza virus, and
- Can be transported to Canada without undue suffering by reason of infirmity, illness, injury, fatigue or any other cause,

2. The date on which the dogs were vaccinated, that the vaccine was licensed by the country of origin of the dogs, and the trade name and serial number of the vaccine, and
3. The date and time of the examination recorded legibly in the veterinarian's handwriting, and are imported into Canada not more than thirty-six (36) hours after the time of the examination.

Special purpose dogs
Assistance dogs that are certified as a guide, hearing, or other service dog are not subject to any restrictions for importation where the person importing the dog is the user of the dog and accompanies the dog to Canada

Fees
Fees are payable for inspection of dogs being imported into Canada from countries other than the United States. In certain cases, dogs imported from the United States will require inspection; inspection fees will apply. Upon arrival at the first port of entry in Canada, the dog and the accompanying paperwork will be inspected. The fee must be paid at the time of inspection.
The current fees are:
- $30.00 + tax for the first animal in the shipment and
- $5.00 + tax for each additional animal in the shipment

If you choose to have a dog vaccinated upon arrival in Canada, the following fees apply:
- $55.00 + tax for the first animal in the shipment and
- $30.00 + tax for each additional animal in the shipment.

If you are importing dogs and the above conditions do not apply, please refer to www.airs-sari.agr.ca/airs-sari.asp.

Importation of Personally Owned Pet Birds from the United States

It is possible to import personally owned pet birds under the following conditions:
1. The birds must accompany the owner to Canada.
2. The birds must be found to be healthy when inspected at the port of entry.
3. The owner must sign a declaration stating that the birds have been in his/her possession for the (90) ninety-day period preceding the date of importation and have not been in contact with any other birds during that time.
4. The owner must sign a declaration stating that the birds are the owner's personal pets and are not being imported for the purpose of re-sale.
5. The owner or any member of the family must not have imported birds into Canada under this pet bird provision during the preceding ninety (90) day period.

The necessary certification to clear Customs will be made by filling out the form, which is available at Customs. Under the above arrangement, no import permit or quarantine period is required. *If these conditions cannot be met, it will be necessary for you to obtain an import permit from the appropriate regional office in the province into which you will be entering.*

The importation of birds into Canada is subject to the control of the Canadian Wildlife Service (Convention on International Trade in Endangered Species - [CITES]). You may contact them by telephone: (613) 997-1840, by fax: (613) 953-6283 or by E-mail: suzanne.vincent@ec.gc.ca.

Importation of Pet Birds from Countries Other than the United States

For import purposes, the expression "pet bird" means a personally owned and cared for bird, and applies only to species commonly known as "caged" birds such as psittacines, love birds, song birds, toucans, canaries, finches, cardinals, etc. The expression does not apply to pigeons, doves, species of wild or domesticated fowl, or game birds.

An import permit issued by the Regional office must accompany the shipment. Before issuance can be considered, you must:
1. Contact the appropriate Import Officer, request an application form, complete the form, and forward it to the regional office with an originally signed declaration of the following:
   - That the birds have been in your possession as personally-owned pets for at least ninety (90) days immediately before applying; and
   - That the birds have not been in contact with any other birds while in your possession; and
   - That neither you nor members of your family have imported pet birds into Canada during the preceding ninety (90) days; and
   - That you will personally accompany the birds from the country of origin to Canada.
2. Arrange for the inspection and approval of your proposed Canadian premises for the quarantine of the birds. To arrange for the inspection of your premises, you should contact the Canadian Food Inspection Agency Regional Office in the province in which you are going to reside

Upon receipt of the above information and a report approving your premises for the quarantine of the birds, the regional office will be in a position to consider issuance of the import permit.

The essential conditions under which such birds are permitted to enter Canada are:
1. The original import permit issued by the regional office must accompany the birds to Canada.
2. The birds must accompany the owner (person having personal possession) to Canada and cannot be shipped unaccompanied.
3. It is recommended that the birds be treated, by the owner, for psittacosis-ornithosis during the quarantine period, which is a minimum of forty-five (45) days.

The importation of birds into Canada is subject to the control of the Canadian Wildlife Service (Convention on International Trade in

Endangered Species - [CITES]). Please contact them at (613) 997-1840 or (819) 953-6283.

Importation of Foxes, Skunks, Raccoons and Ferrets

An import permit issued by the Canadian Food Inspection Agency (CFIA) is required for the import of these animals from all countries, with the exception of ferrets being imported from the United States. Ferrets from the United States may enter Canada without an import permit if a vaccination certificate signed by an accredited veterinarian is presented at the port of entry and attests that these animals have been vaccinated against rabies within the year preceding the date of import.

For personal pets, these animals must have been in the owner's personal possession in the country of origin and accompany the owner to Canada.

Importation of Animals of the Rodentia Family

(Guinea Pigs, Gerbils, Mice, Rats, Chinchillas, Hamsters)

Please be advised that all animals of the Rodentia family are no longer regulated under the *Health of Animals Regulations*. As a result, no Canadian Food Inspection Agency import permit or health certificate is required. Normally, there will be no inspection done at the border. Imports are permitted from any country, for any use, to any destination (In the case of rats, they are not currently permitted entry into the Province of Alberta) in Canada.

The importation of these animals into Canada however, may be subject to the control by other federal or provincial government departments. Please contact the Canadian Wildlife Services (Convention on International Trade in Endangered Species [CITES]) at (613) 997-1840, (819) 953-6283 or their Website at: www.cws-scf.ec.gc.ca/.

Importation of Pet Rabbits

From the United States

Rabbits from the United States need to be presented to Canada Customs for release. No import permits or health certificates are required for entry into Canada.

From countries other than the United States

An import permit issued by a CFIA Area Import Office must accompany the shipment. Before issuance can be considered, you must contact the appropriate CFIA Area Import Office, request an application form and once completed, forward it to the Area Office with an originally signed declaration of the following:
1. That the rabbits have been in your possession as personally-owned pets;
2. That you will personally accompany the rabbits from the country of origin to Canada.

Arrangements must be made for the inspection and approval of your proposed Canadian premises for the quarantine of the rabbits in the province in which you are going to reside.

Upon receipt of the above information and a report approving your premises for the quarantine of the rabbits, the Area Office will be in a position to consider issuance of the import permit. The essential conditions under which such rabbits are permitted to enter Canada are:
1. The original import permit issued by the Area Office must accompany the rabbits to Canada.
2. The rabbits must accompany the owner (person having personal possession) to Canada and cannot be shipped unaccompanied.
3. The rabbits must originate from a premises certified free from myxomatosis. Rabbits being presented for importation must not be vaccinated with myxoma virus.
4. The rabbits must originate from a premises certified free of rabbit viral hemorrhagic disease and either:
    - The rabbits or the source animals must have been born on or resident on the premises of origin for the ninety (90) days immediately preceding the date of export and no case of viral hemorrhagic disease (rabbit calicivirus disease) must have been diagnosed on the premises of origin during the ninety (90) days immediately preceding export, or
    - The rabbits are certified free from rabbit viral hemorrhagic disease (VHD) and the rabbits must have been vaccinated, at least thirty (30) days but not more than ninety (90) days before being exported, with an

inactivated rabbit calicivirus vaccine recognized for that purpose by the central veterinary authority of the country of origin. The name of the vaccine and date of vaccination must be stated on the health certificate and the certificate of vaccination must be appended, or
- The rabbits are certified free from rabbit viral hemorrhagic disease (VHD) and the rabbits must have been tested for VHD using ELISA within the thirty (30) days immediately preceding export.

NOTE: Please apply for a permit at least 30 days in advance of the import.

Endangered Species List

The importation of rabbits into Canada may be subject to the control of the Canadian Wildlife Services (Convention on International Trade in Endangered Species [CITES]). Please contact them at (613) 997-1840, (819) 953-6283 or their Website at www.cws-scf.ec.gc.ca.

Fees

Fees are applicable when applying for an import permit, approval of a quarantine facility, and inspection of animals. The CFIA Area Import Office will advise you on the fees applicable to your particular situation.

If you are importing rabbits and the above conditions do not apply, please refer to www.airs-sari.inspection.gc.ca.

Importation of Pet Primates

(Apes, baboons, chimpanzees, gorillas, mandrills, monkeys, orangutans, and marmosets, etc.)

From The United States

Two (2) or less primates may be imported from the United States for personal use and not for resale. In these circumstances, no certification is required. However, you must check the species against the CITES list (please see below) to determine whether other permits from other agencies are required.

From Countries Other than the United States

It is not permitted to import primates from countries other than the United States for use as personal pets.

Countries of the World

Endangered Species List
The importation of primates into Canada may be subject to the control of the Canadian Wildlife Services (Convention on International Trade in Endangered Species [CITES]). Please contact them at (613) 997-1840, (819) 953-6283 their Website at www.cites.ec.gc.ca/cites/html/eng/sct0/index_e.htm.

If you wish to view the import requirements for primates, please refer to www.airs-sari.inspection.gc.ca.

Importation of Amphibians and Reptiles
Amphibians such as salamanders, frogs, toads, and geckos.
Reptiles such as snakes, crocodiles, caiman, iguanas, turtles, and tortoises.

All Amphibians and Reptiles (Excluding Turtles and Tortoises)
Please be advised that amphibians and reptiles (excluding turtles and tortoises) are no longer regulated under the *Health of Animals Regulations* and as a result, no Canadian Food Inspection Agency import permit is required, nor a health certificate and no inspection will normally be done at the border. Imports are permitted from any country, for any use, to any destination in Canada.

Turtles and Tortoises
An import permit* is required for turtles and tortoises from all countries. For personal pets, these animals must have been in the owner's personal possession in the country of origin and accompany the owner to Canada.

Turtle and Tortoise Eggs
An import permit* is required for turtle and tortoise eggs from all countries, but will only be issued to zoos and research laboratories.
The reason for restrictions on turtles, tortoises, and their eggs is that there is a great danger of transmitting serious diseases, such as salmonella. Until a Risk Assessment demonstrates safety, no permits will be issued for turtle and tortoise eggs for personal use or commercial purposes (i.e. Pet Shops).

*Please, complete an Application for Permit to Import and forward it to the CFIA Area Import Office in the province into which you wish to import the animal(s).

NOTE: Please apply for a permit at least 30 days in advance of the import.

Endangered Species List
The importation of reptiles into Canada may be subject to the control of the Canadian Wildlife Services (Convention on International Trade in Endangered Species [CITES]). Please contact them at (613) 997-1840, (819) 953-6283 or their Website at www.cws-scf.ec.gc.ca.

Fees
Fees are applicable when applying for an import permit, approval of a quarantine facility, and inspection of animals. The CFIA Area Import Office will advise you on the fees that apply to your particular situation.

If you wish to view the import requirements for turtles or tortoises, please refer to www.airs-sari.inspection.gc.ca.

For information on import of animals or for permits to transit Canada contact:
   Client Services
   Animal Health Divion
   Health of Animals Directorate
   Canadian Food Inspection Agency
   59 Promenade Camelot Drive
   Ottawa, Canada K1A OY9

Pet may enter Canada as passenger's baggage in the cabin or as cargo.

Website: www.travelcanada.ca
Website: www.canadatourism.com

Canada office
   Canadian Tourism Commission
   8th Floor West, 235 Queen Street
   Ottawa, ON K1A 0H6, Canada
   Telephone: (613) 946-1000
   Fax: (613) 954-3945 or 954-3964
   E-mail: trdc@ctc-ctc.ca

UK office
   Visit Canada Centre
   P.O. Box 5396
   Northampton NN1 2FA, UK
   Telephone: (0906) 871 5000 (24-hour consumer and tourism enquiries line) calls cost 60p per minute
   Fax: (0870) 165 5665
   E-mail: visitcanada@dial.pipex.com

USA office
   Canadian Tourism Commission
   1251 Avenue of the Americas
   New York, NY 10020
   Telephone: (212) 757-3583
   Telephone: (800) 577-2266 toll-free in USA
   Fax: none
   E-mail: none

Embassy of Canada
501 Pennsylvania Avenue, NW
Washington, DC 20001
Telephone: (202) 682-1740
Fax: (202) 682-7726
E-mail: webmaster@canadianembassy.org
Website: www.canadianembassy.org

Cape Verde

An International Health Certificate is required. Dogs also require an additional rabies inoculation certificate. Contact the Ministry of Agriculture at the address below for more information.
   Ministry of Agriculture
   Dr. David Monteiro
   Veterinary
   Telephone: (238) 64 75 47
   Fax: (238) 64 75 43

Cape Verde office
   Centro de Promoção Turística, do Investimento e das Exportações (PROMEX)
   Avenue OUA

CP 89c
Praia, Santiago, Cape Verde
Telephone: 622 621
Fax: 622 737
E-mail: promex@mail.cvtelecom.cv

Embassy of the Republic of Cape Verde
3415 Massachusetts Avenue, NW
Washington, DC 20007
Telephone: (202) 965-6820
Fax: (202) 965-1207
E-mail: ambacvus@sysnet.net
Website: www.capeverdeusembassy.org/

Cayman Islands

Anyone intending to bring a family pet or other animal into the Islands must direct these enquiries to the Department of Agriculture. Importation of dogs and cats require an import permit or a valid animal passport issued by the Department of Agriculture, and an official health certificate issued by a government-employed or accredited veterinary inspector in the country of origin. Application forms for import permit are available from the Agriculture Department. Applications should be submitted well in advance of travel and must be accompanied by a non-refundable fee of CI$50 (U.S.$61) in the form of a bank draft or an international money order, payable to the Cayman Islands Government.

Further requirements included on the health certificate are:
1. The pet must be free from any communicable disease and free from external parasites.
2. The pet must be treated with a topical preparation for ticks.
3. The pet has not been within 30 miles of an area quarantined for foot and mouth disease during the last 30 days. (This does not apply to dogs and cats arriving directly from the USA, Canada, or the UK).
4. The pet has not been exposed to rabies or has not been present within the last 6 months in an official quarantine rabies area.
5. The pet has all inoculations (including date and type) given within one year of travel to Cayman Islands.

Prohibited breeds include Mallanais, Rottweiler, Japanese Argentino, Fila Brasileiro, Chinese Shar-Pei, Pit Bull Terrier, Japanese Akita, Staffordshire, and Mastiff. Countries of origin that are prohibited are Asia, Central and South America, Cuba, Puerto Rico, Haiti and the Dominican Republic.

Contact:
>   Department of Agriculture-Veterinary Services
>   P. O. Box 459 GT
>   Grand Cayman, Cayman Islands
>   Telephone: (345) 947-3090
>   Fax: (345) 947-2634
>   E-mail: cavo@candw.ky

Website: www.caymanislands.ky
Website: www.divecayman.ky

Canada office
>   Cayman Islands Department of Tourism
>   234 Eglinton Avenue East, Suite 306
>   Toronto, ON M4P 1K5, Canada
>   Telephone: (416) 485-1550
>   Telephone: (800) 263-5805 toll-free in Canada
>   Fax: (416) 485-7578
>   E-mail: info-canada@caymanislands.ky

Cayman Islands office
>   Cayman Islands Department of Tourism
>   The Pavilion, Cricket Square
>   P.O. Box 67 GT
>   Grand Cayman, Cayman Islands
>   Telephone: (345) 949-0623
>   Fax: (345) 949-4053
>   E-mail: cscott@caymanislands.ky

UK office
>   Cayman Islands Department of Tourism
>   6 Arlington Street
>   London SW1 1RE, UK
>   Telephone: 171 491-7771

Telephone: 207-491-7771 toll-free in UK
Fax: 171 409-7773
E-mail: info-uk@caymanislands.ky

USA: California office
Cayman Islands Department of Tourism
3440 Wilshire Avenue, Suite 1202
Los Angeles, CA 90010
Telephone: (213) 738-1968
Telephone: (800) 346-3313 toll-free in USA
Fax: (213) 738-1829
E-mail: none

USA: Florida office
Cayman Islands Department of Tourism
6100 Blue Lagoon Drive, Suite 150
Miami, FL 33126-2085
Telephone: (305) 266-2300
Telephone: (800) 346-3313 toll-free in USA
Fax: (305) 267-2932
E-mail: none

Central African Republic

Dogs and cats must be accompanied by a current International Health Certificate, including:
1. Confirmation of rabies inoculation not less than 2 weeks nor more than 6 months before arrival, and;
2. Statement that no case of rabies has occurred in area of origin for 60 days before shipment.

Central African Republic office
Ministère de l'Industrie du Commerce du Tourisme et de l'Artisanat
BP 655
Bangui, Central African Republic
Telephone: 613 222 or 611 055
Fax: 617 653
E-mail: none

Consulate in Montreal, Canada
E-mail: mail@consultaxe.com
Embassy of the Central African Republic
1618 22nd Street, NW
Washington, DC 20008
Telephone: (202) 483-7800
Fax: (202) 332-9893
E-mail: none
Website: none

Chad

Chad does not require a permit or quarantine. An International Health Certificate and an immunization certificate are required. No translation is required.

Chad office
Direction de la Promotion Touristique
BP 86
N'Djaména, Chad
Telephone: 524 416
Fax: 524 419
E-mail: none

Embassy of The Republic of Chad
2002 R Street, NW
Washington, DC 20009
Telephone: (202) 462-4009
Fax: (202) 265-1937
E-mail: info@chadembassy.org
Website: www.chadembassy.org

Chile

This information is a courtesy of LAN Chile Airlines. Only one dog or one cat or one pair of birds will be allowed per cabin. Pet reservations must be made 48 hrs in advance.

Fares: Except in the case of guide dogs, the fare to be charged will be that for excess baggage.

Documentation: A recent International Health Certificate done by the time of traveling. A vaccination certificate dated less than one year before arrival is also necessary. The certificates require a stamp by the Chilean Consulate.

Website: www.sernatur.cl
Website: www.visitchile.org

Chile office
Servicio Nacional de Turismo (SERNATUR)
Avenida Providencia 1550
P.O. Box 14082
Santiago, Chile
Telephone: (2) 731 8336 or 731 8310 or 731 8337
Fax: (2) 251 8469 or 236 4054
E-mail: info@sernatur.cl

USA: Florida office
Chile Tourist Office
9700 South Dixie Hwy, Suite 640
Miami, FL 33156
Telephone: (800) 995-4888 toll-free in USA
Telephone: (800) 244-5366 toll-free in USA
Telephone: (305) 671-5018
E-mail: infochile@chiletourdesk.com

Embassy of The Republic of Chile
1732 Massachusetts Avenue, NW
Washington, DC 20036
Telephone: (202) 785-1746
Fax: (202) 887-5579
Website: www.embassyofchile.org
Tourism Department (Embassy address)
Telephone: (202) 785-1746, 530-4109, 530-4108
E-mail: ofitur@embassyofchile.org

China

Persons intending to bring animals, plants, and related products or other quarantinable objects into China must submit application forms to the customs, and the frontier quarantine department should examine them. Those who bring animals into China must present quarantine and other certificates issued by the country or region of origin. Each passenger is allowed to bring one pet into China. Such pets should be accompanied by quarantine and rabies-immunization certificates. One-month quarantine is required. Birds are prohibited entry into China. Pets are not permitted in hotels.

Website: www.cnta.com
Website: www.cits.net
Website: www.cnto.org

Canada office
    China National Tourist Office (CNTO)
    480 University Avenue, Suite 806
    Toronto, ON M5G 1V2, Canada
    Telephone: (416) 599-6636
    Telephone: (866) 599-6636 toll-free in Canada
    Fax: (416) 599-6382
    E-mail: cntoyyz@sprint.ca
    E-mail: Toronto@cnta.gov.cn

China office
    China National Tourism Administration (CNTA)
    Department of Marketing and Communications
    9A Jianguomennei Avenue
    Beijing 100740, People's Republic of China
    Telephone: (10) 6520 1114
    Fax: (10) 6512 2096
    E-mail: webmaster@cnta.gov.cn

China office
    China International Travel Service (CITS)
    103 Fuxingmennei Avenue
    Beijing 100800, People's Republic of China
    Telephone: (10) 6601 1122 or 6601 2055
    Fax: (10) 6603 9331
    E-mail: webmaster@cits.net

UK office
China National Tourist Office (CNTO)
4 Glentworth Street
London NW1 5PG, UK
Telephone: (020) 7935 9787
Telephone: (09001) 600 188 (brochure request and general information); calls cost 60p per minute)
Fax: (020) 7487 5842
E-mail: London@cnta.gov.cn
E-mail: weixing.xu@btinternet.com

USA: California office
China National Tourist Office
333 West Broadway, Suite 201
Glendale, CA 91204
Telephone: (818) 545-7505
Fax: (818) 545-7506
E-mail: la@cnta.gov.cn
E-mail: chinanto@aol.com

USA: New York office
China National Tourist Office
350 Fifth Avenue, Suite 6413
New York, NY 10118
Telephone: (212) 760-9700 or 760-8218
Fax: (212) 760-8809
E-mail: cntony@aol.com

Embassy of The People's Republic of China
2300 Connecticut Avenue, NW
Washington, DC 20008
Telephone: (202) 328-2500
Fax: (202) 588-0032
E-mail: webmaster@china-embassy.org
Website: www.china-embassy.org

Colombia

The requirements to import pets into Columbia are to have a health certificate issued by a veterinarian and a recent vaccination certificate. These documents do not require legalization before a Columbian

Consulate. For further information, contact the Consul of Columbia in your jurisdiction.

Columbia office
Columbia Government Tourist Office
Calle 28 No. 13A-15 piso 18
Bogotá, Columbia
Telephone: (57-1) 382 17 00 ext.107
Telephone: (57-1) 382 13 07
Telephone: (57-1) 382 13 11
Fax: (57-1) 352 21 01
E-mail: turismo@mindesa.gov.co
E-mail: turismo02@mindesa.gov.co

USA: New York office
Colombia Government Tourist Office
140 East 57th Street
New York, NY 10022
Telephone: (212) 355-7776
Fax: none
E-mail: none

USA office: NY consulate
General Consulate of Columbia
10 East 46th Street
New York, NY 10017
Telephone: none
Fax: none
E-mail: concolny@idt.net

USA office: DC consulate
Columbia Consulate
1875 Connecticut Avenue, NW
Suite 524
Washington, DC 20009
Telephone: none
Fax: none
E-mail: cnwas@bellatlantic.net

Embassy of Colombia
2118 Leroy Place, NW
Washington, DC 20008
Telephone: (202) 387-8338
Fax: (202) 232-8643
E-mail: emwas@colombiaemb.org
Website: www.colombiaemb.org

Comoros

Dogs and cats need a current International Health Certificate and a vaccination certificate.

Comoros office
>Direction Générale du Tourisme et de l'Hôtellerie
>BP 97
>Moroni, Comoros
>Telephone: 744 265 or 744 242
>Fax: 744 241
>E-mail: dg.tourisme@snpt.km

Embassy of The Federal and Islamic Republic of the Comoros
420 East 50th Street
New York, NY 10022
Telephone: (212) 972-8010
Fax: (212) 983-4712
E-mail: none
Website: none

Congo, Republic of

Vaccination documents are required. I would suggest obtaining the most recent information when inquiring about entry visas. (Whether specifically requested or not, always take an International Health Certificate.)

Congo office
>Ministère du Tourisme et de l'Environnement
>BP 456
>Brazzaville, Congo
>Telephone: 814 031 or 814 030

Fax: none
E-mail: none

Embassy of The Republic of Congo
4891 Colorado Avenue, NW
Washington, DC 20011
Telephone: (202) 726-5500
Fax: (202) 726-1860
E-mail: none
Website: none

Congo, Democratic Republic of (Zaire)

Pets are permitted into the Congo without a quarantine period, but a Certificate of Good Health that includes verification that the pet is free of ticks and has not been exposed to any contagious diseases must accompany them. (Do not obtain the certificate more than fifteen days before departure from the States.)

All dogs and cats must also have a rabies certificate. An inactivated or Kelev vaccine against rabies must be done more than one month but less than twelve months before departure. If an avianzed (flury) vaccine is administered, it must be done thirty-six months before departure.

Do not forget to check on the "in transit" pet rules for all countries you will be connecting through to reach Kinshasa.

There is one clinic, which most in the embassy community calls on exclusively. Two European trained doctors, one Belgian and the other Congolese, staff it. The vets themselves and their staff have been described as competent and caring. Costs are reported to be comparable to or even lower than in the States.

Pet supplies, including food, are very expensive in Congo. It is recommended that you bring as much as possible in your consumables shipment.

Pets may enter as passenger's checked baggage, in the cabin or as cargo.

Website: www.congo2000.com

Canada office
    Embassy of the Democratic Republic of Congo
    18 Range Road
    Ottawa, ON K1N 8J3, Canada
    Telephone: (613) 230-6391
    Fax: (613) 230-1945
    Website: www.ambassadesrdcongo.org

UK office
    Embassy of the Democratic Republic of Congo
    38 Holne Chase
    London N2 0QQ, UK
    Telephone/Fax: (020) 8458 0254
    E-mail: none

Embassy of The Democratic Republic of Congo
1800 New Hampshire Avenue, NW
Washington, DC 20009
Telephone: (202) 234-7690
Fax: (202) 237-0748
E-mail: none
Website: none

Cook Islands
See also: South Pacific Tourism Organization

Cats and dogs may only be imported from Australia, New Zealand, United Kingdom, and Ireland and only if sent as cargo in strong containers.

The Animal Quarantine Supervisor suggested that each traveler contact the Ministry of Agriculture directly for the current regulations because the protocols change from time to time. Contact:
    Ministry of Agriculture
    E-mail: cimoa@oyster.net.ck

Website: www.cook-islands.com/

Canada office
   Cook Islands Tourism Corporation
   Suite 202, 280 Nelson Street
   Vancouver, BC V6B 2E2, Canada
   Telephone: (604) 301-1190
   Telephone: (888) 994-2665 toll-free in USA and Canada
   Fax: (604) 687-3454
   E-mail: cookislands@earthlink.net

Cook Islands office
   Cook Islands Tourism Corporation
   P.O. Box 14
   Rarotonga, Cook Islands
   Telephone: (682) 29435
   Fax: (682) 21435
   E-mail: tourism@cookislands.gov.ck

UK office
   Cook Islands Tourist Bureau
   203 Sheen Lane
   East Sheen
   London SW14 8LE, UK
   Telephone: (020) 8876 1938
   Fax: (020) 8878 9876
   E-mail: none

UK office
   Cook Islands Tourist Bureau
   48 Glentham Road
   Barnes, London SW13 9JJ, UK
   Telephone: (020) 8741 6082
   Fax: (020) 8741 6107
   E-mail: info@spto.org

USA office
   Cook Island Tourism Corporation
   Suite 660
   5757 W. Century Boulevard
   Los Angeles, CA 90045-6407
   Telephone: (310) 641-5621

Telephone: (888) 994-2665 toll-free in USA
Fax: (310) 338-0708
E-mail: cooks@itr-aps.com

The Cook Islands are self-governing "in free association" with New Zealand. New Zealand Embassies and High Commissions represent them in countries with no Consular offices.

Costa Rica

In order to enter Costa Rica with your pet, you will need the following documents:
1. A pet's health certificate issued by a licensed veterinarian and endorsed by a Veterinary Services (VS) veterinarian at the U. S. Department of Agriculture Animal and Plant Health Inspection Service (USDA-APHIS).
2. A personal letter stating your pet's market value or a document that proofs it such as an invoice.
3. Proof of payment of your pet's Custom's duty (if applicable).
4. A pet's quarantine permit issued by the Ministry of Agriculture and Animal Control ("Ministerio de Agricultura y Ganaderia" (MAG)) in Costa Rica.

To expedite your Customs procedures, the Ministry of Agriculture and Animal Control of Costa Rica ("Ministerio de Agricultura y Ganadería") suggests that examination be conducted within two weeks before your departure.

The health certificate must contain the following information:
1. Veterinarian Information:
   - Full Name of the Veterinarian
   - Veterinarian License Number
   - Name of the Pet Hospital/clinic
   - Address
   - Telephone Number
   - E-mail address (if any)
2. Personal Information:
   - Your full name
   - Your passport number
   - Your home address

- Your telephone number
3. Your Pet's Information:
   - Place of origin (City, State, Country)
   - Species
   - Age
   - Sex
   - Family tree (if any)
   - Vaccinations that pet has received
   - Dates of those vaccinations
   - A statement that your pet is healthy and free of any parasites and of any clinical signs of infectious diseases.
4. Health Certificate Required Statements:
   - Required statements depend on the area where you live, the diseases, or parasites that have been reported to occur in your area, and/or your pet's place of origin.
   - It is important that your pet's veterinarian clearly states that your pet is free of any diseases and parasites that have been reported to occur in the area where your pet lives.
   - The following are required statements for different pets. If there are new diseases and/or parasites reported to occur in the country where the pet lives endangering your pet's species, the certificate must clearly list those new diseases and state that your pet is free of them:

Birds: (psittacines, finches, and other soft-billed cage-birds)
The certificate must include the following statements:
- The birds were isolated for at least 30 days.
- The birds were examined and found to be clinically healthy and free of ectoparasites.
- The birds are free of velogenic Newcastle disease and highly pathogenic avian influenza.
- The birds originated from a country, state, county, hatchery, or aviary free of avian salmonellosis (Salmonella pullorum, Salmonella gallinarum).
- Pet birds (psittacines in particular) should be properly identified (band or tattoo), and such identification should appear on the health certificate that is issued by

the licensed veterinarian. If applicable, a C.I.T.E.S. permit must accompany the bird

Dogs and Cats:
It is recommended that a State or Federal (VS Form 18-I) U.S. Interstate and International Certificate for small animals be used including the following statements:
- The cats/dogs were vaccinated against distemper, hepatitis, leptospirosis, and parvovirus.
- If cats/dogs are over 4 months old, they must be vaccinated against rabies and the certificate must state that cats/dogs were vaccinated against rabies.
- If there are any diseases that have been reported to occur in your area, the certificate must list the name of those diseases and clearly state that the cats/dogs are free of those diseases.

Horses:
The certificate must include the following statements:
- The United States is free from African horse sickness, dourine, glanders, epizootic lymphangitis, and Venezuelan equine encephalomyelitis.
- The premises of origin are free of coital exanthema and ulcerative lymphangitis.
- Horses originated from premises where abortion caused by Salmonella abortus equi and clinical cases of equine viral arteritis have not been reported to occur during the 12 months before embarkation.
- Horses were vaccinated for eastern and western encephalomyelitis at least 30 days and no more than 6 months before embarkation. (Name of product and date of vaccination must be included on the health certificate.)
- No clinical cases of equine rhinopneumonitis or influenza were observed on the premises of origin in the 6 months before embarkation and the horses were vaccinated against these diseases on _____ (date) with _____ (killed/modified live) vaccine.

- Horses have been treated for internal and external parasites within the 30 days before embarkation.
- Horses were isolated from animals not tested for exportation to Costa Rica from the first test until embarkation.
- None of the horses in this shipment originated from premises under any type of State of Federal quarantine for contagious equine metritis or any other equine diseases.
- The animals were negative to the following tests within 30 days of embarkation: Equine Infectious Anemia: Agar-gel immunodiffusion (Coggins) test, OR ELISA test.

Additional Information
- Foals under 5 months of age, when accompanying the dam, are not required to be vaccinated or tested before export.
- If horses were vaccinated against Venezuelan encephalitis, indicate product used and date of vaccination on the health certificate.

Others: (Frog, Iguanas, Lizards, etc.)
If there is a disease and/or parasite that has been reported to occur in the city, state, and/or country where your pet lives endangering your pet's species, the certificate must specifically list those diseases and/or parasites and state that your pet is free of them. If there are no diseases/parasites reported to occur in the city, state, and country where your pet lives, it is not necessary to issue any additional statements.

Customs Duty
General Information
When you pass through customs with your pet, a Customs officer will conduct a visual examination of your pet - there is a $1.00US (one U.S. dollar) fee per pet.

If your pet has a highly contagious disease, that puts in threat the fauna of Costa Rica, your pet will not be allowed in the country, and

you will be required to take your pet out of Costa Rica. If you do not take your pet out of the country, your pet will be destroyed. If your pet has a disease that is not highly contagious, your pet will be treated by a veterinarian and must be hosted for 40 days or until the disease is terminated at the Custom Animal Shelter of the Ministry of Agriculture and Animal Control.
You or the Customs broker that you hired will be required to present the pet's health certificate. If your pet does not have this certificate, your pet will not be allowed into the country, and you will have to send it back home.

Then, you will be required to file for a pet's quarantine permit at the Ministry of Agriculture and Animal Control ("Ministerio de Agricultura y Ganaderia"). Once you get this permit, you can take your pet anywhere within Costa Rica without restrictions.

Customs will not release your pet unless you have the pet's quarantine permit. Your pet will remain at Customs or will be transferred to the Ministry of Agriculture and Animal Control ("Ministerio de Agricultura y Ganaderia")'s Customs Animal Shelter in San Jose, Costa Rica until you get the permit - it all depends on how fast you can get the quarantine permit. The shelter is not in the greatest conditions, thus, you might want to bring additional pet accessories to ensure your pet's comfort. The shelter does not offer food, however, you will have a visit schedule where you can come and feed your pet.

Paying Customs Duties
Once Customs accepts your pet's health certificate, you must pay Customs duty based on your pet's market value.

If your pet's market value is below $100.00 (one hundred U.S. dollars), you have not brought pets into the country for the last two years (Customs will check their records) and you are not into the import export business, your pet will be considered to be an import of non-commercial nature and no Customs Duty will be required.

If you come with your pet in the same plane/bus/ship, and you declare it as part of your luggage, or you are traveling with your pet and you will be staying for no more than 30 days, your pet will only need the pet's health certificate and the quarantine permit. No Customs Duties will be required.

Recent invoices are the ideal proof of your pet's market value. However, if you do not have an invoice available, a letter stating your current pet's market value would be enough. Your pet's market value shown in your letter is subject to change at Customs own discretion.

Pet's Quarantine Permit
The quarantine permit must be issued by the Ministry of Agriculture and Animal Control ("Ministerio de Agricultura y Ganaderia"). It costs $22.00US (twenty-two U.S. dollars) per pet. You can file for this permit before your pet's arrival through a Custom Agency, in person if you are already in Costa Rica, or through a third party that represents you.

The government of Costa Rica has appointed an organization called "Ventanilla Unica" (The Only Window) to issue permits associated with importing plants, animals, substances, food, machinery, and others. The "Ventanilla Unica" is located at 40th Street, between 1st and 3rd Avenue in San Jose, inside The Center of Foreign Trade ("Centro de Comercio Exterior") on the Northeast side of the building called "Edificio Colon" in San Jose. Their phone number is 506-256-7111. Ask to speak to the manager Mr. Marvin Salas.

It takes 72 hours to issue the quarantine permit. You need to bring your pet's health certificate, proof of payment of visual examination conducted by Customs - the fee is $1.00US (one U.S. dollar) - and proof of payment of your pet's Customs Duties (if applicable.) This quarantine permit allows you to take your pet with you wherever you go in Costa Rica.

Once you get this permit, you need to take it to Customs or to the Ministry of Agriculture and Animal Control ("Ministerio de Agricultura y Ganaderia")'s Customs Animal Shelter in San Jose, Costa Rica.

A vaccination certificate and an International Health Certificate must be sent to a Consulate for authentication before travel. Upon arrival in Costa Rica, the Zoonosis Department (Part of the Ministry of

Health) must be contacted. Their telephone is 223-0333. The pet will be quarantined for 24 hours while the paper work is completed. If you arrive on a weekend, the pet will be quarantined until the next week.

Website: www.tourism-costarica.com

Costa Rica office
    Instituto Costarricense de Turismo
    (Costa Rica Tourist Board)
    Apartado 777
    1000 San José, Costa Rica
    Telephone: 223 1733
    Telephone: (800) 343-6332 toll free in USA and Canada
    Fax: 223-5452 or 255-4997
    E-mail: info@tourism-costarica.com

Costa Rica office
    Cámara Nacional de Turismo (CANATUR)
    Apartado 828
    1000 San José, Costa Rica
    Telephone: 234 6222
    Fax: 253 8102
    E-mail: canatour@tourism.co.cr
    Website: www.costarica.tourism.co.cr

USA office
    JGR and Associates
    3361 SW 3rd Avenue
    Suite 102
    Miami, FL 33145
    Telephone: (305) 858-7277
    Fax: (305) 857-0071
    E-mail: none

Embassy of Costa Rica
2114 S Street, NW
Washington, DC 20008
Telephone: (202) 234-2945 or 46
Telephone: (800) 343-6332 toll free in USA and Canada
Fax: (202) 265-4795

E-mail: embassy@costarica-embassy.org
Website: costarica-embassy.org
The embassy address also serves as an additional mailing address for the Costa Rica Tourist Board.

Cote d'Ivoire (Ivory Coast)

Cats and dogs accompanying passengers may enter without an import license. Pet owners must hold a rabies inoculation certificate and International Health Certificate, dated not earlier than 3 days before travel commenced and issued by health authorities at the point of origin. Health certificate must indicate that no contagious disease (including rabies) has existed in that territory during previous 6 weeks.

Import license required in addition to above certificates for cats and dogs not accompanying passenger, and for all other pets. EXEMPT are, animals originating in following countries: Benin, Burkina Faso, Central African Republic, Chad, Republic of Congo, France, Gabon, Madagascar, Mali, Mauritania, Niger, and Senegal – certificates as above are sufficient.

Ivory Coast office
    Office Ivoirien du Tourisme et de l'Hôtellerie
    01 BP 8538
    2nd Floor, EECI Building
    place de la République
    Abidjan 01, Côte d'Ivoire
    Telephone: 2020 6500 or 2020 6519
    Fax: 2020 6531
    E-mail: none

USA office
    Tourism Cote d'Ivoire
    2424 Massachusetts Avenue, NW
    Washington, DC 20008
    Telephone: (202) 797-0352
    Fax: (202) 387-6381
    E-mail: none
    This is also the address for the Embassy.

Croatia

To permanently import pets, one needs to obtain authorization from the Ministry of Agriculture and Forestry-Veterinary Deportment. To bring pets temporarily, a tourist or in transit, one must have an "International Pet Passport" which will contain identification information and the vaccination records. Dogs older than 3 months have to be vaccinated against rabies at least 15 days before entering the country but not more than six months.

The Croatian Consulate may also be able to assist you with your plans. Contact them at (212) 599-3066 or E-mail: croatian.consulate@gte.com.

Website: www.htz.hr
Website: www.mint.hr

Croatian office
    Croatian National Tourist Board
    Iblerov Trg 10/IV
    10000 Zagreb, Croatia
    Telephone: (1) 455 6455
    Fax: (1) 455 7827
    E-mail: info@htz.hr

UK office
    Tourist Information
    2, Lanchesters
    162-164 Fulham Palace Road
    London W6 9ER, UK
    Telephone: 20 8563 7979
    Fax: 20 8563 2616
    E-mail: info@cnto.freeserve.co.uk

USA office
    Croatian National Tourist Office, Inc.
    350 Fifth Avenue, Suite 4003
    New York, NY 10118
    Telephone: (212) 279-8672 or 279-8674
    Telephone: (800) 829-4416 toll-free in USA

Fax: (212) 279-8683
E-mail: cntony@earthlink.net

Embassy of Croatia
2343 Massachusetts Avenue, NW
Washington, DC 20008
Telephone: (202) 588-5899
Fax: (202) 588-8936
E-mail: amboffice@croatiaemb.org
E-mail: consular@croatiaemb.org
Website: www.croatiaemb.org

Cuba

Cats, dogs, birds, and ornamental fishes must be accompanied by veterinarian (government) certificate of good health issued at the point of origin. Dogs must also be accompanied by rabies inoculation certificate. All Certificates to be issued by the Cuban consul in country of origin. Any pet will be quarantined (free of charge) for a period not longer than 2 weeks.

The official response stated that pets are not allowed in hotels, so tourists should not generally travel with pets.

Website: www.cubatravel.cu (in Spanish)

Canada office
  Bureau de Tourisme de Cuba
  440 boul Dorchester Ouest, #1402
  Montreal, QC H2Z 1U7, Canada
  Telephone: (514) 875-8004
  Fax: none
  E-mail: none

Cuba office
  Ministerio de Turismo
  Calle 19, No 710
  Entre Paseo y A, Vedado
  Havana, Cuba
  Telephone: (7) 334 319

Fax: (7) 334 086
E-mail: promo@mintur.mit.cma.net

UK office
Cuba Tourist Board
154 Shaftesbury Avenue
London WC2H 8JT, UK
Telephone: (020) 7240 6655
Fax: (020) 7836 9265
E-mail: cubatouristboard.london@virgin.net

Cuba Interests Section
2630 and 2639 16th Street, NW
Washington, DC 20009
Telephone: (202) 797-8518
Fax: (202) 986-7283
E-mail: cubaseccion@igc.apc.org
Website: none

Curacao

Pets are required to be accompanied with a current International Health Certificate.

Website: www.curacao-tourism.com

Curaçao office
Curaçao Tourism Development Bureau
Pietermaai 19
P.O. Box 3266
Willemstad, Curaçao, NA
Telephone: (9) 461 6000
Fax: (9) 461 5017
E-mail: ctdbcur@attglobal.net

UK office
Curaçao Tourism Development Bureau
c/o Axis Sales & Marketing Ltd
421A Finchley Road
London NW3 6HJ, UK
Telephone: (020) 7431 4045

Fax: (020) 7431 7920
E-mail: curacao@axissm.com

USA: Florida office
Curaçao Tourism Development Bureau
330 Biscayne Boulevard
Miami, FL 33132
Telephone: (305) 374-5811
Telephone: (800) 445-8266 toll-free in USA
Fax: (305) 374-6741

USA: New York office
Curaçao Tourism Development Bureau
475 Park Avenue, Suite 2000
New York, NY 10016
Telephone: (212) 683-7660
Telephone: (800) 270-3350 toll-free in USA
Fax: (212) 683-9337
E-mail: ctdbny@ctdb.com

Embassy of Curacao
4200 Linnean Avenue, NW
Washington, DC 20008
Telephone: (202) 244-5300
Fax: (202) 362-3430
E-mail: none
Website: none

Cyprus

Dogs and cats shall not be landed in Cyprus unless and until there is delivered to a Veterinary Officer at the port/airport of import an Animal Health Certificate issued by a duly authorized Veterinary Officer of the Government of the exporting country attesting that the animals:
1. Were clinically examined not more than 72 hours before exportation and found to be in good health and free from signs of rabies and any other infectious or contagious disease.

OR

2. Were kept since birth or for the six months before shipment in the exporting country where no case of rabies was officially reported during the past two years.

OR

Were kept for six months before shipment in premises where no cases of rabies was officially reported during that period.

OR

3. Either has not been vaccinated against rabies.

OR

Were vaccinated against rabies using a vaccine complying with the standards of the W.H.O. Expert Committee on rabies and approved by the O.I.E. not less than one month and not more than one year before shipment (in this case, the certificates shall comply with the requirements set out in the model O.I.E. / W.H.O. /F.A.O. International Certificate of Vaccination against Rabies given in Part 6 International Zoosanitary Code, Fifth Edition, 1986). Vaccination certificates for rabies and any other vaccinations, which the animal has been given, should be attached.

4. Were treated against echinococcosis-hydatidosis before shipment and that the treatment used is recognized as being efficient.

5. Were treated with an insecticidal preparation against ectoparasites before shipment.

A permit regarding the animal to be imported is required and may be obtained from the Cyprus Tourist Organization. Additional information can be obtained from:
Ministry of Agriculture, Natural Resources & Environment
Department of Veterinary Services
1417
Cyprus
Telephone: (02) 805201
Fax: (02) 332803
E-mail: vetservices@cytanet.com.cy

Website: www.cyprustourism.org

UK office
 Cyprus Tourist Office

17 Hanover Street
London W1R OHB, UK
Telephone: (0171) 5698800
Fax: (0171) 4994935
E-mail: ctolon@ctolon.demon.co.uk

USA office
Cyprus Tourist Organization
13 East 40th Street
New York, NY 10016
Telephone: (212) 683-5280
Fax: (212) 683-5282
E-mail: gocyprus@aol.com

Embassy of The Republic of Cyprus
2211 R Street, NW
Washington, DC 20008
Telephone: (202) 462-5772
Fax: (202) 483-6710
E-mail: cypembpow@sysnet.net
Website: cyprusembassy.org

Czech Republic

The Czech Republic requires a vaccination certificate dated 30 days to one year before travel and a current International Health Certificate. There is no permit required (unless the pet stays longer than 3 months). No quarantine will be imposed. For animals other than cats and dogs, check with the Embassy in Washington, additional documentation may be required. The embassy's Website www.mzv.cv/washington/sons/vetinary.htm has more information.

Website: www.czech.cz
Website: www.visitczechia.cz
Website: www.czechcenter.com

USA: New York office
Czech Tourist Authority
1109 Madison Avenue
New York, NY 10028
Telephone: (212) 288-0830

Fax: (212) 288-0971
E-mail: nycenter@pop.net
E-mail: travelczech@pop.net

Embassy of The Czech Republic
3900 Spring of Freedom Street, NW
Washington, DC 20008
Telephone: (202) 274-9100
Fax: (202) 966-8540
E-mail: washington@embassy.mzv.cz
Website: www.czech.cz/washington

Denmark

When traveling directly from countries considered free from rabies (Faroe Islands, Iceland, Norway, Sweden, Ireland, Great Britain, Japan, New Zealand, and Australia) dogs and cats can be imported into Denmark via any border control post without any restrictions.

When traveling from other countries, dogs, and cats can be imported to Denmark via any border control post as long as they are vaccinated against rabies at least 30 days and not more than 12 months before entry. A vaccination certificate must be demonstrated at request.

Dogs and cats being 3 and 4 months of age must be vaccinated against rabies as well. If the period between vaccination and entry is shorter than 30 days, a health certificate is required. This certificate must be issued by a veterinary surgeon no more than 10 days before entry.

Dog and cats being less than 3 months of age can be imported into Denmark without being vaccinated against rabies. A health certificate as mentioned above is required.

There is no mandatory quarantine and no permit is required. Pets from the U.S. are required to have a USDA stamp.

Additional information may be obtained from the Danish Ministry of Agriculture and Fisheries.

    Danish Ministry of Agriculture and Fisheries
    Holbergsade 2
    DK-1057 Copenhagen K

Denmark
Telephone: +45 33 92 33 01
E-mail: fvm@fvm.dk

Website: www.visitdenmark.com

UK office
   Danish Tourist Board
   55 Sloane Street
   London SW1X 9SY, UK
   Telephone: 171 259 5959
   Fax: 171 259 5955
   E-mail: dtb.london@dt.dk
   Website: www.dtb.dt.dk

USA office
   Danish Tourist Board
   655 Third Avenue, 18th Floor
   New York, NY 10017
   Telephone: (212) 885-9700
   Fax: (212) 885-9726
   E-mail: info@goscandinavia.com

Royal Danish Embassy
3200 Whitehaven Street, NW
Washington, DC 20008
Telephone: (202) 234-4300
Fax: (202) 328-1470
E-mail: wasamb@wasamb.um.dk
Website: www.denmarkemb.org

Djibouti
Pets may be imported into Djibouti with an International Health Certificate and a vaccination certificate. There is no quarantine. No permits are required.

Djibouti office
   Office National du Tourisme de Djibouti (ONTD)
   BP 1938

Djibouti, Djibouti
Telephone: 353 790 or 352 800
Fax: 356 322
E-mail: onta@intnet.dj

Embassy of The Republic of Djibouti
1156 15th Street, NW
Suite 515
Washington, DC 20005
Telephone: (202) 331-0270
Fax: (202) 331-0302
E-mail: usdjibouti@aol.com
Website: none

Dominica

Pets may enter the country if accompanied by a valid International Health Certificate and an importation permit. Obtain the permit from:
Veterinary Officer of the Ministry of Agriculture
Botanical Gardens, Roseau
Commonwealth of Dominica
Telephone: (767) 448-0414
Fax: none
E-mail: none

Website: www.dominica.dm

Dominica office
National Development Corporation - Division of Tourism
P.O. Box 293
Valley Road
Roseau, Commonwealth of Dominica
Telephone: 448 2045
Fax: 448 5840
E-mail: ndc@cwdom.dm

UK office
Dominica Tourist Office
1 Collingham Gardens
London SW5 0HW, UK
Telephone: 171-835-1937 or 370-5194

Fax: none
E-mail: none

UK office
Dominica Tourist Office
MKI Ltd, Mitre House
66 Abbey Road, Bush Hill Park
Enfield, Middlesex EN1 2QE, UK
Telephone: (020) 8350 1004
Fax: (020) 8350 1011
E-mail: liz@ttg.co.uk

USA office
Dominica Tourist Office
800 2nd Avenue, Suite 1802
New York, NY 10017
Telephone: (212) 949-1711
Telephone: (800) 645-5637
Fax: (212) 949-1714
E-mail: dominicany@msn.com

Embassy of The Commonwealth of Dominica
3216 New Mexico Avenue, NW
Washington, DC 20016
Telephone: (202) 364-6781/2
Fax: (202) 364-6791
E-mail: Embdomdc@aol.com
Website: none

Dominican Republic

When traveling with your pet, it is necessary to submit to the Department of Animal Health the following documents:
Cats:
1. Anti-rabies vaccine certificate, with inoculation 30 days before the arrival date of the animal.
2. Health certificate issued within the 15 days before the arrival date of the animal.

Dogs:
1. Anti-rabies vaccine, triple vaccine (distemper, leptospirosis, hepatitis), and parvovirus vaccine certificates showing inoculations 30 days before the arrival date of the animal.
2. Health certificate issued within the 15 days before the arrival date of the animal.

If these requirements are not met, your pet will be quarantined from 8 to 30 days, depending on the country of origin. For other animal species, Direccion General de Ganaderia, issues authorization. Telephone: 532-2858

On departure, be sure to obtain a health certificate at the Office of Animal Health, Telephone: 542-0132, valid for 72 hours.

Website: www.dominicana.com.do
Website: www.dominicanrepublic.com

Canada office
   Dominican Republic Tourist Board
   2080 rue Crescent
   Montréal, QC H3G 2B8, Canada
   Telephone: (514) 499-1918
   Fax: (514) 499-1393
   E-mail: republiquedominicaine@op-plus.net

Dominican Republic office
   Secretaría de Estado de Turismo (Ministry of Tourism)
   Apdo 497
   Santo Domingo, Dominican Republic
   Telephone: 221 4660
   Fax: 682 3806
   E-mail: sectur@codetel.net.do

UK office
   Dominican Republic Tourist Board
   18-21 Hand Court
   High Holborn
   London WC1V 6JF, UK
   Telephone: (020) 7242 7778

Fax: (020) 7405 4202
E-mail: domrep.touristboard@virgin.net

USA: Florida office
Dominican Republic Tourist Office
2355 Salzedo Street, Suite 307
Coral Gables, Miami, FL 33134
Telephone: (888) 358-9594 toll-free in USA
Fax: (305) 444-4845
E-mail: domrep@herald.infi.net

USA: New York office
Dominican Republic Tourist Office
136 East 57th Street, Suite 803
New York, NY 10022
Telephone: (888) 374-6361) toll-free in USA
Telephone: (212) 588-1012
Fax: (212) 588-1015
E-mail: dr.info@ix.netcom.com
E-mail: newyork@sectur.gov.do

Embassy of The Dominican Republic
1715 22nd Street, NW
Washington, DC 20008
Telephone: (202) 332-6280
Fax: (202) 265-8057
E-mail: embdomrepusa@msn.com
Website: www.domrep.org

East Timor

East Timor became fully independent on May 20, 2002. Dogs, cats, and birds, may enter East Timor without quarantine. An International Health Certificate and a current vaccination certificate are required. These documents should be dated less than 7 days prior to travel.

East Timor Government
Website: www.gov.east-timor.org

UN Mission of Support in East Timor (UNMISET)
Dili, East Timor

Website: www.un.org/peace/timor/timor.htm

UN Development Programme (UNDP)
UN Agency House
Caicoli Street
Dili, East Timor
Fax: (390) 312 408
E-mail: registry.tp@undp.east-timor.org
Website: www.undp.east-timor.org

British Embassy
PO Box 194
Dili, East Timor
Telephone: (0061) 408 010 991
E-mail: dili.fco@gtnet.gov.uk

US Embassy/Consulate
Avenida do Portugal
Farol
Dili, East Timor
Telephone: (390) 324 684
Fax: (390) 313 206

Ecuador

The following regulations pertain to household cats and dogs being imported into Ecuador.

Cats: The animal or animals will be presented with a certificate from an official authority of animal sanity of the United States, which will require the following:
1. The animals have been vaccinated within sixty days before departure, against the following diseases: panleukopenia felina and rabies (for the animals older than three months).
2. The animals have been treated against parasites, externally and internally, at least thirty days before embarkation.
3. The animals have been inspected and identified at the moment of embarkation by an official veterinarian, who will find them in normal health condition, without tumors, fresh wounds or in the process of healing, or without any

quarantined transferable diseases or the presence of ectoparasites.
4. They also must be placed in special cages or boxes that have been cleaned and disinfected before being used.

Dogs: The animal or animals will be presented with a certificate from an official authority of animal sanity of the United States, which will require the following:
1. The animals have been vaccinated within at least sixty days before departure against the following diseases: distemper, canine hepatitis, leptospirosis, parvovirus, influenza, and rabies (for the animals less than three months old). (In each case, proof of these immunizations will include the date received, the type and trademark of the product used)
2. The animals have been treated against parasites, externally and internally, at least thirty days before embarkation.
3. The animals have been inspected and identified at the moment of embarkation by an official veterinarian, who will find them in normal health condition, without tumors, flesh wounds or in the process of healing, or without any quarantined transferable diseases or the presence of ectoparasites.
4. They also must be placed in special cages or boxes that have been cleaned and disinfected before being used.

The documents will require authentication by the Ecuador Consulate. The fee is U.S. $50.

Website: www.captur.com
Website: www.ecuador.org

Ecuador office
 Ministerio de Turismo
 Avenida Eloy Alfaro N32-300 and Carlos Tobar
 Quito, Ecuador
 Telephone: (2) 507 562 or 228 304/5
 Fax: (2) 229 330
 E-mail: rvazmtour@ec-gov.net

Ecuador office
   Camara Provincial de Turismos (CAPTUR)
   Avenida 6 de Diciembre 1424 y Carrión
   Quito, Ecuador
   Telephone: (2) 224 074 or 509 860
   Fax: (2) 507 682
   E-mail: captur@captur.com

USA office
   Ecuador Tourist Information
   7270 NW 12th Street, Suite 400C
   Miami, FL 33126
   Telephone: (305) 477-0041
   Telephone: (800) 553-6673 toll-free in USA
   Fax: (305) 577-0531
   E-mail: none

Embassy of Ecuador
2535 15th Street, NW
Washington, DC 20009
Telephone: (202) 234-7200
Fax: (202) 667-3482
E-mail: embassy@ecuador.org
Website: www.ecuador.org

Egypt
Traveling with cats/dogs (other pets):
Certificate from the veterinarian (country of origin).
   1. Certificate must show that pet is free from any transmitted disease and is in good health condition.
   2. A current vaccination certificate showing the following vaccines: distemper, hepatitis, leptospirosis, parvovirus, canine parainfluenza, rabies carnivirus enteritis and bordetella bronchiseptica.
   3. The pet will be under supervision for up to three months (pet will remain with owner at all times).
   4. Administrative fees to be paid upon arrival.

Traveling with birds:
   1. Certificate from the veterinarian (country of origin).

2. Endangered species will not be allowed in the country, only the species that are covered by the international treaty.
3. Certificate must show that pet is free from any transmitted disease such as psittacus erithcus.
4. Pet birds will be under supervision for 15 days (pet will stay with owner at all times)
5. Administrative fees to be paid upon arrival.

Before departure:
The tourist must take the pet to the Quarantine Office at the Airport 48 hours before departure and a health certificate and a permit will be issued for the pet before leaving the country. There are fees involved.

For Hospital and Animal Shelter info call:
El-Sha'b Hospital and Animal Shelter
Cairo, Egypt
Telephone (011-2-02) 482-2294

Animal Rights Society
Dr. Ahmed Samir Salem, Chairman
Abu Wafya Street - Sharabeya
Cairo, Egypt
P.O. Box 166 Ramses
Telephone (011-2-02) 235-2098
Fax (011-2-02) 231-0062

Website: www.touregypt.net
Website: www.egypttourism.org

Canada office
Egyptian Tourist Authority
1253 McGill College Avenue, Suite 250
Montreal, QC H5B 2Y5, Canada
Telephone: (514) 861-4420
Fax: (514) 861-8071
E-mail: eta@total.net

UK office
Egyptian Tourist Authority
Egyptian House

170 Piccadilly
London W1V 9DD, UK
Telephone: 171-4935282
Fax: 171-4080295
E-mail: none

USA: California office
Egyptian Tourist Authority
Wilshire San Vicente Plaza
8383 Wilshire Boulevard, Suite 215
Beverly Hills, CA 90211
Telephone: (323) 653-8815
Telephone: (877) 773-4978 toll-free in USA
Fax: (323) 653-8961
E-mail: Egypt@etala.com

USA: Chicago office
Egyptian Tourist Authority
645 North Michigan Avenue, Suite 829
Chicago, IL 60611
Telephone: (312) 280-4666
Telephone: (877) 773-4978 toll-free in USA
Fax: (312) 280-4788
E-mail: none

USA: New York office
Egyptian Tourist Authority
630 Fifth Avenue, Suite 1706
New York, NY 10111
Telephone: (212) 352-2570
Telephone: (877) 773-4978 toll-free in USA
Fax: (212) 956-6439
E-mail: egypttoursp@aol.com

Embassy of the Arab Republic of Egypt
3521 International Court, NW
Washington, DC 20008
Telephone: (202) 966-6342
E-mail: egypt-embassy@usa.net

E-mail: embassy@egyptembdc.org
Website: www.embassyofegyptwashingtondc.org

El Salvador

There are two methods of obtaining the proper documentation for bringing pets into El Salvador.
1. The International Health Certificate is notarized by a county official (County Clerk) and then forwarded to the Consulate office to be legalized. There is a $20 fee.
2. The International Health Certificate can be taken to the Department of State within each of the U.S. states and given an Apostille Seal. This process bypasses the Consulate office.

Website: www.elsalvadorturismo.gob.sv

El Salvador office
    Corporacion Salvadoreña de Turismo (CORSATUR) (Salvadorian Tourism Corporation)
    Bvd del Hipódromo 508
    Col. San Benito
    San Salvador, El Salvador
    Telephone: 243 7835
    Fax: 243 0427
    E-mail: corsatur@salnet.net

Canada office
    Consulate General of El Salvador
    1080 Cote du Beaver Hall, Bureau 1604
    Montreal, QC H2Z 1S8, Canada
    Telephone: (514) 861-6515
    Fax: (514) 861-6513
    E-mail: none

Embassy of the Republic of El Salvador
2308 California St, NW
Washington, DC 20008
Telephone: (202) 265-9671 / 72 / 75
Fax: (202) 234-3834

E-mail: correo@elsalvador.org
Website: www.elsalvador.org

England
See also: United Kingdom

Website: www.travelengland.org.uk/

UK office
English Tourist Board
Thames Tower
Black's Road
Hammersmith
London W6 9EL, UK
Telephone: 0800 192 192 toll-free in England
E-mail: travelinfo@bta.org.uk

Equatorial Guinea
A rabies inoculation certificate must accompany pets. All animals are subject to examination by a Customs Veterinarian (clearance may be delayed after office hours and on weekends).

Embassy of The Republic of Equatorial Guinea
1712 I Street, N.W., Suite 410
Washington D.C. 20006
Telephone: (202) 296-4174
Fax: (202) 296-4195
E-mail:
Website: www.equatorialguinea.org

Eritrea
A veterinarian good health certificate issued at the point of origin must accompany dogs, cats, and other pets. At the entry point, both the Health Officer of Quarantine and the Ministry of Agriculture Quarantine Officer will request the health certificate.

Eritrea office
Ministry of Tourism
P.O. Box 1010

Asmara, Eritrea
Telephone: (1) 126 997 or 123 941 or 122 999
Fax: (1) 126 949
E-mail: ona12@eol.com.er

Embassy of Eritrea
1708 New Hampshire Avenue, NW
Washington, DC 20009
Telephone: (202) 319-1991
Fax: (202) 319-1304
E-mail: veronica@embassyeritrea.org
Website: www.embassyeritrea.org

Estonia

Only clinically healthy cats and dogs older than 10 weeks may be imported into the Republic of Estonia. Cats and dogs should be vaccinated against rabies with internationally accepted vaccine at least 30 days and not more than 12 months before entering Estonia. The International Health Certificate or the international passport of the pet should state the name of the vaccine and date of vaccination by the veterinary official. Documents may be in Estonian, English, or Russian. All such certificates must be certified by the Secretary of State where the document was issued and legalized at the Consulate General of the Republic of Estonia in New York. The legalization fee is $12.00 per document.

For more information contact the Veterinarian Border Inspection, Telephone 372-6-380181 or 372-6-380177.

Estonia Veterinary contact:
E-mail: vet@vet.agri.ee

Website: www.tourism.ee
Website: www.visitestonia.com
Website: www.tallinn.ee/turismiinfo

Estonia office
Estonian Tourist Board
Roosikrantsi 11

10119 Tallinn, Estonia
Telephone: +372 6279 770
Fax: +372 6279 777
E-mail: info@visitestonia.com
E-mail: tourism@eas.ee

Consulate General of the Republic of Estonia
600 Third Avenue, 26th Floor
New York, NY 10016
Telephone: (212) 883-0636
Fax: (212) 883-0648
E-mail: none

Embassy of Estonia
1730 M Street, NW
Suite 503
Washington, DC 20008
Telephone: (202) 588-0101
Fax: (202) 588-0108
E-mail: Emb.Washington@mfa.ee
E-mail: info@estemb.org
Website: www.estemb.org

Ethiopia

A current International Health Certificate issued at the point of origin must accompany cats and dogs.

Website: www.visitethiopia.org

Ethiopia office
   Ethiopian Tourism Commission
   P.O. Box 2183
   Addis Ababa, Ethiopia
   Telephone: (1) 517 470 or 512 310
   Fax: (1) 513 899
   E-mail: tour-com@telecom.net.et

Embassy of Ethiopia
3506 International Drive NW
Washington, DC 20008

Telephone: (202) 364-1200
Fax: (202) 686-9551
E-mail: info@ethiopianembassy.org
Website: www.ethiopianembassy.org

Falkland Islands

At present, only cats and dogs from UK, New Zealand, and Australia are permitted to be imported. If they are brought here from the UK by boat, they must undergo a 2-week house confinement upon arrival. If they arrive by plane from any of those three countries, they must undergo 4 weeks house confinement upon arrival. Other animals, or from any other country, will be dealt with on an individual basis by the veterinary department. You may contact a veterinarian directly by E-mail: spointing@doa.gov.fk or klawrence@doa.gov.fk.

Website: www.tourism.org.fk
Website: www.falklandislands.com

Falkland Islands office
Falkland Islands Tourist Board
West Hillside, Stanley, Falkland Islands
Telephone: (500) 22215
Fax: (500) 22619
E-mail: jettycentre@horizon.co.fk

UK office
Falkland Islands Tourist Board
Falkland House
14 Broadway, Westminster
London SW1H 0BH, UK
Telephone: 171 222 2542
Fax: 171 222 2375
E-mail: manager@figo.u-net.com

USA office
Falkland Islands Tourist Board
Tread Lightly Travel
37 Juniper Meadow Road
Box 329
Washington Depot, CT 06794

Telephone: (860) 868-1710
Fax: (860) 868-1718
E-mail: patread@aol.com

The Falkland Islands is a British Overseas Territory represented abroad by British Embassies. See also: United Kingdom.

Faroe Islands

Importing pets to the Faroe Island by tourists is prohibited. The commercial importation of pets to the Faroe Islands has to follow the rules laid down in the EU Directive 97/78/EC that has been implemented in the Faroese legislation. Currently, the legislation on importation of pets is under revision. The FUTURE rules are the following:
1. Pet animals can only be imported by residents on the Faroe Islands or who are moving to the Faroe Islands. Tourists are not allowed to bring their pets with them.
2. Importation of dangerous animals (Pit Bull Terriers, poisonous snakes, or invertebrates, etc.) is forbidden.
3. Importation of dogs and cats from countries or areas with rabies shall be vaccinated against rabies not later than one month before the arrival and no earlier than one year before they arrive.
4. Dogs and cats shall be vaccinated against common viral and bacterial diseases and treated against endo and ectoparasites.
5. A health certificate issued by a veterinarian no earlier than one week before the arrival shall accompany pets intended for importation to the Faroe Islands.

For more information contact:
 Bjorn Harlou
 Chief Veterinary Officer
 Ministry of Trade and Industry
 Veterinary Department
 Portulalio, Tinganes
 P.O. Box 139
 FO-110 Torshavn
 Faroe Islands
 E-mail: cvo@vmr.fo

Fiji

A permit is required for all pets. Pets will require quarantine on arrival, unless from Australia, Canada, New Zealand, United Kingdom or United States (including Hawaii). The country of origin will determine the length of quarantine.

Make inquiries to:
>Director of Animal Health and Production
GP.O. Box 15829, Suva
Telephone: 679 315322
Fax: 679 301368

Website: www.BulaFiji.com
Website: www.bulafiji-americas.com

Fiji office
>Fiji Visitors Bureau
P.O. Box 92
Thomson Street
Suva, Fiji
Telephone: (679) 302 433
Fax: (679) 300 970 or 302 751 or 300 986
E-mail: infodesk@fijifvb.gov.fj
E-mail: marketing@fijivb.gov.fj

UK office
>Fiji Visitors Bureau
34 Hyde Park Gate
London SW7 5BN, UK
Telephone: 171-584-3661
Fax: 171-584-2838
E-mail: fijirepuk@compuserve.com

USA: California office
>Fiji Visitors Bureau
5777 West Century Boulevard, Suite 220
Los Angeles, CA 90045
Telephone: (310) 568-1616
Telephone: (800) 932-3454 toll-free in USA
Fax: (310) 670-2318

E-mail: infodesk@bulafiji-americas.com
This office also deals with inquires from Canada.

Embassy of Fiji
2233 Wisconsin Avenue, NW
Suite 240
Washington, DC 20007
Telephone: (202) 337-8320
Fax: (202) 337-1996
E-mail: fijiemb@earthlink.net
Website: none

Finland

Dogs and cats can be imported to Finland; however, they need to be vaccinated against rabies. A certificate issued by a qualified veterinary surgeon in the country of export must state that the animal has been vaccinated at least 30 days and not more than 12 months before importation. The certificate must state the name and batch number of the rabies vaccine. The document/certificate must be in English, Finnish, Swedish, Danish, German, or Norwegian. Dogs and cats imported from rabies-free countries do not need the rabies vaccination mentioned above, if the animals have not visited a rabies-country during transportation. The International Health Certificate must be current. No import permit is required. There is no mandatory quarantine.

Traveling with pets in Finland
Rail: Long distance rail service. There is a special car for the travelers with pets. Reservations are necessary. For sleeping cars, you need to reserve a whole compartment. There is a separate charge for a seat and sleeping car reservation.
Local rail service: There are special cars for the travelers with pets. There is no extra charge. It is recommended to avoid the rush hours.
Bus: Pets are allowed on long distance buses. However, if there is a passenger already in the bus with allergies then the pet is not allowed to travel in that bus. Pets and pet owners are directed to travel in the back of the bus.
Hotels: Most of the hotels accept pets; you need to mention it when making the reservation. Hotels have limited number of rooms for the travelers with pets. Pets are not allowed in restaurants in Finland.

Website: www.mek.fi
Website: www.thekingsroad.com
Website: www.finland-tourism.com
Website: www.finlandkingsroad.com

UK office
 Finnish Tourist Board
 PO Box 33213
  London W6 8JX, UK
  Telephone: 20-8600 5680
  Fax: 20-8600 5681
  E-mail: mek.lon@mek.fi

USA office
 Finnish Tourist Board
 655 Third Avenue
 New York, NY 10017
 Telephone: (212) 885-9737
 Telephone: (800) 346-4636 toll-free in North America
 Fax: (212) 885-9739
 E-mail: mek.usa@mek.fi

Embassy of Finland
3301 Massachusetts Avenue, NW
Washington, DC 20008
Telephone: (202) 298-5800
Fax: (202) 298-6030
E-mail: info@finland.org
Website: www.finland.org

France

This information is from the French Embassy.

Dogs and Cats
Travelers may bring their dogs and cats from the United States into France or transit in France, under the following conditions:
- Each family is limited to 5 animals. Every animal must be at least 3 months old. If it is younger, it must be traveling with its mother.

- Every animal must be identified by a microchip or a tattoo.
- Every animal must be accompanied with a valid rabies vaccination certificate.
- A health certificate (in French) executed no more than 10 days before the arrival of the pet(s) into France must accompany the pet(s).

WARNING: The health certificate requires that the pets have had shots for the following diseases:
- For cats: feline leucopenia
- For dogs: canine distemper, viral hepatitis, leptospirosis, and canine parvovirus.

Moreover, for dogs and cats, a blood test to confirm the rabies vaccination anti-body level must be done at least **3 months** before arrival into France. The dosage must also be done at least 30 days after the pet has been vaccinated against rabies for the first time.
There is no need to revaccinate the pet if the vaccination is still valid.
There is no need to do a new blood test if one has already been done on the pet.

Domestic pet rodents (rabbits, hamsters, mice...)
You may bring into France a maximum of 5 domestic rodents. A health certificate (in French), executed not more than **ten days** prior to arrival into France by a national licensed veterinarian of the country of export (i.e., in the US, a USDA certified veterinarian), must accompany the rodent.

Pet reptiles not intended for sale
You may bring into France a maximum of 5 pet reptiles (by family), provided:
- They are not sold under any circumstances;
- They are accompanied by a health certificate executed not more than ten days prior to arrival and bearing the signature of a licensed veterinarian of the country of export (i.e., in the US, a USDA certified veterinarian);
- They must be free of evidence of disease (in particular, of lesions of the skin).

Pet birds
Pet birds may be brought into France, although one family is only allowed to bring 2 birds of the Psittaciformes (parrots) order and 10 birds of other small species.

The following requirements must be fulfilled:
- A valid health certificate, executed by a licensed veterinarian in the country of export within ten days before the arrival and showing that the animal is free of evidence of disease, should accompany the bird;
- The following written pledge should also be submitted to Customs, in French at the port of entry. "Je soussigné (nom, prénom du propriétaire), certifie être le propriétaire du/des oiseaux (descritpion:race, couleur, taille, âge,). Je m'engage à ne pas les revendre et j'accepte tout contrôle que les services vétérinaires estimeraient nécessaires d'effectuer à l'adresse suivante (adresse du propriétaire). Date: Signature:
- English version: "I, (owner's Full Name), certify I am the owner of this/these bird(s) (description: breed, color, size, age). I undertake not to sell them and to accept any sanitary visit considered necessary by the Veterinarian services at the following address: (owner's address in France). Date: Signature:

WARNING: Many birds are registered as "Endangered Species" according to the Washington Convention. In such case, a specific permit is required in the country of departure and in the country of arrival. Please check our page "Endangered Species."

Other species
For other pets than those mentioned above or pets listed above but intended to be exported to France in greater quantities than those allowed for under the standards regulation, please call the French Embassy (202) 944-6375.

WARNING: France is party to the Convention on International Trade in Endangered Species of Wild Fauna and Flora. International trade in species listed by the Convention is unlawful unless authorized by permit. This includes, for example, wild birds, reptiles, crustaceans, fish as well as any part or product (such as skins, feathers, eggs) and products and articles manufactured from wildlife and fish. Permits to export from Canada or re-export certificates are issued by Environment Canada (Convention Administrator, Canadian Wildlife Service, Ottawa, ON K1A 0H3). Permits to export from the US or re-export certificates are issued by the US Fish and Wildlife Service (Office of Management Authority, Department of the Interior, Washington, DC 20240). Permits to import into France are issued by the Ministère de l'aménagement du territoire et de l'environnement (direction de la nature et des paysages - sous-direction de la chasse, de la faune et de la flore sauvages - bureau des échanges internationaux d'espèces protégées - 20, avenue de Ségur 75302 Paris 07 SP - France).

The application for such a permit must be filed, in French.
For more information, contact the Agricultural Service at the French Embassy in Washington, DC, telephone: 202-944-6341/6358, fax 202-944-6303. The Website: www.info-france-usa.org/customs has additional information on pets. The application to import is also available online.

Website: www.franceguide.com
Website: www.francetourism.com
Website: www.fgtousa.org

Canada office
    Maison de la France
    1981 av. McGill College, Suite 490
    Montreal, QC H3A 2W9, Canada
    Telephone: (514) 288-4264
    Fax: (514) 845-4868
    E-mail: mfrance@attcanada.net

UK office
    Maison de la France
    178 Piccadilly
    London W1V 0AL, UK
    Telephone: 207 399 3500
    Fax: 207 493 6594

USA: California office
French Government Tourist Office
9454 Wilshire Boulevard, Suite 715
Beverly Hills, CA 90212-2967
Telephone: (310) 271-6665
Fax: (310) 276-2835
E-mail: fgto@gte.net

USA: Illinois office
French Government Tourist Office
676 North Michigan Avenue, Suite 3360
Chicago, IL 60611-2819
Telephone: (312) 751-7800
Fax: (312) 337-6339
E-mail: fgto@mcs.net

USA: New York office
French Government Tourist Office
444 Madison Avenue
New York, NY 10022-6903
Telephone: (212) 838-7800
Fax: (212) 838-7855
E-mail: info@francetourism.com

French Embassy
4101 Reservoir Road, NW
Washington, DC 20007
Telephone: (202) 944-6000
Fax: (202) 944-6072
E-mail: info@ambafrance-us.org
Website: www.ambafrance-us.org

French Guiana

Also known as Guyane.
See also: France

The policies to import pets are the same as France.

Website: www.guyanetourisme.com
Website: www.tourisme-guyane.gf

French Guiana office
   Comite du Tourisme de la Guyane
   12 rue Lallouette
   B.P. 801
   97338 CAYENNE Cedex
   Telephone: 0594 29 65 00
   Fax: 0594 29 65 01
   E-mail: ctginfo@tourimse-guyane.gf

French Guiana is an Overseas Department of the Republic of France and does not maintain overseas missions/embassies. See also: France.

French Polynesia

There is no quarantine of pets coming from Hawaii. The importation of pets from the continental United States is strictly forbidden. As a derogation you can obtain an importation permit if:
1. Your pet spends one month in an authorized quarantine station in one of the following countries: Australia, State of Hawaii, Ireland, Iceland, New Caledonia, New Zealand, or United Kingdom. There is no authorized quarantine station in French Polynesia.
2. Your pet stayed continuously in the U.S. for the six months immediately preceding their departure to the quarantine station. A dosage of antibodies against rabies was practiced at least three months after first vaccine injection and three months before departure to quarantine station. The antibodies titer must be ≥ 0.5 IU/ml.

At importation time in French Polynesia, your pet must be correctly vaccinated against rabies and:
- Dogs: canine distemper, viral hepatitis, leptospirosis, and canine parvovirus.
- Cats: feline panleukopenia, calicivirus, and rhinotracheitis.

When the antibody dosage is completed and you have made a firm reservation in a quarantine station, please write again to ask for entry for your pet. Your letter must enclose all the items of the following list.

1. Officially authorized copy of the pet's vaccination book.
2. Officially authenticated copy of the pet's vaccination certificate for rabies.
3. Officially authenticated copy of the pet's identification card. Only skin tattoo and microchip ISO 11784 of operating frequency 134.2 kHz are agreed by French Polynesia. Identification is compulsory.
4. A veterinarian's statement that the pet has been staying continuously in the U.S. during the six months immediately preceding their departure to the quarantine station.
5. Officially authenticated copy of the pet's antibody dosage bearing the identification number of the pet.
6. Officially authenticated copy of our reservation in the quarantine station.

Website: www.gototahiti.com
Website: www.tahiti-tourisme.com
Website: www.cia.gov/cia

Tahiti office
    Tahiti Tourisme
    P. O. Box 65
    Papeete, Tahiti
    Telephone: (689) 50 57 00
    Fax: (689) 43 66 19
    Email: tahiti-tourisme@mail.pf

UK office
    Tahiti Tourisme
    c/o CIB Group
    1 Battersea Church Road
    London SW11 3LY, UK
    Telephone: (020) 7771 7023
    Fax: (020) 7771 7059
    E-mail: tahiti@cibgroup.co.uk

USA office
    Tahiti Tourisme
    300 Continental Boulevard, Suite 160
    El Segundo, CA 90245

Telephone: (310) 414-8484
Fax: (310) 414-8490
E-mail: tahiti-tourisme@mail.pf
E-mail: tahitilax@earthlink.net

French Polynesia (Tahiti) is an Overseas Territory of the Republic of France and does not maintain overseas missions/embassies. See also: France.

Gabon

Gabon requires an International Health Certificate and vaccination certificates to enter the country. These documents should be translated into French. Pets are allowed on trains, buses, and the airline system but small pets will need to be in proper kennels. Most hotels, restaurants, and places of business do not allow pets, so contact your hotel before leaving home.

Additional information:
Airways
- A vaccination book with all recent vaccinations.
- An international good health certificate provided after the veterinary consultation. It should be established less than 72 hours before the day of departure.
- Pets cannot travel before three months old.
- If it is the first travel, vaccinations must be made one month ahead. Vaccinations against rabies and others usual diseases (concerning dogs and cats) are the most important. Rabies vaccination must be dated more than one month and less than one year.

Railway
- "Transgabonais" is the national and unique railway company.
- Travel by train is permitted for pets only if it is in a cage.
- The price depends on the distance.

Hotels
- The Maïsha Hotel Residency: pets are just accepted outside. Not in bedrooms;
- Okoume Palace Intercontinental: pets are not accepted.

- Atlantic Hotel: only non aggressive pets are permitted but it must be kept on a lead during the stay;
- Monts de Cristal hotel: pets are not permitted. Except at the subsoil and put into a cage;
- Rapotchombo: pets in a cage are accepted with a daily tax of CFA Francs 5000 (FF 50);
- Meridien Ré-Ndama: only small pets, as dachshund or poodle, are accepted in a cage.

Internal airline companies
- Air Gabon: pets under 5kg weight are allowed in the cabin. From 5kg it go into a cage;
- Air Service Gabon: pets are weighed (CFA Francs 800/ kg)
- Gabon Fret: pets are weighed. The price of weight depend on destination;
- Air Inter Gabon: pets are weighed (CFA Francs 700 / kg) and put into a cage.
- Gabon Express: pets go into a cage. When the weight is under 10kg, the price is CFA Francs 5000. Beyond this, the price is fixed on CFA Francs 470 / kg);
- Gabon Air Transport: pets are not carried.
- Avirex: pets are weighed (CFA Francs 1500 / kg) and put into a cage;
- Air Affaires Gabon: pets are not carried;
- Transair: pets are put into a cage and pay all-in price.

Website: www.internetgabon.com/tourisme

Canada office
GABONTOUR
4 Range Road
P.O. Box 368
Ottawa, ON KIN 8J5, Canada
Telephone: (613) 232-5301 / 232-5302
Fax: (613) 232-6916
E-mail: none

Gabon office
  Centre Gabonais de Promotion Touristique (GABONTOUR)
  BP 2085
  Libreville, Gabon
  Telephone: 728 504 or 723 949
  Fax: 728 503
  E-mail: gabontour@internetgabon.com
  E-mail: men@internetgabon.com

UK office
  GABONTOUR
  27 Elvaston Place
  London SW7 5NL, UK
  Telephone: 171 823 99 86
  Fax: 171 584 00 47
  E-mail: none

USA office
  GABONTOUJR
  347 Fifth Avenue, Suite810
  New York, NY 10016
  Telephone: (212) 447-6700
  Fax: (212) 447-1532
  E-mail: LTT1NYC@aol.com

  Embassy of The Gabonese Republic
  2034 20th Street, NW
  Suite 200
  Washington, DC 20009
  Telephone: (202) 797-1000
  Fax: (202) 332-0668
  E-mail: consulategabon@aol.com
  Website: none

Gambia

A current International Health Certificate issued at the point of origin must accompany cats and dogs. The day after arrival, pets have to be registered at the Gambian Veterinary Department to obtain an import permit. Telephone: 220-472727. Pets may enter as passenger's checked baggage, in the cabin or as cargo.

Website: www.gambia.com

Gambia office
    The Gambia National Tourist Office
    Ministry of Tourism and Culture
    The Quadrangle
    Banjul, The Gambia
    Telephone: (220) 228 496
    Fax: (220) 227 753
    E-mail: gntohq@gamtel.gm

UK office
    The Gambia National Tourist Office
    The Gambia High Commission Building
    57 Kensington Court
    London W8 5DG, UK
    Telephone: 20 7376 0093
    Fax: 20 7937 9095
    E-mail: info@thegambia-touristoff.co.uk

Embassy of The Gambia
1155 15th Street, NW
Suite 1000
Washington, DC 20005
Telephone: (202) 785-1399
Fax: (202) 785-1430
E-mail: gamembdc@gambia.com
Website: none

Georgia

Georgia requires an International Health Certificate. Upon arrival, your pet may require an examination by a Georgian veterinarian. If you have any endangered species of animal, you must have a license from the appropriate department in your country, although Customs may detain you until the appropriate Georgian Department is notified.

Georgia office
    State Department of Tourism and Resorts
    Prospekt Chavchavadze 80

380062 Tbilisi, Georgia
Telephone: (32) 226 125
Fax: (32) 294 052
E-mail: none

Embassy of the Republic of Georgia
1615 New Hampshire Avenue NW
Suite 300
Washington, DC 20009
Telephone: (202) 387-2390
Fax: (202) 393-4537
E-mail: none
Website: www.georgiaemb.org
The embassy will also deal with inquires from Canada.

Germany

Dogs and cats need a current International Health Certificate, issued by a licensed veterinarian more than 30 days but less than 12 months before entry, plus a notarized German translation of the document. There is no quarantine. No import permit is required. The International Health Certificate must have a USDA stamp if the pet is from the U.S.

The German Consulate submitted the following information.

REGULATIONS REGARDING THE IMPORTATION AND TRANSIT OF CERTAIN DOMESTIC ANIMALS INTO THE FEDERAL REPUBLIC OF GERMANY FROM THIRD COUNTRIES

The following German regulations under epizootic law should be observed for the importation and transit of domestic animals.

Dogs and Domestic Cats
Internal Market Epizootic Protection Ordinance promulgated March 31, 1995 (BGBl. I, p. 431) as amended.

Principle
A permit under epizootic law shall be required for the importation and transit of dogs and domestic cats from the highest veterinary authority of the *Land*, which you enter first.

Exceptions
A permit shall not be required for the importation and transit of dogs and domestic cats:
1. Which are imported or transported in transit by travelers or being imported for reasons of moving to Germany provided
   a. Not more than three animals are involved, in the case of falls of dogs or domestic cats the dam and the entire fall under three months
   b. These animals are not intended to be handed over to a third person, and
   c. It is proved that each animal has been vaccinated against rabies - or in case of litters the mother - and that the vaccination
      - Occurred at least 30 days but not more than 12 months before entering the Federal Republic of Germany.
      - Was renewed within 12 month of the previous vaccination against rabies but no more than 12 month before entering the Federal Republic of Germany.

A veterinarian must certify the vaccination. A valid International Vaccination Certificate or a veterinary vaccination certificate **must be issued in the German language** or must be accompanied by an officially certified German translation. If the documents are multilingual, including German, an official certification is not necessary. The seal or stamp must clearly state the agency or the address of the veterinary surgeon.

2. Which are in transit between locations of a neighboring third country across the territory of the Federal Republic of Germany or between locations in Germany across the territory of a neighboring third country if there is an agreement between the Federal Republic of Germany and this third country to facilitate transit traffic;

3. Which are used for artistic performances;
4. Dogs
   a. Which are used as guide dogs and official dogs of the Federal Armed Forces, the Federal Border Guard, customs authorities or the police or in the rescue service;
   b. Sledge dogs for the purposes of participating in races accompanied by a written confirmation of participation from the organizer of the race;
   c. Transported within or imported into the European Union accompanied by a vaccination certificate in accordance with paragraph 1.

A permit from the highest veterinary authority of the Land, which you enter first, is required for the importation of dogs and domestic cats not vaccinated against rabies regardless of age. This applies to pets not traveling with a person or handed over to a third person.

Parrots and Parakeets
Internal Market Epizootic Protection Ordinance promulgated March 31, 1995 (BGBl. I, p. 431) as amended.

Principle
A permit under epizootic law shall be required for the importation and transit of parrots and parakeets from the highest veterinary authority of the Land, which you enter first.

Exceptions
A permit shall not be required for the importation and transit of parrots and parakeet,
1. Which are imported or transported in transit by travelers or being imported for reasons of moving to Germany provided
   a. Not more than three animals are involved,
   b. These animals are not intended to be handed over to a third person;
2. Which are accompanied by an International Health Certificate issued no more than 10 days before departure. The health certificate should also state that the animals have been found healthy and no diseases communicable to parrots

and parakeets have been notified within the last 30 days in their stock of origin;
3. Which are in transit between locations of a neighboring third country across the territory of the Federal Republic of Germany or between locations in Germany across the territory of a neighboring third country if there is an agreement between the Federal Republic of Germany and this third country to facilitate transit traffic;
4. Which are used for artistic performances.

Domestic and Wild Fowl
Internal Market Epizootic Protection Ordinance promulgated March 31, 1995 (BGBl. I, p. 431) as amended

Principle
A permit under epizootic law shall be required for the importation and transit of domestic wild fowl from the highest veterinary authority of the Land, which you enter first.

Exceptions
A permit shall not be required for carrier pigeons if they are imported in special containers for being released.

Scope:
- Domestic fowl: ducks, geese, hens including guinea fowls and turkeys, flat-chested birds;
- Wild fowl: capercaillies, black-grouse game, pheasants, sand grouses, hazel hens, red grouses, moor-grouses, hybrid grouses, partridges, snow-grouses, snipes, swans, rock partridges, bustards, wild turkeys, coots, wild ducks, wild geese, quails, peacocks, wild pigeons, peacocks, doves.

Hares and Domestic Rabbits
Internal Market Epizootic Protection Ordinance promulgated March 31, 1995 (BGBl. I, p. 431) as amended.

Principle
A permit under epizootic law shall be required for the importation and transit of live hares and rabbits from the highest veterinary authority of the Land, which you enter first.

Exceptions
A permit shall not be required for the importation and transit of hares and domestic rabbits
1. Which are imported or transported in transit by travelers or being imported for reasons of moving to Germany provided
   a. Not more than three animals are involved
   b. These animals are not intended to be handed over to a third person.
2. Which are in transit between locations of a neighboring third country across the territory of the Federal Republic of Germany or between locations in Germany across the territory of a neighboring third country if there is an agreement between the Federal Republic of Germany and this third country to facilitate transit traffic;
3. Which are used for artistic performances.

Monkeys
Internal Market Epizootic Protection Ordinance promulgated March 31, 1995 (BGBl. I, p. 431) as amended

Principle
A permit under epizootic law shall be required for the importation and transit of monkeys and prosimians from the highest veterinary authority of the Land, which you enter first.

Others
Reptiles, Aquarium Fishes, Gold Fishes, Hamsters, or Guinea Pigs are not subject to any import restrictions under epizootic law.

In consideration of the epizootic conditions in the countries of origin, the regulations governing the importation of animals not specified above vary from country to country. Please be advised to consult in any case the responsible veterinary authority of the Land you will enter.

In accordance with the legal requirements of the European Union and of the Federal Republic of Germany, also the Washington Convention on International Trade in Endangered Species of Wild Fauna and Flora must continue to be observed for the importation of domestic

animals. For questions on this matter, please contact the responsible German authority:
   Bundesamt für Naturschutz
   Konstantinstr 110
   D-53179 Bonn
   Telephone: (0228) 9543-453/441/458
   Fax: (0228) 9543-470

Website: www.germany-tourism.de

Canada office
   German National Tourist Office
   North Tower, Suite 604
   175 Bloor Street East
   Toronto, ON M4W 3R8, Canada
   Telephone: (416) 968-1570
   Fax: (416) 968-1986
   E-mail: germanto@idirect.com

UK office
   German National Tourist Office
   P.O. Box 2965
   London W1A 3TN, UK
   Telephone: 09001 600100 24 hour brochure request service
   Fax: 020 7495 6129
   E-mail: gntolon@d-z-t.com

USA: Los Angeles office
   German National Tourist Office
   P. O. Box 641009
   Los Angeles, CA 90062
   Telephone: (212) 661-7200
   Fax: (212) 661-7174
   E-mail: gntolax@aol.com

USA: New York office
   German National Tourist Office
   52nd Floor
   122 East 42nd Street

New York, NY 10168-0072
Telephone: (212) 661-7200
Fax: (212) 661-7174
E-mail: gntony@aol.com

Embassy of Germany
4645 Reservoir Road, NW
Washington, DC 20007-1998
Telephone: (202) 298-4000
Fax: (202) 298-4249 or 333-2653
E-mail: gic1@germany-info.org
Website: www.germany-info.org

Ghana

An International Health Certificate and a current rabies vaccination certificate must be presented upon entering Ghana. There is no quarantine. They may enter as passenger's checked baggage either in the cabin or as cargo.

USA office
   Ghana Permanent Mission to the United Nations
   (Visas and Tourist Information)
   19 East 47th Street
   New York, NY 10017
   Telephone: (212) 832-1300
   Fax: (212) 751-6743
   E-mail: ghanaperm@aol.com

Embassy of Ghana
3512 International Drive, NW
Washington, DC 20008
Telephone: (202) 686-4520-4526
Fax: (202) 686-4527
E-mail: ghemwash@cais.com
E-mail: infocon@cais.com
Website: ghana-embassy.org

Gibraltar

Cats and dogs may be imported only directly from the United Kingdom or via the UK from the Channel Islands, Isle of Man, or Ireland provided at least 4 months of age and accompanied by:
1. A certificate from a veterinarian stating that they have been vaccinated against rabies not less than 28 days before importation, and
2. A certificate from the British Ministry of Agriculture stating that the animal has been resident for 6 months, or since birth, and that rabies has not existed in one of the areas mentioned above during the previous 12 months. The animals will be re-inoculated on arrival.

Website: www.gibraltar.gi

Gibraltar office
    Gibraltar Tourist Board
    Duke of Kent House
    Cathedral Square
    Gibraltar
    Telephone: +350 74950
    Fax: +350 74943
    E-mail: tourism@gibraltar.gi

USA office
    Gibraltar Tourist Board
    1156 15th Street, NW
    Suite 1100
    Washington, DC 20005
    Telephone: (202) 452-1108
    Fax: (202) 452-1109
    E-mail: gibinfobur@msn.com

Greece

Cats and dogs require health and rabies inoculation certificates issued by a veterinary authority in the country of origin not more than 12 months (cat six months) and not less than six days before arrival. Singing birds that have come from varieties and regions, which have been clear of parrot fever for not less than six months, may be imported. Parrots may be imported, provided they are not intended for resale. In the particular case of parrots, the health certificate must state that, at the time they were shipped, they were not suffering from parrot fever, and that their country of origin was not infected with parrot fever. Note: Keep birds under surveillance for six months after arrival. There is no quarantine or import permit.

Website: www.gnto.gr

Canada: Toronto office
Greek National Tourism Organization (GNTO)
1300 Bay Street, Main Level
Toronto, ON M5R 3K8, Canada
Telephone: (416) 968-2220
Fax: (416) 968-6533
E-mail: grnto.tor@sympatico.ca

Canada: Montreal office
Greek National Tourist Organization
1170 Place du Frere Andre, Suite 300
Montreal, QC H3B 3C6, Canada
Telephone: (514) 871-1535
Fax: (514) 871-1498

UK office
Greek National Tourist Organization
4 Conduit Street
London W1R ODJ, UK
Telephone: (00411) 2210105
Fax: (00411) 2871369
E-mail: greektouristoffice@btinternet.co.uk

USA: California office
Greek National Tourist Organization
611 West Sixth Street, Suite 2198
Los Angeles, CA 90017
Telephone: (213) 626-6696
Fax: (213) 489-9744

USA: New York office
   Greek National Tourist Organization
   645 Fifth Avenue Olympic Tower
   New York, NY 10022
   Telephone: (212) 421-5777
   Fax: (212) 826-6940
   E-mail: gnto@greektourism.com

Embassy of Greece
2221 Massachusetts Avenue, NW
Washington, DC 20008
Telephone: (202) 939-5800
Fax: none
E-mail: nycons@greekembassy.org
Website: www.greekembassy.ca

Greenland

Bringing pets to Greenland is not always possible. It is prohibited to bring pets (especially dogs) above the Arctic Circle and on the East Coast, as these are the sled dogs regions. To ensure the strength (and thereby survival) of the Greenland sled dogs, these cannot be crossbred. Some pets are allowed in the regions below the Arctic Circle, usually with some kind of quarantine. Check the government Website of www.gh.gl or call the Home Rule Government Office in Copenhagen +299 3369 3400. Special rules apply for Seeing Eye dogs.

Website: www.greenland.com
Website: www.greenland-guide.gl
Website: www.visitgreenland.com
Website: www.visitdenmark.com

Denmark office
   Greenland Tourism Copenhagen
   The National Tourist Board of Greenland
   Kalaallit Nunaanni Takornariaqarnermik Siunnersuisoqatigiit
   Pilestræde 52
   P.O. Box 1139
   DK-1010 Copenhagen K, Denmark
   Telephone: +45 33 69 32 00

Fax: +45 33 93 38 83
E-mail: info@greenland.com

Greenland office
The National Tourist Board of Greenland
Kalaallit Nunaanni Takornariaqarnermik Siunnersuisoqatigiit
P.O. Box 1615
DK-3900 Nuuk
Greenland
Telephone: (+299) 34 28 34
Mobil/cell telephone: (+299) 55 11 88
Private telephone: (+299) 31 11 55
Fax: (+299) 32 68 77
E-mail: jke@gt.gl
E-mail: info@greenland.com

UK office
Danish Tourist Board
55 Sloane Street
London SW1X 9SY, UK
Telephone: (020) 7259 5959
Fax: (020) 7259 5955
E-mail: dtb.london@dt.dk

USA office
Danish Tourist Board
655 Third Avenue, 18th Floor
New York, NY 10017
Telephone: (212) 885-9700
Fax: (212) 885-9726
E-mail: info@goscandinavia.com
Website: www.goscandinavia.com
This office also deals with enquiries relating to Canada.

Greenland is part of the Kingdom of Denmark and is represented abroad by Danish Embassies. See also: Denmark.

Grenada

Grenada has forms for the importation of pets such as dogs and cats. These forms are available at the Veterinary Division of the Ministry of Agriculture, which is located at the Ministerial Complex, in Tanteen, St. George's, Grenada. Sometimes, the Grenada Board of Tourism obtains the forms on behalf of those who have written to them requesting it.

The animal will need to be vaccinated against rabies, distemper, hepatitis, leptospirosis, parvovirus, and parainfluenza in the last months before arrival and with a certificate of proof. The animal will also require an International Health Certificate issued two (2) weeks before arrival. The permit must be presented at the time of arrival and the Government Veterinary Officer needs to be notified before arrival.

Website: www.grenadagrenadines.com
Website: www.spiceisle.com

Canada office
    Consulate General of Grenada
    Phoenix House
    439 University Avenue, Suite 930
    Toronto, ON M5G 1Y8, Canada
    Telephone: (416) 595-1343
    Fax: (416) 595-8278
    E-mail: grenadator@sympatico.ca
    E-mail: tourism@grenadaconsulate.com
    E-mail: info@grenadaconsulate.com
    Website: www.grenadaconsulate.com

Grenada office
    Grenada Board of Tourism
    P.O. Box 293
    Burns Point
    St George's, Grenada
    Telephone: 440 2001 or 440 2279
    Fax: 440 6637
    E-mail: gbt@caribsurf.com

UK office
    Grenada Board of Tourism
    1 Battersea Church Road

London SW11 3LY, UK
Telephone: 020 7771 7016
Fax: 020 7771 7059
E-mail: grenada@cibgroup.co.uk

USA office
Grenada Board of Tourism
c/o Richartz Fliss Clark & Pope
317 Madison Avenue, Suite 1522
New York, NY 10017
Telephone: (212) 687-9554
Telephone: (800) 927-9554 toll-free in USA
Fax: (212) 573-9731
E-mail: noel@rfcp.com

Embassy of Grenada
1701 New Hampshire Avenue, NW
Washington, DC 20009
Telephone: (202) 265-2561
Fax: (202) 265 2468
E-mail: grenada@oas.org
Website: none

Guadeloupe

Cats and dogs above the age of 3 months are admitted temporarily as pets. Visitors must have a certificate of origin and good health and/or a current rabies certificate, issued by a licensed veterinarian from the country of shipment.

Website: www.frenchcaribbean.com
Website: www.franceguide.com

Canada office
Maison de la France
1981 av. McGill College, Suite 490
Montreal, QC H3A 2W9, Canada
Telephone: (514) 288-4264
Fax: (514) 845-4868
E-mail: mfrance@attcanada.net

Guadeloupe office
  Office du Tourisme
  BP 422
  5 square de la Banque
  97181 Pointe-à-Pitre, Guadeloupe
  Telephone: (590) 82 09 30
  Fax: (590) 83 89 22
  E-mail: office.tourisme.guadeloupe@wanadoo.fr

Guadeloupe office
  The Tourist Bureau of BasseTerre
  Masion du Port
  97100 Basse-Terre, Guadeloupe
  Telephone: (590) 81 61 54 or 81 24 83
  Fax: (590) 81 18 10
  E-mail: otb@outremer.com

UK office
  Maison de la France (French Government Tourist Office)
  178 Piccadilly
  London W1J 9AL, UK
  Telephone: (09068) 244 123 (information line; calls cost 60p per minute)
  Fax: (020) 7493 6594
  E-mail: info@mdlf.co.uk

USA: California office
  French Government Tourist Office
  9454 Wilshire Boulevard, Suite 715
  Beverly Hills, CA 90212-2967
  Telephone: (310) 271-6665
  Fax: (310) 276-2835
  E-mail: fgto@gte.net

USA: Illinois office
  French Government Tourist Office
  676 North Michigan Avenue, Suite 3360
  Chicago, IL 60611-2819
  Telephone: (312) 751-7800

Fax: (312) 337-6339
E-mail: fgto@mcs.net

USA: New York office
French Government Tourist Office
444 Madison Avenue
New York, NY 10022-6903
Telephone: (212) 838-7800
Fax: (212) 838-7855
E-mail: info@francetourism.com

Guadeloupe is an Overseas Department of the Republic of France and is represented abroad by French Embassies. See also: France.

Guam

The following requirements are for obtaining an entry permit for cats and dogs:
1. A completed entry permit application by the owner of the animal or his authorized representative with the payment of the required fee of $60.00 per pet. Send a certified check or money order (payable to the Treasurer of Guam) to: Department of Health and Social Services, P.O. Box 2816, Agana, Guam 96910. The number for the animal shelter in Yigo is: (671) 653-2474/6717. The number for the Animal Control & Quarantine (Division of Environmental Health under the Dept of Public Health and Social Services) is (671) 735-7226. Please also verify the requirements below if they are still accurate.
2. A health certificate with veterinarian's signature dated not more than fourteen (14) days before shipment.
3. A rabies vaccination certificate with veterinarian's signature for animals over three months old, dated no less than thirty days, and not more than one year before shipment.
4. A certificate of immunization with veterinarian's signature against distemper, adenovirus, parainfluenza, parvovirus, corona virus, hepatitis, leptospirosis, and bordetella for dogs.
5. A certificate of immunization with veterinarian's signature against feline viral rhinotracheitis, calici virus, panleukopenia and feline leukemia for cats.

6. A confirmed reservation at one of Guam's government approved commercial quarantine facilities if originating from an area other than Hawaii, Australia, New Zealand, or the United Kingdom.

There is a minimal quarantine period before any animal will be allowed to enter Guam. Animals originating from Japan, Hong Kong, Oceania, and the continental United States (excluding counties contiguous to the United States-Mexico border, such as certain counties in California, Arizona, New Mexico, and Texas) can be quarantined on Guam. Animals originating from areas outside this list must be quarantined in Hawaii before being allowed on island.

There are no government quarantine areas on Guam, so pets must be kept in a private kennel. You must have a reservation with a government-approved kennel before shipping your pet to Guam. Currently, there is only one approved kennel on island. Ask your sponsor to contact the kennel for more information, or contact: Harper Valley Boarding & Quarantine at the village of Chalan Pago (671)-734-4543 Fax (671)-734-0151

If you have an exotic bird or other unusual pet, you must get an import permit to bring it to Guam. If you have any questions, please check with Guam's Department of Agriculture to see if your pet will be allowed on the island. Contact the department by writing:
Animal Industries Division
Department of Agriculture
P.O. Box 2950
Agana, Guam 96910
Telephone: (671)-734-3942/3
Fax: (671)-6569

Please be sure to contact them to verify that the statements above are correct or have been changed. Note: Information regarding Department of Agriculture Permits is available by calling: (671)-734-3965. The Department of Agriculture Veterinarian can be reached at (671)-734-3940.

Should you require further information, contact the Bureau of Animal Vector Control at Telephone: (671) 735-7204/7223 or Fax: (671) 734-5556. The Website: www.gov.gu/pets.html is also helpful.

All pets coming from the U.S. (except Hawaii) and Canada will be quarantined for 120 days.

Website: www.visitguam.org

Guam office
   Guam Visitors Bureau
   401 Pale San Vitores Road
   Tumon, GU 96913, Guam
   Telephone: 646-5278/9

   Fax: 646-8861
   E-mail: guaminfo@visitguam.org

USA office
   Guam Visitors Bureau
   1336-C Park Street
   Alameda, CA 94501
   Telephone: (800) 873-4826 toll-free in USA and Canada
   Telephone: (510) 865-0366
   Fax: (510) 865-5165
   E-mail: guam@avisoinc.com

Guam is an External Territory of the United States of America and is represented abroad by U.S. Embassies.

Guatemala

In order to bring your pet into Guatemala, your veterinarian needs to fill out the health certificate, which is then taken to the Department of Agriculture and then to the consulate to be legalized. Before sending any document to the Consular Section, it has to be notarized, authenticated by the County Court where the notary is registered (if applicable), and authenticated by the corresponding Secretary of State. Bring along a vaccination certificate that is less than one year old. Then your pet is legal in Guatemala.

Please note that you must pay with cash, certified check or through a money order payable to the Embassy of Guatemala. The fee is $10 per document. Also, note that along with your documents and proper payment, you must enclose a brief cover letter and a prepaid self-addressed envelope or airway bill. Documents may be dropped off in person or by courier Monday through Friday, from 10:00 am to 1:00 pm. There is no "while you wait" service. For further information, please contact the Consular Section Telephone: (202) 745-4952 Ext. 101, 106, 107.

Website: www.travel-guatemala.org.gt
Website: www.guatemala.travel.com.gt
Website: www.inguat.net

Guatemala office
  Guatemala Tourist Commission (INGUAT)
  7a Avenida 1-17, zona 4
  Centro Cívico
  Guatemala City, Guatemala
  Telephone: 331 1333
  Telephone: (888) 464-8281 toll-free number USA only
  Telephone: (801) 464-8281 toll-free number Guatemala only
  Fax: 331 4416 or 331 8893
  E-mail: infoINGUAT@intelnet.net.gt

UK office
  Embassy of The Republic of Guatemala
  13 Fawcett Street
  London SW10 9HN, UK
  Telephone: (020) 7351 3042 (embassy and consular section)
  Telephone: (020) 7349 0346 (tourism section)
  Fax: (020) 7376 5708 (embassy and consular section)
  Fax: (020) 7349 0331 (tourism section)
  E-mail: embagranbretana@minex.gob.gt
  Website: www.guatemalafzs.com

Embassy of The Republic of Guatemala
2220 R Street, NW
Washington, DC 20008
Telephone: (202) 745-4952

Fax: (202) 745-1908
E-mail: info@guatemala-embassy.org
E-mail: embestadosunidos@minex.gob.gt
E-mail: consulate@guatemala-embassy.org
Website: www.guatemala-embassy.org

Guernsey

See also: United Kingdom

Potential visitors to Guernsey wanting to bring their pets will need to travel either through St Malo or via Britain. There are currently no air carriers that fly direct to Guernsey and only one sea carrier (Emeraude), which is taking part in the scheme.

Details of air carriers participating in the scheme to London Heathrow:

Amsterdam (Schipol)	British Midland Airways
Brussels	British Midland Airways
Madrid	British Midland Airways
Majorca	British Midland Airways
Paris (Guide dogs only)	British Midland Airways
Helsinki	Finnair
Frankfurt	Lufthansa

When traveling by ferry, pets must be traveling in a vehicle and must stay in the vehicle during the journey. This scheme applies to cats and dogs only.

To qualify for the scheme, pets must (in this order):
- Be fitted with a microchip
- Be vaccinated against rabies
- Be blood tested
- Be issued with an official PETS certificate
- Be treated against ticks and tapeworm
- Have relevant documentation

Pet owners must ensure that they receive an official document issued by the country in which the treatment is carried out. No other documents are acceptable.

Depending on which qualifying country or countries to be visited, pet owners may have to obtain an export health certificate (this currently includes France and the Netherlands).

Upon arrival in the Guernsey, (or Great Britain if traveling via) pets, and documentation will be checked. If any of the checks are failed, a pet will have to either go into quarantine or return to the country from which it came.

Guernsey's Agriculture Committee does not currently have a Website however; Britain's Ministry of Agriculture has a Website where the appropriate forms and further information about the scheme can be downloaded. Website: www.maff.gov.uk

Guernsey's Committee of Agriculture advises that persons wishing to travel to Guernsey with their pet should contact their local Ministry of Agriculture for advice as rules of the scheme can vary from country to country.

It should be noted that it is against the law to bring certain dangerous dogs into Guernsey. These are Pit Bull Terriers and Japanese Tosa. If traveling through Great Britain it should be noted that the following dogs are banned in Great Britain: Pit Bull Terrier, Japanese Tosa, Dogo Argentino, and Fila Brasileiro.

For further information, please contact the Agriculture and Countryside Board:
    Telephone: 1481 235741 or 1481 236501
    Telephone: 1481 257261 (quarantine premises)
    Fax: 1481 235015
    E-mail: imports@agriculture.guernsey.gg
    E-mail: admin@agriculture.guernsey.gg
    Website: www.agriculture.guernsey.gg

Website: www.guernseytouristboard.com
Website: www.guernseytourism.gov.gg

Canada office
    Telephone: (888) VISIT UK (847-4885)
    Website: www.visitbritain.com/ca

Guernsey office
  Guernsey Tourist Board
  P.O. Box 23
  St Peter Port
  Guernsey, Channel Islands GY1 3AN, UK
  Telephone: (01481) 723 552
  Fax: (01481) 714 951
  E-mail: enquiries@tourism.guernsey.net

USA office
  British Tourist Authority
  Telephone: (800) 462-2748
  E-mail: travelinfo@bta.org.uk
  Website: www.travelbritain.org

Guinea

A current International Health Certificate and rabies inoculation certificate, issued at the point of origin, must accompany cats and dogs.

Website: www.guinee.gov.gn (French only)

Guinea office
  Office National du Tourisme
  BP 1275
  6 Avenue de la République
  Immeuble Al-Aman
  Conakry, Guinea
  Telephone: 455 161/62/62
  Fax: 455 164
  E-mail: none

Embassy of the Republic of Guinea
2112 Leroy Place, NW
Washington, DC 20008
Telephone: (202) 483-9420
Fax: (202) 483-8688
E-mail: emgui@sysnet.net
Website: none

Guinea-Bissau

A current International Health Certificate is required for pets to enter Guinea-Bissau.

The Embassy in Guinea-Bissau remains closed. U.S. citizens who plan to enter Guinea-Bissau despite the Travel Warning are encouraged to register with the Consular Section of the U.S. Embassy at Avenue Jean XXIII, Dakar, Senegal. The mailing address is B.P. 49, Dakar, Senegal. The telephone number is (221) 823-4296 and fax (221) 822-5903. The E-mail address is consulardakar@state.gov.

Guinea-Bissau office
    Centro de Informação e Turismo
    CP 294
    Bissau, Guinea-Bissau
    Telephone: 213 905 or 212 844 (government office)
    Fax: none
    E-mail: none

Embassy of The Republic of Guinea-Bissau
P.O. Box 33813
Washington, DC 20033
Telephone: (301) 947-3958
Fax: none
E-mail: none
Website: none

Guyana

Pets are permitted to enter Guyana after the following procedure has been completed:
1. Persons wishing to import live animals or birds into Guyana should first consult the Veterinary Authority, Ministry of Agriculture, Animal Services Division, Regent & New Garden Streets, Georgetown, Guyana to ascertain in the first place if--
    - The particular species of animal or bird is accepted into Guyana,
    - The import of animals is at all permitted from the country in question.

2. If the importation of live animals or birds is allowed, a written permit, under the hand of the Veterinary Authority or any veterinarian so authorized by him/her, will be issued detailing the health requirements and other conditions that are to be met by the exporting country.
3. The permit should then be sent to the Veterinary Authority of the exporting country who will inform the importer if the requisite conditions/requirements can be satisfied.
4. If these cannot all be satisfied, the Veterinary Authority in Guyana will then decide whether the animal (s) or bird (s) will be accepted under the circumstances.
5. Where import licenses are required, it will also be necessary to have these endorsed by the Veterinary Authority of Guyana. Licenses and import permits will normally be ready within two (2) days of application.

Arrangements for importation should be made only after completion of the above formalities.

6. An International Health Certificate duly signed by the Veterinarian so authorized must accompany animals or birds arriving in Guyana. The certificate should be issued no longer than one (1) day before departure of the animals or birds.
7. The Veterinary Authority of Guyana must be notified of arrivals at least twenty-four (24) hours before entry so that arrangements could be made for veterinary examination at the port of entry.

A Veterinary Officer at the port of entry must examine all animals or birds.

8. Animals or birds arriving in Guyana without an International Health Certificate or without a Ministry of Agriculture permit will be returned to the country of origin or destroyed at the port of entry.
9. All dogs and cats, (except those arriving from Australia, Great Britain, New Zealand, Northern Ireland, Republic of Ireland, Antigua, Dominica, Jamaica, Montserrat, St Kitts, St Lucia, St Vincent, Barbados, and Trinidad or any other country known to be free of rabies), will be quarantined for a period of at least three (3) months. Special arrangements are in place for animals traveling with a circus etc.

10. The imposition of quarantine of any form other than in the case of rabies (see 9), will be entirely at the discretion of the Veterinary Authority, will be influenced by the pattern of disease prevailing in the area of origin, at the time of export.

Website: www.exploreguyana.com

Guyana office
Tourism & Hospitality Association of Guyana
157 Waterloo Street
North Cummingsburg
Georgetown, Guyana
Telephone: 225 0807
Fax: 225 0817
E-mail: tag@solutions2000.net

UK office
Caribbean Tourism Organisation
42 Westminster Palace Gardens
Artillery Row
London SW1P 1RR, UK
Telephone: (020) 7222 4335
Fax: (020) 7222 4325
E-mail: cto@carib-tourism.com
Website: www.doitcaribbean.com

Embassy of Guyana
2490 Tracy Place, NW
Washington, DC 20008
Telephone: (202) 265-6900
Fax: (202) 232-1297
E-mail: guyanaembassy@hotmail.com
Website: www.guyana.org

Haiti

This information was obtained from the embassy. Tourists may not stay more than 90 days; pets would likely obey their masters on this one. Not too many people bring pets to Haiti. French translation of documentation would be helpful. It is advisable to have a recent rabies certificate (issued not less than 21 days and not more than 11 months before arrival). An International Health Certificate issued not more than 7 days prior to arrival is necessary. Check with your accommodations before planning to bring your pet. Pets are not allowed in restaurants.

Website: www.haititourisme.com
Website: www.haiti.org

Canada office
>Haitian National Office of Tourism
>50 Blvd Cremazie Ouest, Suite 617
>Box 344
>Montreal, PQ H2P 2T3, Canada
>Telephone: (514) 389-3577
>Fax: none
>E-mail: none

Haiti office
>Secrétariat d'Etat au Tourisme
>8 rue Légitime
>Port-au-Prince, Haiti
>Telephone: 223 2143 or 223 5631
>Fax: 221 0161
>E-mail: none

USA: New York office
>Haitian National Office of Tourism
>18 East 41st Street, Suite 1602
>New York, NY 10017
>Telephone: (212) 779-7177
>E-mail: none

USA: Miami office
>Haitian National Office of Tourism
>7270 NW 12th Street, Suite 2
>Miami, FL 33126
>Telephone: (305) 471-0607
>Fax: none
>E-mail: none

Embassy of The Republic of Haiti
2311 Massachusetts Avenue, NW
Washington, DC 20008
Telephone: (202) 332-4090
Fax: (202) 745-7215
E-mail: embassy@haiti.org
Website: www.haiti.org

Honduras

Entry into Honduras will require a certificate of vaccination issued by a veterinarian and this will have to be authenticated at the USDA office. Then you may apply for a permit to import the pet with a permit obtained from the Consulate. You may call the consulate for more information. You may also contact the Agriculture Ministry at (504) 232-5007 or by fax at (504) 232-9338. Additional information may be obtained by contacting the Honduras Information Office at (800) 410-9608 or E-mail: gohondurastourism@compuserve.com. The permit must be in Spanish and can be provided by the Embassy or Consulate of Honduras. There is no quarantine in Honduras.

Website: www.hondurasinfo.com
Website: www.letsgohonduras.com

Honduras office
   Instituto Hondureño de Turismo
   P.O. Box 3261
   Edificio Europa
   5to Piso, Colonia San Carlos
   Avenida Ramon Cruz
   Tegucigalpa, Honduras
   Telephone: 220 1600
   Fax: 238 2102
   E-mail: info@iht.hn

USA office
   Honduras Tourism Institute
   2100 Ponce de Leon Boulevard, Suite 1175
   Coral Gables, FL 33134
   Telephone: (800) 410-9608 toll-free in USA

Fax: none
E-mail: none

Embassy of Honduras
3007 Tilda Street, NW
Suite 4M
Washington, DC 20008
Telephone: (202) 966-7702
Fax: (202) 966-9751
E-mail: embhondu@aol.com
E-mail: consul.hondurasdcusa@verizon.net (Consular Section)
Website: www.honduaemb.org

Hong Kong

Pets may enter Hong Kong with a special permit. The special permit fee depends on the kind of imported animal. Include a full description of the animal or bird, date of arrival, means of transportation, scientific name of animals, etc. The length of quarantine will depend on the country of origin.

In general, an International Health Certificate and proper vaccinations are required. The permit may be obtained from:
Permit Issuing Desk (Counter #10)
5th Floor, Agriculture, Fisheries, and Conservation Department
Cheung Sha Wan Government Offices
303 Cheung Sha Wan Road
Kowloon, Hong Kong
Telephone: Permit Issuing Desk (852) 2150 7057
Import Control Section (852) 2150 7070
Website: www.afcd.gov.hk/web/index_e.htm (Click "Public Information" from the left side of screen, then choose "Animals" for information on importation of animals)
E-mail: icsenquiry@afcd.gov.hk

Website: www.hktb.org
Website: www.discoverhongkong.com

Canada office
Hong Kong Tourism Board
Hong Kong Trade Centre

9 Temperance Street, 3rd Floor
Toronto, ON M5H 1Y6, Canada
Telephone: (416) 366-2389
Fax: (416) 366-1098
E-mail: hktbyyz@hktb.org
E-mail: yyzwwo@hktourismboard.com

Hong Kong office
Hong Kong Tourism Board
9-11th Floor, Citicorp Centre
18 Whitfield Road
North Point, Hong Kong
Telephone: (852) 28 07 65 43 or 25 08 12 34
Fax: (852) 28 06 03 03
E-mail: info@hktourismboard.com

UK office
Hong Kong Tourism Board
6 Grafton Street
London W1S 4EQ, UK
Telephone: (20) 7533 7100
Fax: (20) 7533 7111
E-mail: lonwwo@hktourismboard.com

USA: Illinois office
Hong Kong Tourism Board
401 North Michigan Avenue, Suite 1640
Chicago, IL 60611
Telephone: (312) 329-1828
Fax: (312) 329-1858
E-mail: chiwwo@hktourismboard.com

USA: San Francisco office
Hong Kong Tourism Board
130 Montgomery Street
San Francisco, CA 94104
Telephone: (415) 781-4587
Fax: (415) 392-2964
E-mail: sfowwo@hktourismboard.com

USA: New York office
Hong Kong Tourism Board
115 East 54th Street, 2nd Floor
New York, NY 10022-4512
Telephone: (212) 421-3382
Telephone: (800) 282-4582 toll-free in USA
Fax: (212) 421-8428
E-mail: nycwwo@hktourismboard.com

On July 1, 1997, Hong Kong became a Special Administrative Region of China. Operating under a "one country, two systems policy," Hong Kong maintains its own economical, social, and political systems. English remains an official language and Hong Kong's border with China still exists. See also: China.

Hungary

Pets must have health and vaccination certification dated no more than one week before arrival. The certificate must state that the animal is free of diseases and has been properly vaccinated for rabies and distemper. It must also state that there has been no case of rabies within 20 km of the point of origin and there is no objection to the animal traveling. There is no imposed entry permit or quarantine.

Pets may enter as passenger's checked baggage, in cabin or as cargo.

Website: www.hungarytourism.hu
Website: www.gotohungary.com

UK office
Hungarian National Tourist Office
46 Eaton Place
London SW1X 8AL, UK
Telephone: (020) 7823 1032 or 7823 1055
Fax: (020) 7823 1459
E-mail: htlondon@hungarytourism.hu

USA office
Hungarian National Tourist Office
150 East 58th Street
New York, NY 10155-3398

Telephone: (212) 355-0240
Fax: (212) 207-4103
E-mail: info@hungarytourism.hu
E-mail: hnto@gotohungary.com

Embassy of the Republic of Hungary
3910 Shoemaker Street, NW
Washington, DC 20008
Telephone: (202) 362-6730
Fax: (202) 686-6412
E-mail: office@huembwas.org
Website: www.hungaryemb.org

Iceland

All pets that come to Iceland must be sent to a quarantine station on an island north of Iceland and kept there for 6-8 weeks depending on the country of export. The cost is about $1,000-$1,400 USD and the waiting list is always considerable long, usually 5-6 months.

Pets are not allowed on buses in Iceland. Pets are not allowed in restaurants because of health inspection laws and no hotels welcome them unless it is a farm holiday visit. Farm holiday is where people stay on farms, usually a very nice accommodation with everything a good hotel room would offer, and farmers are doing this all over the country.

IMPORTATION OF PETS INTO ICELAND

In accordance with Act no. 54/1900 regarding the importation of animals, it is unlawful to import into Iceland any type of living animal, domestic or wild, nor their genetic material. The Icelandic Ministry of Agriculture, however, is authorized, on receipt of the recommendation of the Chief Veterinary Officer, to grant an exception to this provision of the law, on condition that the terms for granting such an importation are strictly complied with.

Given the location of the country, animals in Iceland (wild animals, livestock and other animals) have been protected for a long time against most illnesses found in animals in other countries. Icelandic stocks are therefore extremely sensitive to illnesses that can come with imported animals and their genetic material or by other means. A high value is placed on the cleanliness and health of Icelandic stocks, and emphasis is therefore placed on preserving the stocks as best possible. This applies to pets as well as to other animals. Strict terms have therefore been set concerning the importation of animals into Iceland and full compliance is required.

Conditions for the importation of pets into Iceland
1. Import Permit from the Ministry of Agriculture.
2. Quarantine at the Pet Quarantine Station on Hrísey Island.
3. Certificates of Health and of Vaccination on the forms provided by the Ministry of Agriculture.
4. Identification marking with a mark that fulfils ISO standard 11784 or Annex A with ISO standard 11785. A tattoo shall not be considered valid.
5. Vaccinations:
Dogs and cats:
- Rabies- with a minimum blood antibody rate against rabies of 0.5IE/ml. (Does not apply to dogs and cats from Norway, Sweden, Finland, the Faroes, Britain, Australia, New Zealand, and Hawaii).

Dogs:
- Canine distemper
- Parvovirus
- Hepatitis Contagiosa Canis

Cats:
- Panleukopenia
- Rhinotracheitis virus
- Calici virus

(See the form for vaccinations from the Ministry of Agriculture.)
6. Treatment 24-72 hours before departure for Iceland for:
- Tapeworm (Echinococcus multilocularis) with the active ingredient praziquantel (Droncit) and
- External application for parasites with Frontline/Exspot.

(See the form for the Certificate of Health from the Ministry of Agriculture)
7. It is unlawful to import into Iceland puppies or kittens younger than four months of age, a pregnant bitch, a pregnant cat, a bitch with puppies or a cat with kittens, as well as dogs of the following breeds: Akita Inu, Staffordshire Bull Terrier, American Staffordshire Terrier, Bull Terrier, Pit

Bull Terrier, Fila Brasileiro, Toso Inu, Dogo Argentino, or any crossbred dogs which are in part any of the aforesaid breeds or any crossbred dogs which are part wolf.
8. Pets must be healthy on admission to quarantine and may not have recently undergone treatment or surgery that requires examination or subsequent treatment of any kind.
9. Dogs and cats may only be transported to Iceland by plane and only via the airport at Keflavík. The animal shall arrive on a weekday. Arrival on a weekend shall only be permitted under special conditions.
10. On arrival of the animal the Import Permit together with the properly completed originals of the Certificates of Health and Vaccination shall be presented to the Customs authorities (see item 3).

Responsibility of the owner
The owner shall be responsible for all costs and for all care for the animal while, it is quarantined, including:
1. Transportation costs to and from the Pet Quarantine Station on Hrísey Island,
2. The cost of food and supervision, blood samples and any medicines, if needed,
3. In addition, the cost of any damage caused by the animal while in quarantine.

The importer of the dog obligates him/herself to comply with all conditions and terms set by the Ministry and the Chief Veterinary Officer regarding the importation of a pet and its quarantine at the Pet Quarantine Station on Hrísey Island, and confirms this obligation by his/her signature on the application for a permit to import a pet.

Revocation of permit
Should the above conditions not be fully complied with in all respects on the arrival of the animal in Iceland, the Import Permit shall be instantly invalidated and the animal returned at once to the country from which it was sent, if possible, or otherwise the animal will be put down.

Instructions for Importing Dogs and Cats into Iceland

The importation of dogs and cats into Iceland is prohibited by Act no. 54/1990. The Icelandic Ministry of Agriculture, however, is authorized to grant an exception on compliance with specific conditions. It is necessary to apply formally for an Import Permit to the Ministry of Agriculture, Sölvhólsgata 7, 150 Reykjavík. All information and necessary forms may be obtained at the Ministry or on the Ministry's Website: www.stjr.is.

What is required?
1. A formal application to the Icelandic Ministry of Agriculture for a permit to import a dog or cat, using the form supplied by the Ministry.
    Ministry of Agriculture
    Sölvhólsgata 7
    150 Reykjavík, Iceland
    Telephone: (354) 560-9750
    Fax: (354) 552-1160
    E-mail: postur@lan.stjr.is
    Website: www.landbunadarraduney.is
    Office hours are daily from 08:30 – 16:00. If there is no special delay, applications are generally dealt with about one week after receipt by the Ministry.
2. When the Ministry has dealt with the application, the applicant will be sent a notice advising that an Import Permit has been granted. Then a verification fee of ISK 12,000 must be paid for each animal covered by the permit, which is a prepayment applied to the cost of quarantining the animal. The verification fee is not refundable in case the import is cancelled. The verification fee shall be paid before the specified date. A photocopy of the Receipt of Payment must be sent to the Ministry of Agriculture, Fax: (354) 552-1160.
3. When the Verification Fee has been paid, the applicant will be sent an Import Permit together with forms for the Certificate of Health and the Certificate of Vaccination, the originals of which a veterinarian in the country of origin must fill out and sign. The Import Permit and the correctly completed Certificate of Health and Certificate of Vaccination must accompany the pet on its arrival in Iceland. At the same time that the Import Permit is issued the Pet

Quarantine Station on Hrísey Island will be notified that a permit has been issued. Home quarantine is not permitted in Iceland.

4. It is important to read over all the import conditions carefully, detailing what has to be done and when. If any condition is not completely fulfilled in every respect, the animal will not be allowed to enter Iceland.
5. As there is a waiting list of several months for a place, it is safest to contact the Quarantine Station as soon as the permit has been issued to find out the permitted, planned date of arrival of your pet. The Station telephone number is (354) 466-1781. Telephone hours are from 9.30 -10.30 a.m. and 15.30-16.30 p.m. on weekdays.
Fax: (354) 466-3030
E-mail: einangrun@hotmail.com

What should be done first when the Import Permit has been obtained?

Dogs and cats:
1. Identifying mark
   - It is necessary to give the animal an identifying mark that fulfils ISO standard 11784 or Annex A for ISO standard 11785. The number of the mark shall be entered in the appropriate space on the Certificate of Health and the Certificates of Vaccination.
   - Note that a tattoo is not a valid mark.
2. Vaccinations:
   Dogs and cats:
   Rabies- Dogs and cats must be vaccinated for rabies with a killed vaccine and the amount of antibody in the blood against rabies (0.5IE/ml) must be measured. (Does not apply to dogs or cats from Norway, Sweden, Finland, the Faroes, Britain, Australia, New Zealand, or Hawaii.)
   - If the animal has been vaccinated before (during the preceding 12 months), it must be taken to a veterinarian, who shall the take a blood sample and send it to a recognized laboratory *(see the list on the back of the Certificate of Health).*

- Thirty days must have passed since the vaccination before a blood sample may be taken.
- If the antibody level is not sufficiently high (at least 0.5IE/ml), the animal must be revaccinated and the antibody level measured again after 30 days.
- Dogs and cats must be older than 3 months to be vaccinated.

The dog or cat must be marked with an identifying mark *before* it is vaccinated for rabies.

Dogs:

- Canine Distemper- The dog must be vaccinated more than 30 days before arrival in Iceland but not more than 12 months before arrival.
- Hepatitis Canis Contagiosa- The dog must be vaccinated more than 30 days before arrival in Iceland but not more than 12 months before arrival.
- Parvovirus- The dog must be vaccinated more than 30 days before arrival in Iceland but not more than 12 months before arrival.

Cats:

- Feline Panleukopenia- The cat must be vaccinated more than 30 days before arrival in Iceland but not more than 12 months before arrival.
- Rhinotracheitis virus- The cat must be vaccinated more than 30 days before arrival in Iceland but not more than 12 months before arrival.
- Calici virus- The cat must be vaccinated more than 30 days before arrival in Iceland but not more than 12 months before arrival.

Air travel

When the transport day has been decided, it is necessary to reserve space on the plane and to buy a container/cage that is suitable for the dog or cat. The animal shall be transported in a plastic container/cage. The cage will be cleaned and sterilized in the Quarantine Station and the animal sent home in it at the end of the quarantine period.

Parasites
> 24-72 hours before departure the dog or cat must be taken to a veterinarian and be given medicine (Praziquantel/Drontal) for tapeworm (*E. multilocularis, E. granulosus*) and treated for external parasites (Frontline or Exspot). The veterinarian shall at the same time fill out a Certificate of Health and confirm that the animal has received the medicine for external parasites and that it shows no sign of contagious disease.

Send the forms to the Pet Quarantine Station on Hrísey Island
> Copies of all documents that must be presented to Customs on arrival in Iceland must be sent to the Pet Quarantine Station on Hrísey Island by fax at least three full days (72 hrs.) before the date of arrival. These documents are Import Permit, Certificate of Health, Certificate of Vaccination, and a copy of the invoice for the animal if the owner has had it for less than 12 months before arrival in Iceland.

Cost of quarantining pets
According to the rate schedule issued in May 2001 the daily charge for the Quarantine Station is ISK 900.00 for each cat and ISK 1,100.00 - 1,400.00 for each dog, depending on weight. The pet owner must also pay the cost of transport from Keflavík to Hrísey Island and return (the amount varies according to the destination after the quarantine and whether the animal is picked up on Hrísey Island), any costs incurred with administration of medicine and analysis of tests, cost of the services and supervision of a veterinarian, and any special medical treatment, as applicable. The quarantine period is 6 weeks for animals from Norway, Sweden, Finland, UK, Republic of Ireland, and Ireland; and 8 weeks from any other country. It can be expected that the total cost, including VAT, for quarantining a cat will be approximately ISK 92 – 108,000 and for a medium-sized dog approximately ISK 115 – 136,000. The full invoice will be presented 14 days before the end of the quarantine.

The owner/importer shall also pay to the Customs authorities VAT on the cost of an animal, which the owner has had for less than one year. It is therefore necessary that the invoice for purchase of the animal accompany the animal on its arrival in Iceland. The VAT shall be paid at least 10 days before the animal returns home after being quarantined.

Care of pets in quarantine
The employees and veterinarian at the Quarantine Station make every effort to see to it that the animals are well cared for during the quarantine period. Effort is made to keep the animal's coat clean and in good condition. Unfortunately, there are no facilities for clipping or trimming the coat of animals for exhibition in accordance with the requirements for showing the animal.

On arrival on Hrísey Island animals are examined by the Station veterinarian, weighed, and blood and stool samples taken for testing. Stool samples are taken twice and tested during the quarantine period. The veterinarian regularly follows the health of the animals and they are weighed when they leave. A file is kept on each animal with, among other things, information about its weight on arrival and departure, how much and what type of food it has eaten, other details concerning bathing and care, administration of deworming medicine, dates of taking samples and the test results, as well as treatment of any diseases, as applicable. Those pet owners who request it may have a copy of the file at the end of the quarantine period.

It should be remembered that, on arrival at the Quarantine Station, the articles that accompanied the animal, such as a rug/blanket, bed, bone to gnaw on or toys, will be destroyed.

It is preferable to let the employees of the Quarantine Station know what type of food you wish your dog/cat to receive and an effort will be made to comply with your request as far as it is feasible.

It is permissible to visit an animal after it has been quarantined at the Station for 14 days, after consultation with the quarantine veterinarian and the Station's employees, and after that once a week. It is not possible to receive visitors during a weekend.

Have you remembered to?
- Apply for an import permit from the Icelandic Ministry of Agriculture?

- Pay the verification fee once notified of importation being granted?
- Contact the Quarantine Station on Hrísey Island to see when they can receive your pet?
- Mark your pet for identification?
- The number marked shall be entered in the appropriate space on the Certificate of Health and the Certificate of Vaccination from the Ministry of Agriculture.
- Vaccinate your dog for rabies? (The vaccine must be killed.)
- Have a blood sample taken 30 days later to test for antibodies to rabies? (Make certain that the blood sample is sent to an authorized research lab – see list on the back of the Certificate of Vaccination)
- Were the results of the antibody test for rabies acceptable, i.e., the minimum antibody level is 0.5IE/ml?
- Check when your dog/cat was last vaccinated for other viral diseases (parvovirus, canine distemper, hepatitis/panleukopenia, and cat influenza/calicivirus)?
- The vaccination must not have been given more than 12 months before expected arrival nor more recently than 30 days before arrival.
- Reserve a place for your dog/cat on a flight to Iceland?
- Buy a suitable traveling container for your dog/cat, which must be of plastic?
- Make a reservation with your veterinarian for treatment for tapeworm and external parasites and to let him/her fill out the Certificates of Vaccination and of Health? This must be done more than 24 hours before departure and within 72 hours of departure.
- Talk to the veterinarian about a tranquillizer for your dog/cat for the coming trip?
- Send an E-mail to the Quarantine Station for pets on Hrísey Island (at least 3 days before the arrival of your dog/cat) along with:
    - Exact information as to the flight number and arrival time of the plane to Keflavík,
    - Copies of all documents that must be presented to customs on arrival of your dog/cat in Iceland, i.e.: Import Permit, Certificate of Vaccination, properly

completed forms attesting health examination, confirmation of vaccination, and the invoice showing the purchase price of the animal, if the owner purchased it less than 12 months before arrival in Iceland.

Website: www.iceland.org
Website: www.goiceland.org
Website: www.icetourist.is
Website: www.icelandair.co.uk
Website: www.icelandtouristboard.com

Iceland office
    Icelandic Tourist Board
    Laekjargata 3, 101 Reykjavík, Iceland
    Telephone: 535 5500
    Fax: 535 5501
    E-mail: info@icetourist.is
    E-mail: tourinfo@tourinfo.is
    E-mail: tourinfo@simnet.is

UK office
    Icelandic Tourist Information Office/Icelandair
    3rd Floor, 172 Tottenham Court Road
    London W1P 0LY, UK
    Telephone: (020) 7874 1019 or 7874 1000
    Fax: (020) 7387 5711
    E-mail: london@icelandair.is

USA office
    Icelandic Tourist Board
    655 Third Avenue
    New York, NY 10017
    Telephone: (212) 885-9700
    Fax: (212) 885-9710
    E-mail: info@icelandtouristboard.com

Embassy of Iceland
1156 15th Street, NW
Suite 1200
Washington, DC 20005-1704

Telephone: (202) 265-6653
Fax: (202) 265-6656
E-mail: icemb.wash@utn.stjr.is
Website: www.iceland.org

India

Plants and domestic pets, dogs, cats, birds, etc. may be imported. Import of plants, animals, and birds is governed by strict health certificate regulations and quarantine. The health certificate is not a customs matter. Please inquire with your airline or travel agent or Embassy for details on this matter.

One dog and other domestic pets like cats and birds in limited numbers can be imported on furnishing the following health certificates to the customs authorities:
 1. Dog: A health certificate from a veterinary officer authorized to issue a valid certificate by the Government in the country of export to the effect that the dog imported is free from Aujossky's disease, distemper, rabies, leishmaoiasis, and leptospirosis.
 2. Cat: A health certificate from a veterinary officer authorized to issue a valid certificate by the Government in the country of export to the effect that the cat imported is free from distemper and rabies.

In the case of import of dogs and cats originating from countries where rabies infection is known to exist, a health certificate containing a record of vaccination, vaccine used, brew of the vaccine and the name of the production laboratory and to the effect that the dog/cat was vaccinated against rabies more than one month, but within 12 months before actual embarkation with nervous tissue vaccine or within 36 months with chicken embryo vaccine, both the vaccines having previously passed satisfactory potency tests.
 3. Parrots: In the case of parrots, a certificate to the effect that the parrots were subjected to a compliment fixation test for psittacosis with negative results within 30 days before actual embarkation.

Website: www.tourisminindia.com/
Website: www.tourismofindia.com

Website: www.indiatouristoffice.org
Website: www.tourindia.com/

Canada office
>Government of India Tourist Office 60 Bloor Street
>Suite 1003
>Toronto, ON M4 W3 B8, Canada
>Telephone: (800) 962-3787 toll-free in Canada
>Fax: (416) 962-6279
>E-mail: india@istar.ca

India office
>Government of India Tourist Office (GITO)
>88 Janpath
>New Delhi 110 001, India
>Telephone: (11) 332 0342 or 332 0005 or 332 0008
>Fax: (11) 332 0109
>E-mail: goitodelhi@tourism.nic.in

UK office
>Government of India Tourist Office
>7 Cork Street
>London, WIX 2AB, UK
>Telephone: 171 437-3677
>Fax: none
>E-mail: info@indiatouristoffice.org

USA: California office
>Government of India Tourist Office
>3550 Wilshire Boulevard, Room 204
>Los Angeles, CA 90010
>Telephone: (800) 422-4634 toll-free in USA
>Fax: (213) 380-6111
>E-mail: none

USA: New York office
>Government of India Tourist Office
>1270 Avenue of the Americas, Suite 1808
>New York, NY 10020
>Telephone: (800) 953-9399 toll-free in USA

Fax: (212) 582-3274
E-mail: goitony@tourindia.com

Embassy of India
2107 Massachusetts Avenue, NW
Washington, DC 20008
Telephone: (202) 939-7000
Fax: (202) 265-4351
E-mail: info2@indiagov.org
Website: www.indianembassy.org

Indonesia

Birds (other than parrots and parakeets), cats and dogs must be accompanied by health certificate (AND photo copy) issued in country of origin within 5 days before shipment stating that the animals are free from disease and have not been in a Yellow Fever infected area for a period of at least 5 days before shipment. Inspection upon arrival at the airport for which carrier's office must previously be advised so that a veterinarian will be available at the airport.

Furthermore, pets must be accompanied by:
1. Import license, to be obtained before arrival from:
    The Ministry of Agriculture
    Animal Health
    Jl Salemba Raya 16/P O Box 1402, Second Floor
    Jakarta, Pusat, Indonesia 10014
    Telephone: (021) 3142838 / 3142979
    Fax: (021) 3143937
2. Copy of animal passport; and
3. Copy of passport of owner; and
4. Certificate from the Dept. of Agriculture, Directorate

Cats, dogs, and monkeys: Additional rabies inoculation certificate showing that vaccination was affected within 1 year before departure.

Pets may enter as passenger's checked baggage, in the cabin or as cargo.

PROHIBITED:
1. Parrots and parakeets;
2. Birds, cats, dogs, monkeys, and other animals are strictly prohibited in the districts of Bali West Nusa Tenggara, East Nusa Tenggara, Irian Jaya, Madura, Maluku, Timor, Timur, West Kalimantan, and the small islands surrounding the main island of Sumatra. Failure to comply will result in the immediate destruction of the animal concerned.

Website: www.goindo.com
Website: www.tourismindonesia.com
Website: www.indonesiatourism.com

Indonesia office
Indonesia Tourism Promotion Board (ITPB)
Wisma Nugra Santana Building, 9th Floor
Jalan Jend Sudirman Kav 7-8
Jakarta 10220, Indonesia
Telephone: (21) 570 4879
Fax: (21) 570 4855
E-mail: info@itpb.or.id

UK office
Indonesia Tourist Promotion Office (ITPO)
38 Grosvenor Square
London W1K 2HW, UK
Telephone: (020) 7499 7661
Fax: (020) 7491 4993
E-mail: none

USA: California office
Indonesian Tourist Promotion Office
3457 Wilshire Boulevard
Los Angeles, CA 90010
Telephone: (213) 387-2078
Fax: (213) 380-4876
E-mail: none

USA: New York office
   Consulate General of Indonesia
   5 East 68th Street
   New York, NY 10021
   Telephone: (212) 879-0600
   Fax: (212) 570-6206
   E-mail: none

Embassy of the Republic of Indonesia
2020 Massachusetts Avenue, NW
Washington, DC 20036
Telephone: (202) 775-5200
Fax: (202) 775-5365
E-mail: indonsia@dgs.dgsys.com
Website: www.kbri.org

Iran

Entrance of domestic animals such as dogs, cats, and birds to Islamic Republic of Iran is subject to the following regulations:
1. Animals that are entered for non-commercial use can accompany passengers if the animal has an official health certificate, an identification card, and a vaccination card from the veterinary officials of the originating country.
2. Passengers can release the animal after having the vaccination card certified by the veterinary guarantee stationed at the entrance port.

Pets may be transported as passenger's checked baggage, in the cabin or as cargo.

Website: www.irantourism.org

Iran office
   Iran Touring and Tourism Organisation (ITTO)
   Hajj and Pilgrimage Building
   Roudaki Avenue
   Azadi Street
   Tehran, Iran
   Telephone: (21) 643 2098 or 643 2099

Fax: (21) 643 2088 or 643 2099
E-mail: moezi@sr.co.ir

Iran office
Iran Tourist Company
257 Motahari Avenue
Tehran 15868, Iran
Telephone: (21) 873 4512 or 873 9819
Fax: (21) 873 6158
E-mail: none

Iranian Interests Section
c/o The Embassy of Pakistan
2209 Wisconsin Avenue, NW
Washington, DC 20007
Telephone: (202) 965-4990
Fax: (202) 965-1073
E-mail: none
Website: www.daftar.org

Iraq

A current International Health Certificate must accompany cats and dogs.

Iraq office
E-mail: iraqmail@uruklink.net
Website: www.uruklink.net/tourism

Permanent Mission of Iraq to the United Nations
E-mail: iraq@un.int
Website: www.iraqi-mission.org/

Iraqi Interests Section
1801 P Street, NW
Washington, DC 20036
Telephone: (202) 483-7500
Fax: (202) 462-5066
E-mail: iraqyia.london@talk21.com (Iraq Interest Section in UK)

Ireland

Pets from Great Britain, the Channel Islands, and the Isle of Man are permitted entry. All other pets are quarantined for six months. The owner is responsible for all fees and costs associated with the quarantine. The vaccinations must be less than 6 months before entry and the International Health Certificate must be current. No import permit is required.

Travelers with pets, before departure for Ireland, should confirm that the information is valid by either contacting the Irish Embassy in Washington, D.C. or the Irish Department of Agriculture, Food & Rural Development in Dublin, Telephone: +353-1-607-2000. Their Website may also be informative: www.irlgov.ie/daff

Website: www.ireland.travel.ie
Website: www.irelandtravel.co.uk

Ireland office
    Bord Fáilte Eireann
    Baggot Street Bridge
    Dublin 2, Ireland
    Telephone: (1) 602 4000
    Fax: (1) 602 4100
    E-mail: info@irishtouristboard.ie

UK office
    Irish Tourist Board/Bord Fáilte
    150 New Bond Street
    London W1S 2AQ, UK
    Telephone: (020) 7518 0800 or (0800) 039 7000 (travel enquiries)
    Fax: (020) 7493 9065
    E-mail: info@irishtouristboard.co.uk

USA office
    Irish Tourist Board / Bord Failte
    345 Park Avenue
    New York, NY 10154
    Telephone: (212) 418-0800
    Telephone: (800) 223-6470 toll-free in USA
    Fax: (212) 371-9052

E-mail: info@irishtouristboard.com
Website: www.irelandvacations.com
This office also deals with inquires from Canada.

Embassy of Ireland
2234 Massachusetts Avenue, NW
Washington, DC 20008
Telephone: (202) 462-3939
Fax: (2020) 232-5993
E-mail: Ireland@irelandemb.org
Website: www.irelandemb.org

Israel

Dogs and cats accompanying visitors must be over fours months old, inoculated against rabies, and bear a valid International Health Certificate from the country of origin. The vaccination should be between one month and 12 months before embarkation. There is no mandatory quarantine. No import permit is required. Cats and dogs under the age of 3 months are prohibited.

Website: www.infotour.co.il
Website: www.goisreal.com

Canada office
   Israel Government Tourist Office
   180 Bloor Street
   Toronto, ON M5S2V6, Canada
   Telephone: (416) 964-3784
   Fax: (416) 964-2420
   E-mail: igto@idirect.com

Israel office
   Ministry of Tourism
   P.O. Box 1018
   King George Street 24
   Jerusalem, Israel
   Telephone: (2) 675 4811 or 567 8777
   Fax: (2) 625 7955
   E-mail: none

UK office
   Israel Government Tourist Office
   UK House
   180 Oxford Street
   London W1D 1NN, UK
   Telephone: (020) 7299 1111
   Fax: (020) 7299 1112
   E-mail: information@igto.co.uk

USA: California office
   Israel Government Tourist Office
   6380 Wilshire Boulevard, Suite 1700
   Los Angeles, CA 90048
   Telephone: (213) 658-7462
   Fax: (213) 658-6543
   E-mail: none

USA: Illinois office
   Israel Government Tourist Office
   5 South Wabash Avenue
   Chicago, IL 60603-3073
   Telephone: (800) 782-4306 toll-free in USA
   Telephone: (312) 782-4306
   Fax: (312) 782-1243
   E-mail: igtochigo@aol.com

USA: New York office
   Israel Government Tourist Office
   800 Second Avenue, 16th Floor
   New York, NY 10117
   Telephone: (212) 499-5600
   Telephone: (888) 77-ISRAEL toll-free in USA
   Fax: (212) 499-5665
   E-mail: Info@Goisrael.com

Embassy of Israel
3514 International Drive, NW
Washington, DC 20008
Telephone: (202) 364-5500
Fax: (202) 364-5423

E-mail: ask@isrealemb.org
Website: www.israelemb.org

Italy

An International Health Certificate must be presented with a cat or dog stating that the animal is in good health and has been vaccinated against rabies between 20 days and 11 months before entry into Italy. The certificate is valid for 30 days. Forms for certification are available from all Italian diplomatic and consular representatives and from the Italian Government Tourist Board. Dogs must be on a leash or muzzled when in public.

Psittacine birds (Parrots and parakeets) require an International Health certificate stating that the country of origin is free from psittacosis or the birds have been kept for a period of six months prior to departure under State veterinary control in a breeding park or zoological garden and that in the area within a 20 km radius no case of psittacosis occurred during that period.

Small pets other than dogs, cats, and psittacine birds (such as canaries, small fish, hamsters, turtles, etc.) may be imported in suitable packing, free from any Veterinary Service formality.

Website: www.enit.it
Website: www.piuitalia2000.it/
Website: www.italiantourism.com

Canada office
    Italian Government Tourist Board
    1 Place Villa Marie, Suite 1914
    Montreal, QC H3B 2C3, Canada
    Telephone: (514) 866-7668
    Fax: (514) 392-1429
    E-mail: none

UK office
    Italian State Tourist Board (ENIT)
    1 Princes Street
    London W1R 8AY, UK
    Telephone: 171 408 1254

Telephone: 0891 600 280 24-hour brochure request
Fax: 171 493 6695
E-mail: enitlond@globalnet.co.uk

USA: California office
Italian Government Tourist Board
12400 Wilshire Boulevard, Suite 550
Los Angeles, CA 90025
Telephone: (310) 820-1898
Fax: (310) 820-6357
E-mail: none

USA: Chicago office
Italian Government Tourist Board
500 North Michigan Avenue, Suite 2240
Chicago, IL 60611
Telephone: (312) 644-0996
Fax: (310) 644-3019
E-mail: none

USA: New York office
Italian Government Tourist Board
630 Fifth Avenue, Suite 1565
New York, NY 10111
Telephone: (212) 245-5618
Fax: (212) 245-4822
E-mail: info@italiantourism.com

Embassy of Italy
3000 Whitehaven Street, NW
Washington, DC 20008
Telephone: (202) 612-4400
Fax: (202) 518-2154
E-mail: stampa@itwash.org
Website: www.italyemb.org

Ivory Coast
See: Cote d'Ivoire

Jamaica

Unfortunately, cats and dogs are not allowed into Jamaica from the U.S. All pets must have an Import Permit issued by the Veterinary Division of the Ministry of Agriculture, Kingston, Jamaica.

Dogs and Cats (may arrive only as manifested cargo):
1. Born and bred in the UK; and
2. No transit en route; and
3. Holding additional health certificate stating that the animals inoculated against rabies at least 6 months prior to exportation.
4. All pets must be accompanied by an Import permit and inspected by a veterinarian upon arrival.

Birds: Birds may be imported from the U.S. if accompanied by the required Health Certificate.

Website: www.jamaicatravel.com/

Canada office
    Jamaica Tourist Board
    1 Eglinton Avenue East, Suite 616
    Toronto, ON M4P 3A1, Canada
    Telephone: (416) 482-7850
    Fax: (416) 482-1730
    E-mail: none

Jamaica office
    Jamaica Tourist Board (JTB)
    64 Knutsford Boulevard
    Kingston 5, Jamaica
    Telephone: 929 9200
    Fax: 929 9375
    E-mail: jamaicatrv@aol.com

UK office
    Jamaica Tourist Board
    1-2 Prince Consort Road
    London SW7 2BZ, UK
    Telephone: 207 224 0505

Fax: 207 224 0551
E-mail: jtb_uk@compuserve.com

USA: California office
Jamaica Tourist Board
3440 Wilshire Boulevard, Suite 805
Los Angeles, CA 90010
Telephone: (213) 384-1123
Telephone: (800) JAMAICA toll-free in USA
Fax: (213) 384-1780
E-mail: none

USA: Florida office
Jamaica Tourist Board
1320 South Dixie Highway, Suite 1100
Coral Gables, FL 33146
Telephone: (305) 665-0557
Telephone: (800) JAMAICA toll-free in USA
Fax: (305) 666-7239
E-mail: none

USA: Illinois office
Jamaica Tourist Board
500 North Michigan Avenue, Suite 1030
Chicago, IL 60611
Telephone: (312) 527-1296
Telephone: (800) JAMAICA toll-free in USA
Fax: (312) 527-1472
E-mail: none

USA: New York office
Jamaica Tourist Board
801 Second Avenue
20th Floor
New York, NY 10017
Telephone: (212) 856-9727
Telephone: (800) JAMAICA toll-free in USA
Fax: (212) 856-9730
E-mail: none

Embassy of Jamaica
1520 New Hampshire Avenue, NW
Washington, DC 20036
Telephone: (202) 452-0660
Fax: (202) 452-0081
E-mail: emjam@sysnet.net
E-mail: emjam@frontiernet.net
Website: www.emjam-usa.org

Japan

Pets must be accompanied with an International Health Certificate and a rabies vaccination certificate. A Veterinary Services veterinarian must endorse these certificates. The rabies vaccination certificate should include the vaccination date, which should be given between 1 and 12 months before arrival to the pet's arrival in Japan. If the rabies vaccine was administered outside these guidelines, your pet could be quarantined between 14 and 180 days.

As of January 2000, dogs and cats must receive a quarantine examination upon arrival in Japan. Any dog or cat brought to Japan must be accompanied by the following two certificates issued by U.S. Department of Agriculture.
1. Health certificate stating that the dog/cat is not infected or is not suspected of being infected with rabies or Leptospirosis;
2. Rabies vaccination certificate showing the date of the last rabies vaccination and the type of the vaccine used.

The length of quarantine required for a dog and a cat can be generally determined by the following criteria.
1. Rabies certificate stating a vaccination date exceeding 30 days before arrival in Japan and the arrival date falls within the effective period of the vaccination - 14 days.
2. Rabies certificate stating a vaccination date not exceeding 30 days before arrival in Japan - 45 days minus the number of days since vaccination upon arrival in Japan.
3. If there is no rabies certificate; or, effective period of vaccination has expired before arrival in Japan-180 days.

Note: There may be changes in the detailed quarantine requirements for dogs and cats by the time quarantine inspection actually commence. Please inquire at the:
Department of the Planning and Coordination of Animal Quarantine Station
Yokohama Head Office
(Telephone: 81-45-751-5921)

Monkeys may be imported from USA, People's Republic of China, Republic of Indonesia, Republic of the Philippines, Socialist Republic of Viet Nam, Republic of Guyana, and Republic of Suriname. Monkeys from other areas are strictly prohibited. Before bringing a monkey to Japan from any of the above countries, a detention inspection period of 30 days or longer under the surveillance of a government agency in the exporting county is required. Upon arrival in Japan, it is also necessary to present a certificate issued by a government agency n the exporting country containing a statement to the effect that the monkey in question has undergone such detention. In addition, the monkey will have to receive an additional detention inspection upon arrival in Japan for a minimum of 30 days in order to assure that it is not infected by the Ebola or Marburg virus.

Monkeys may only be imported at two locations, the New Tokyo International Airport (Narita Airport) and the Kansai International Airport.

A quarantine inspection will be required for small pet birds that are brought into Japan when entering from a foreign country. The inspection of small pet birds will be completed if no abnormalities are recognized in the inspection at the time of arrival. However, small pet birds recognized to have abnormalities as well as all chickens, ducks, turkeys, quail and geese will be subject to an inspection in detention.

Animal quarantine inspections are not required upon arrival in Japan for frogs (amphibians), snakes (reptiles), fish, and so forth that you bring with you from abroad.

Additional information may be obtained from the Animal Quarantine Service, Ministry of Agriculture, Forestry, and Fisheries at: www.animal-quarantine-service.go.jp

Website: www.jnto.go.jp
Website: www.japantravelinfo.com

Japan Rail Pass
Website: www.jreast.co.jp/jrp/index.htm

Canada office
   Japan National Tourist Organization
   165 University Avenue
   Toronto, ON M5H 3B8, Canada
   Telephone: (416) 366-7140
   Fax: (416) 366-4530
   E-mail: jnto@interlog.com
   E-mail: info@jntoyyz.com

Japan office
   Japan National Tourist Organisation (JNTO)
   Overseas Promotion Department
   2-10-1, Yuraku-cho
   Chiyoda-ku
   Tokyo 100-0006, Japan
   Telephone: (3) 3216 1902
   Fax: (3) 3216 1846
   E-mail: none

Japan office
   Tourist Information Centre
   B1, Tokyo International Forum
   3-5-1 Marunouchi
   Chiyoda-ku
   Tokyo 100-0005, Japan
   Telephone: (3) 3201 3331
   Fax: (3) 3201 3347
   E-mail: none
   Office also in: Kyoto (Telephone: (75) 371 5649)

UK office
   Japan National Tourist Organization
   20 Savile Row
   London W1X 1AE, UK

Telephone: 171 734 9638
Fax: 171 734 4290
E-mail: jntolon@dircon.co.uk
E-mail: info@jnto.co.uk

USA: New York office
Japan National Tourist Organization
One Rockefeller Plaza, Suite 1250
New York, NY 10020
Telephone: (212) 757-5640
Fax: (212) 307-6754
E-mail: jntonyc@interport.net
E-mail: visitjapan@jntonyc.org

USA: Los Angeles office
Japan National Tourist Organization
515 South Figueroa Street, Suite 1470
Los Angeles, CA 90071
Telephone: (213) 623-1952
Fax: (213) 623-6301
E-mail: info@jnto-lax.org

USA: San Francisco office
Japan National Tourist Organization
360 Post Street, Suite 601
San Francisco CA 94108
Telephone: (415) 989-7140
Fax: (415) 398-5461
E-mail: sfjnto@webjapan.com

USA: Illinois office
Japan National Tourist Organization
401 North Michigan Avenue, Suite 770
Chicago, IL 60611
Telephone: (312) 222-0874
Fax: (312) 222-0876
E-mail: jntochi@mcs.net

Embassy of Japan
2520 Massachusetts Avenue, NW

Washington, DC 20008
Telephone: (202) 238-6700
Fax: (202) 328-2187
E-mail: none
Website: www.embjapan.org

Jersey

See also: United Kingdom

If you are visiting Jersey from the British Isles or the Republic of Ireland, you can bring your pet with you - provided of course that pets are allowed at your holiday accommodation. If arriving from other countries, "Pet Travel Scheme" regulations apply. Please note from May to September, dogs must be on a lead while on the beach between the hours of 10:30 AM and 6:00 PM.

Website: www.jersey.com
Website: www.jtourism.com

Jersey office
    Jersey Tourism
    Liberation Square
    St Helier
    Jersey JE1 1BB, UK
    Telephone: 1534 500 700
    Fax: 1534 500 808
    E-mail: info@jersey.com

USA office
    Jersey Tourism
    Alice Marshall Public Relations
    780 Madison Avenue
    New York, NY 10021
    Telephone: (212) 861-4031
    E-mail: alice@alicemarshal.com

Jordan

Jordan does not require quarantine or permits. An International Health Certificate and a vaccination certificate are required.

Additional information may be obtained directly from the Ministry of Health, Veterinary section. They can be contacted by E-mail: info@nic.gov.jo or Fax: 962 6 5688373

Website: www.seejordan.com
Website: www.seejordan.org
Website: www.tourism.jo

Jordan office
    Jordan Tourism Board
    P.O. Box 830688
    Amman 11183, Jordan
    Telephone: (6) 567 8294
    Fax: (6) 567 8295
    E-mail: jtb@nets.com.jo

UK office
    The Jordan Tourism Board
    Brighter Resolutions
    Lee House, 2nd Floor
    109 Hammersmith Road
    London W14 OQH, UK
    Telephone: 20 7371 6496
    Fax: 20 7603 2424
    E-mail: info@jordantourismboard.co.uk

USA office
    Jordan Tourism Board North America
    2000 Courthouse Place
    North 14th Street, Suite 770
    Arlington, VA 22201
    Telephone: (877) See-Jordan toll-free in USA
    Telephone: (703) 243-7404
    Fax: (703) 243-7406
    E-mail: info@seejordan.org

Embassy of The Hashemite Kingdom of Jordan
3504 International Drive, NW
Washington, DC 20008

Telephone: (202) 966-2664
Fax: (202) 966-3110
E-mail: HKJEmbassyDC@aol.com
Website: www.jordanembassyus.org

Kazakhstan

Cats, dogs and other animals, birds (except pigeons) and fish must be accompanied by current International Certificate of Health bearing the seal of local Board of Health and not be issued over ten days before arrival. Pigeons are prohibited entry. Pets may enter as passenger's checked baggage, in the cabin or as cargo. Generally, pets are not permitted in hotels.

Website: www.kaztour.kz

Kazakhstan office
  Department of Tourism
  4, Republic Square
  Almaty 4860065, Kazakhstan
  Telephone/Fax: (3272) 620 030
  E-mail: dep_tour@nursat.kz

Embassy of the Republic of Kazakhstan
1401 16th Street, NW
Washington, DC 20036
Telephone: (202) 232-5488
Fax: (202) 232-5845
E-mail: kazakhembusa@earthlink.net
E-mail: kazakh.consul@verizon.net (Consular Section)
Website: www.kazakhembus.com/
The embassy also deals with inquires from Canada.

Kenya

Kenya requires a vaccination between 30 days and one year old. A current International Health Certificate is also required. There is no quarantine in Kenya. An import permit is required. This can be obtained from the Kenya Embassy.

Website: www.kenyatourism.org
Website: www.magicalkenya.com

UK office
Kenya National Tourist Office
25 Brook's Mews, off Davies Street
London W1Y 1LG, UK
Telephone: 171 355 3144
Fax: 171 495 8656
E-mail: none

USA: California office
Kenya Tourist Office
9150 Wilshire Boulevard, Suite 160
Beverly Hills, CA 90212
Telephone: (310) 274-6635
Fax: (310) 859-7010
E-mail: none

USA: New York office
Kenya Tourist Office
424 Madison Avenue
New York, NY 10017
Telephone: (212) 486-1300
Fax: (212) 688-0911
E-mail: none

Embassy of Kenya
2249 R Street, NW
Washington, DC 20008
Telephone: (202) 387-6101
Fax: (202) 462-3829
E-mail: info@kenyaembassy.com
Website: www.kenyaembassy.com

Kiribati

See also: South Pacific Tourism Organization

Cats and dogs may only be imported from Australia, Fiji, and New Zealand. An import permit obtained at least one month in advance of shipment must accompany them. Cats and dogs in transit are not permitted to leave the aircraft.

Pet owner must apply to the Agricultural Office for a permit. The contact address is:
    Chief Agricultural Officer
    Division of Agriculture
    P.O. Box 267
    Tanaea, Tarawa
    Republic of Kiribati

Kiribati office
    Kiribati Visitors Bureau
    P. O. Box 510
    Betio, Tarawa
    Republic of Kiribati
    Telephone: (686) 26 157/26 158
    Fax: (686) 26 233
    E-mail: commerce@tskl.net.ki
    E-mail: info@nouvellecaledonietourisme-sud.com

Consulate of Kiribati
850 Richards Street, Suite 503
Honolulu, Hawaii 96813
Telephone: (808) 521-7703
Fax: (808) 253-0824
E-mail: none

Korea, North (Democratic People's Republic of Korea)

The UN office states that the regulations require a recent International Health Certificate and a current rabies vaccination certificate to enter North Korea. There is no quarantine. No special permits are needed.

Korea office
    The National Directorate of Tourism of the DPRK
    Central District
    Pyongyang, DPR Korea
    Telephone: (2) 381 8901 or 381 8111 (operator)

Fax: (2) 381 7607
E-mail: none

Korea office
Kumgangsan International Tourist Company
Central District
Pyongyang, DPR Korea
Telephone: (2) 31562 or 35431
Fax: (2) 812 100
E-mail: none

UK office
BESTravel Ltd
Savoy Chambers, 1-3 Wellington Street
Stockport
Cheshire SK1 3RP, UK
Telephone: (0161) 480 3829
Fax: (0161) 480 3827
E-mail: none
Website: www.BESTravel.co.uk

Permanent Representative of the Democratic People's Republic of Korea to the United Nations
515 East 72nd Street, 38-F
New York, NY 10021
Telephone: (212) 972-3105
Fax: (212) 972-3154
E-mail: prkun@undp.org
Website: www.dprkorea.com

Korea, South (Republic of Korea)

The people of Korea are very fond of their pets and welcome your pet. An International Health Certificate and vaccination certificate are required. Fees will be incurred. Your pet needs to be crated during train travel. Documents do not require translation.

1. Dogs and cats imported from Australia, Taiwan, Cyprus, Fiji, Guam, Iceland, Ireland, Jamaica, Japan, New Zealand, Portugal, Singapore, United Kingdom, U.S. (Hawaii and American Samoa) do not require quarantine provided they

are accompanied by an International Health Certificate or a certificate issued by a Quarantine Authority.
2. Dogs and Cats form other countries can be imported without quarantine if accompanied by an International Health Certificate and provided the following conditions be met:
- In case the pet is under 90 days, it should be described on health certificate tat the pet is healthy and no symptoms of disease is found;
- when it is older than 90 days, the inoculation date should be clearly specified on the health certificate and the date is at least 30 days elapsed from vaccination, otherwise rabies vaccination certificate should be supplementary required and this certificate should prove that such pet have been vaccinated at least 30 days previously. In case of import before 30 days elapsed time, pets shall be quarantined until 30 days are passed from vaccination.
3. Birds imported from China (People's Republic) and Italy are prohibited. Import from other countries is subject to various and complicated regulations varying from country to country according to the required hygienic standard. Prior contact with Korean Quarantine Office should be made to acquire more details.
4. In principle, 21 days of quarantine period is applied to all cats imported from Australia and Malaysia. For exemptions and more information prior contact with Korean Quarantine Office should be made as it depends on situations of each state and country.

Pets may travel either as checked passenger's baggage in the cabin or as cargo.

Please note: A maximum of nine dogs is allowed without prior permission. If you wish to import more than nine dogs, you must submit a request to the Korean Quarantine Office at Incheon International Airport.

Website: www.nvrqs.go.kr (National Veterinary Research & Quarantine Service of Korea)

Website: www.korea.net
Website: www.knto.or.kr
Website: www.visitkorea.org.kr
Website: www.tour2korea.com
Website: www.goodwillguide.com

Canada office
Korea National Tourism Organization (KNTO)
700 Bay Street, Suite 1903
Toronto, ON M5G 1Z6, Canada
Telephone: (416) 348-9056
Telephone: (800) 868-7567 toll-free in USA and Canada
Fax: (416) 348 9058
E-mail: toronto@knto.ca

Korea office
Korea National Tourism Organisation (KNTO)
10 Ta-dong
Chung-gu
Seoul 100-180, Republic of Korea
Telephone: (2) 729 9600
Fax: (2) 757 5997
E-mail: kntotic@www.knto.or.kr

UK office
Korea National Tourism Organization (KNTO)
3rd Floor, New Zealand House
Haymarket
London SW1Y 4TE, UK
Telephone: (020) 7321 2535
Fax: (020) 7321 0876
E-mail: koreatb@dircon.co.uk
Website: www.visitkorea.co.uk

USA: Los Angeles office
Korea National Tourism Organization
4801 Wilshire Boulevard, Suite 103
Los Angeles, CA 90010
Telephone: (323) 634-0280
Telephone: (800) 868-7567 toll-free in USA

Fax: (323) 634-0281
E-mail: kntola@mail.wcis.com

USA: New York office
Korea National Tourism Organization
1 Executive Drive, Suite 100
Fort Lee, NJ 07024
Telephone: (201) 585-0909
Telephone: (800) 868-7567 toll-free in USA
Fax: (201) 585-9041
E-mail: kntony@ring3.net

Embassy of the Republic of Korea
2450 Massachusetts Avenue, NW
Washington, DC 20008
Telephone: (202) 939-5600
Fax: (202) 797-0595
E-mail: Emcormex@inetcorp.net.mx
Website: www.mofat.go.kr/en_usa.htm

Kuwait

A valid International Health Certificate and an import certificate from the Animal Health Department in Kuwait are necessary to import a pet. Telephone: (965) 473-0867, Fax: (965) 472-2417. The embassy will legalize documents that are certified. It is best to contact the embassy to assure compliance with all the formalities. A visa is required to enter Kuwait

Website: www.kuwaitinfo.org.uk

Kuwait office
Touristic Enterprises Company of Kuwait
P.O. Box 23310
Safat 13094
Kuwait City, Kuwait
Telephone: 565 2775 or 565 3771
Fax: 565 2367
E-mail: none

UK office
   Kuwait Information Centre
   Hyde Park House
   60-60A Knightsbridge
   London SW1X 7JX, UK
   Telephone: (020) 7235 1787
   Fax: (020) 7235 6912
   E-mail: kuwait@dircon.co.uk

Embassy of the State of Kuwait
2600 Virginia Ave, Suite 404
Washington, DC 20037
Telephone: (202) 966-0702
Fax: (202) 364-2868
E-mail: info@embassyofkuwait.com
Website: www.embassyofkuwait.com

Kyrgyz Republic

To export-import pets, it is required to have documented confirmation about all inoculations for the pet, like veterinary certificate and certificate against rabies. You must know that all of these documents have established dates. The International Health Certificate must not be dated more than 10 days prior to arrival. Pigeons are prohibited entry.

Pets will be considered as overweight baggage and will not be free of charge, even if the passenger has no other luggage. The fee will be 1% of the tariff of the first class ticket. It does not matter if your luggage is overweight or not. Dogs with deaf, blind, and disabled persons are excluded from this category. They are transported free of charge, but one thing should be mentioned: such dog must have a dog's lead and muzzle. Pets are accepted for transportation, if the passenger is fully responsible for them. Ferrymen are not responsible for damages, illnesses, and death of pets, in a case of refusal to enter or leave the country.

If the traveler is planning to take a pet to Kyrgyz Republic, they must do the followings:

1. To visit the veterinary department of his country. They must contact the State department of veterinary management and ask for fixed form №1 and permission to enter Kyrgyz Republic with the pet. Fixed form №1 includes all required certifications about the health of pet and the route. After receiving this certification, the traveler must talk with the air carrier regarding the conditions of transportation.
2. After arriving in Kyrgyz Republic, he must make a note in a fixed form №1, that the pet is healthy, at the State department of the veterinary of Kyrgyzstan.

Generally, pets are welcome in hotels if the owner makes prior arrangements.

Kyrgyz Republic office
State Committee for Tourism, Sport, and Youth Policy
720033 Bishkek
Togolok Moldo 17, Kyrgyz Republic
Telephone: (312) 220 657 or 226 397
Fax: (312) 212 845
E-mail: gatiskr@bishkek.gov.kg

Embassy of the Kyrgyz Republic
1732 Wisconsin Avenue, NW
Washington, DC 20007
Telephone: (202) 338-5141
Fax: (202) 338-5139
E-mail: Embassy@kyrgyzstan.org
E-mail: consul@kyrgyzstan.org (Consular Section)
Website: www.kyrgyzstan.org/

Laos

Several requests to the Ministry of Agriculture and Forestry in Laos as well as to the Ministry of Justice went unanswered. The reader is advised to contact the Ministry of Agriculture and Forestry in Laos by Telephone: (856 21) 412 340 or Fax: (856 21) 412 343/344. The Ministry of Commerce and Tourism may also be helpful. Contact them by Telephone: (856 21) 412 000 or 412 001, Fax: (856 21) 412 434.

Website: visit-laos.com

Laos's office
    Lao National Tourism Authority
    P.O. Box 3556
    avenue Lanxang
    Vientiane, Laos
    Telephone: (21) 212 251
    Fax: (21) 212 769
    E-mail: none

Embassy of the Lao People's Democratic Republic
2222 S Street, NW
Washington, DC 20008
Telephone: (202) 332-6416
Fax: (202) 332-4923
E-mail: laoemb@erols.com
Website: www.laoembassy.com/
The embassy will address tourist issues.

Latvia

An International Pet Passport with information concerning vaccinations against rabies (hydrophobia) is required when importing domestic animals. A veterinary certificate (issued by an authorized veterinarian of the country from which the animal is being exported) and import license (issued by the State Veterinary Department, Riga, 2 Republikas Square, telephone: + (371) 7027475) are required when importing domestic animals for commercial purposes. In case of transit, veterinary certificate and consent from the veterinary service of the country of import are necessary.

Website: www.latviatravel.com

Latvia office
    Latvia Tourism Development Agency
    Pils laukums 4
    LV-1050 Riga, Latvia
    Telephone: 722 9945
    Fax: 750 8468
    E-mail: tda@latviatourism.lv

Embassy of Latvia
4325 17th Street, NW
Washington, DC 20011
Telephone: (202) 726-8213
Fax: (202) 726-6785
E-mail: Embassy@Latvia-USA.org
Website: www.latvia-usa.org

Lebanon

Lebanon requires an International Health Certificate indicating that the pet has received all necessary vaccinations. Additional information may be obtained directly from the Lebanon Embassy.

Website: www.lebanon-tourism.gov.lb

Lebanon office
    Ministry of Tourism
    P.O. Box 11-5344
    Beirut, Lebanon
    Telephone: (01) 340940-4
    Fax: (01) 745407
    E-mail: mot@Lebanon-Tourism.gov.lb

Embassy of Lebanon
2560 28th Street, NW
Washington, DC 20008
Telephone: (202) 939-6300
Fax: (202) 939-6324
E-mail: info@lebanonembassy.org
Website: www.lebanonembassy.org/

Lesotho

Domestic pets and livestock may be imported without payment of customs or sales duty, subject to quarantine restrictions. Details concerning the latter aspects can be obtained from the Permanent Secretary, Ministry of Agriculture Co-operatives and Marketing, P.O. Box MS 24 Maseru, Lesotho. NOTE: (Transit permits issued by the Director of Veterinary Services, Private Bag 138, Pretoria, South

Africa must be applied for in respect to all pets and livestock transported through the Republic of South Africa).

An International Health Certificate and rabies inoculation certificate must accompany cats and dogs.

Website: www.lesotho.gov.ls

Embassy of the Kingdom of Lesotho
2511 Massachusetts Avenue, NW
Washington, DC 20008
Telephone: (202) 797-5533
Fax: (202) 234-6815
E-mail: none
Website: none

Liberia

An import permit issued by the Ministry of Agriculture, a current International Health Certificate, and rabies inoculation certificate issued at the point of origin must accompany cats and dogs.

Liberia office
    Ministry of Information, Cultural Affairs and Tourism
    P.O. Box 10-9021
    Capitol Hill, 1000
    Monrovia, Liberia
    Telephone: 226 078
    Fax: 226 269
    E-mail: none
    Website: www.micat.gov.gro

Embassy of the Republic of Liberia
5201 16th Street, NW
Washington, DC 20011
Telephone: (202) 723-0437
Fax: (202) 723-0436
E-mail: info@liberiaemb.org
Website: www.liberiaemb.org/

Libya

Libya requires legalized vaccination certificates and International Health Certificates for pets to enter their country.

Website: www.home.earthlink.net/~dibrahim

Permanent Mission of the Socialist People's Libyan Arab Jamahiriya to the United Nations
309-315 East 48th Street
New York, NY 10017
Telephone: (212) 752-5775
Fax: (212) 593-4787
E-mail: info@libya-un.org
Website: www.libya-un.org

Liechtenstein

The Principality of Liechtenstein is in a customs union with Switzerland. This is the reason why Swiss Animal Health and to some extent other Swiss legislations as well as border provisions are applicable for Liechtenstein too. The requirements are the same as for Switzerland.

Owners of pets (dogs and cats) must have an International Health Certificate with the attestation of vaccination against rabies. The vaccination has to be done at least 30 days before entering Liechtenstein, but not more than 1 year. For animals boostered (re-vaccinated) within 1 year the 30 day rule does not apply.

The vaccination certificate may be written in German, French, Italian, or English with the following wording:
1. Name and address of owner;
2. Description of the animal (race, sex, color, age and special marks);
3. An attestation that the animal has been investigated by a veterinarian and found healthy before vaccination;
4. The date of vaccination against rabies, kind of vaccine, name, producer and LOT number.

Without a vaccination certificate, you can import:
1. Pets (dogs and cats) with Swiss or Liechtenstein origin, which have been temporary abroad accompanying their owner, as well as dogs and cats coming from rabies-free countries where vaccination is forbidden; control authorities (border control) have to inform the competent official veterinarian responsible for the destination;
2. An International Health Certificate accompanies pets younger than 5 months when they are coming from a country without urban rabies. For the countries see the Website of the Swiss Federal Veterinary Office: www.bvet.admin.ch

Dogs must not be imported if they have been abroad and treated in a way forbidden in Switzerland or Liechtenstein. The import of dogs with cut ears or tails is forbidden, when the animals are younger than 5 months. There is no import restriction for dogs of foreigners coming for holiday or temporary stay in Switzerland or Liechtenstein or when they come with their owners in context with change of domicile.

Website: www.tourismus.li

Liechtenstein office
Liechtenstein Tourismus (National Tourist Office)
Stadtle 37
Postfach 139
FL-9490 Vaduz, Liechtenstein
Telephone: 239 63 00
Fax: 239 63 01
E-mail: touristinfo@liechtenstein.li

Lithuania

The requirements to bring pets to Lithuania are quite liberal and are mostly compatible with European standards. The requirements are:
1. Not more than two pets at one time can be brought to Lithuania in non-commercial aims.
2. Every animal must have a health certificate/passport with vaccination information from its veterinarian made 10 days before travel. Dogs need a 5-valency vaccination and for cats, the main requirement is a vaccine from rabies.

3. A certificate may be provided in languages as follows: English, German, Russian, or Lithuanian.

For more information, contact:
> The State Food and Veterinary Service of the Republic of Lithuanian
> Siesiku 19
> Lt- 2010 Vilnius, Lithuania
> Telephone: (00) 370 5 404361
> Fax: (00) 370 5 404362
> E-mail: vvt@vet.lt
> Website: vetlt1.vet.lt/English/english.htm

Website: www.tourism.lt
Website: www.inyourpocket.com
Website: www.travel.lt

Lithuania office
> Lithuanian State Department of Tourism
> Vilniaus 4
> LT-2600 Vilnius, Lithuania
> Telephone: (00) 370 5 622 610
> Fax: (00) 370 5 226 819
> E-mail: vtd@tourism.lt

USA office
> Vytis Tours
> 40-24 235th street
> Douglaston, NY 11363
> Telephone: (718) 423-6161
> Telephone: (800) 778-9847 toll-free in USA
> Fax: (718) 423-3979
> E-mail: vyttours@gnn.com

Embassy of Lithuania
2622 Sixteenth Street, NW
Washington, DC 20009-4202
Telephone: (202) 234-5860
Fax: (202) 328-0466

E-mail: admin@ltembassyus.org
Website: www.ltembassyus.org

Consulate General of Lithuania to USA in Chicago
211 E. Ontario, Suite 1500
Chicago, IL 60611
Telephone: (312) 397-0382
Fax: (312) 397-0385
E-mail: kons.cikaga@urm.lt

Luxembourg

Dogs, cats, and other carnivore are admitted into the territory of the Grand-Duchy of Luxembourg only if they have been inoculated against rabies. Their owners must present a rabies vaccination certificate issued by a veterinarian endorsed by the Animal Health Division of the U.S. Department of Agriculture.

Vaccine Type
In the certificate, the veterinarian has to state that the rabies vaccine used, is controlled and officially approved by the country of manufacture, in this case the U.S. The rabies vaccine used must fall under the following types:

Dogs:
1. Vaccine inactivated on the base of nervous tissues;
2. Live vaccine of the Flury type "High Egg passage (HEP)";
3. Live vaccine of the Flury type "Low Egg passage (HEP)" to be used for dogs over three (3) months of age;
4. Tissue culture vaccine on the base of E.R.A. stock;
5. Inactivated vaccine on the base of virus stock Flury (LEP) multiplied on tissue cultures;
6. Inactivated vaccine on the base of virus stock 'GS 57 Wistar' multiplied on tissue cultures
    - Lyophilized
    - Liquid and adjuvanted by alumna hydroxide.

Cats:
1. Vaccine inactivated on the base of nervous tissues;
2. Live vaccine of the Flury type "High Egg passage (H EP)";
3. Tissue culture vaccine on the base of E.R.A. stock;

4. Inactivated vaccine on the base of virus stock Flury (LEP) multiplied on tissue cultures;
5. Inactivated vaccine on the base of virus stock 'GS 57 Wistar' multiplied on tissue cultures
   - Lyophilized
   - Liquid and adjuvanted by alumina hydroxide

Validity/Time-Limits for Vaccinations

For dogs, the certificate is valid only if the vaccination was administered at least 30 days before the entry into Luxembourg, but not more than:
1. Six months before entry for dogs vaccinated before the age of three months;
2. One year before entry for dogs vaccinated after the age of three months by one of the following vaccines
   - Inactivated vaccine on the base of nervous tissues
   - Live vaccine of the Flury type 'High Egg passage (HEP)'
   - Inactivated vaccine on the base of virus stock Flury (LEP) multiplied on tissue cultures
   - Inactivated vaccine on the base of virus stock 'GS 57 Wistar" multiplied on tissue cultures
     - Lyophilized
     - Liquid and adjuvanted by alumina hydroxide;
3. Two years before entry for dogs vaccinated after the age of three (3) months by one of the following vaccines
   - Vaccine of the type Flury LEP
   - Tissue culture vaccine on the base of E.A. stock
   - Inactivated vaccine on the base of virus stock 'GS 57 Wistar' multiplied on tissue cultures
     - Lyophilized
     - Liquid and adjuvanted by alumina hydroxide.

For Cats, the certificate is valid only if the vaccination was administered within a period of not more than six (6) months and at least 30 days before entry.

Other Certificate Information Required
1. Date of vaccination;
2. Type of vaccine used;

3. Date of expiration of vaccine used;
4. Name of the vaccine's manufacturer;
5. Production batch number of vaccine used;
6. Date of expiration of certificate;
7. Description of animal;
   - Sex
   - Age
   - Breed
   - Color
   - Type and spots of pelt;
8. Name of owner of animal.

If the dogs or cats have been revaccinated, the certificate is valid only if the revaccination respects the time limits mentioned above.

Website: www.etat.lu/tourism
Website: www.ont.lu
Website: www.vistitluxembourg.com

Luxembourg office
   Office National du Tourisme (ONT)
   BP 1001
   L-1010 Luxembourg-Ville, Luxembourg
   Telephone: 4282 8210
   Fax: 4282 8238
   E-mail: info@ont.lu
   Website: www.agendalux.lu

UK office
   Luxembourg National Tourist Office
   122 Regent Street
   London W1B 5SA, UK
   Telephone: (0) 20 7434 2800
   Fax: (0) 20 7734 1205
   E-mail: tourism@luxembourg.co.uk
   Website: www.luxembourg.co.uk

USA office
   Luxembourg National Tourist Office
   17 Beekman Place

New York, NY 10022
Telephone: (212) 935-8888
Fax: (212) 935-5896
E-mail: luxnto@aol.com

Embassy of the Grand Duchy of Luxembourg
2200 Massachusetts Avenue, NW
Washington, DC 20008
Telephone: (202) 265-4171
Fax: (202) 328-8270
E-mail: info@luxembourg-usa.org
Website: www.luxembourg-usa.org

Macau
See also: China

Cats and dogs are required to have an import permit and must be accompanied by a Veterinary Health Certificate issued and signed by the appropriate government veterinary authority of the exporting country. Cats and dogs must also be vaccinated against rabies, however, not less than 14 days and not more than one year before export. Cats and dogs under two months old must not be imported. Animals will be subject to inspection on arrival.

For more information, contact:
General Office for Civil & Municipal Affairs
Telephone: 882049
E-Mail: webmaster@gov.mo

Immigration Service can provide additional information. Please contact:
Travessa de Amigade, Macau
Telephone: (853) 725488
Fax: (853) 7967300
E-mail: info@fsm.gov.mo
Website: www.fsm.gov.mo (Chinese & Portuguese)

Website: www.macautourism.gov.mo

Macau office
    Direcção dos Serviços de Turismo
    (Macau Government Tourist Office)
    Largo do Senado 9
    Ritz Building, Macau
    Telephone: 315 566 or 513 355
    Fax: 510 104
    E-mail: mgto@macautourism.gov.mo

UK office
    Macau Government Tourist Office
    1 Battersea Church Road
    London SW11 3LY, UK
    Telephone: (020) 7771-7000 or 7006
    Fax: (020) 7771-7059
    E-mail: macau@cibgroup.co.uk
    E-mail: Bernstein@cibgroup.co.uk

USA office
    Integrated Travel Resources, Inc.
    5757 West Century Boulevard, Suite 660
    Los Angeles, CA 90045-6407
    Telephone: (310) 568-0009
    Telephone: (800) 622-2800 toll-free in USA
    Fax: (310) 338-0708
    E-mail: mgto@itr-aps.com or mgto_na@altavista.com

Embassy of the People's Republic of China
2300 Connecticut Avenue, NW
Washington, DC 20008
Telephone: (202) 328-2500
Fax: (202) 328-2582
E-mail: chinaembassy_us@fmprc.gov.cn
Website: www.china-embassy.org

The People's Republic of China resumed exercise of sovereignty over Macau effective December 20, 1999.

Macedonia

Macedonia does not require permits or quarantine for pet entry. The only requirements are an International Health Certificate and a vaccination certificate. Further information is available from the Consulate General in New York City: telephone (212) 317-1727.

Embassy of the Republic of Macedonia
130 Albert Street
Ottawa, ON K1M 5G4, Canada
Telephone: (613) 234-3882
Fax: (613) 233-1852
E-mail: emb.macedonia.ottawa@sympatico.ca

Embassy of the Republic of Macedonia
3050 K Street, NW
Suite 210
Washington, DC 20007
Telephone: (202) 337-3063
Fax: (202) 337-3093
E-mail: rmacedonia@aol.com
Website: none

Madagascar

The Madagascar Tourist Office was very helpful and friendly. The representative said that the policy is fairly straightforward and simple. The pet will require an International Health Certificate and a certificate of vaccination. For dogs over 3 months and cats over 6 months, the certificate must further specify they have been vaccinated against rabies (more than 1 month and less than 1 year previously for cats, and for dogs between 3 and 6 months; more than 1 month and less than 3 years previously for dogs over 6 months). She also added that dogs are very welcome in public places, much like France. No translation or certification of documents is necessary.

Website: www.airmad.com

USA office
    Madagascar Tourist Office (Air Madagascar representative)
    124 Lomas Santa Fe Drive, Suite 206

Solana Beach, CA 92075
Telephone: (800) 854-1029 toll-free in USA
Telephone: (619) 792-6999
Fax: (619) 481-7474
E-mail: info@cortez-usa.com

Embassy of Madagascar
2374 Massachusetts Avenue, NW
Washington, DC 20008
Telephone: (202) 265-5525
Fax: (202) 265-3034
E-mail: malagasy@embassy.org
Website: www.embassy.org/madagascar

Malawi

The only requirements for importation of pets into Malawi is that they must have a valid rabies vaccination certificate and must clinically be certified free of major diseases such as distemper, hepatitis, leptospirosis, etc. An import permit must be obtained from the Malawi Animal Health (Veterinary) Department. The permit will state all the conditions for bringing pets into Malawi. For further information contact:
Dr. G. B. Matita
Head-Veterinary Field Services
Telephone: 867 163
E-mail: agric-dahi@malawi.net

Travel in Malawi with pets
- To travel by passenger train, the passenger must secure the pet with a chain or must place it in a cage.
- To travel by passenger ship there is provision for pets in the economy class. For cabins or first class deck, a special arrangement must be made.
- There is no provision for pets when traveling by bus.
- Generally bringing pets in a hotel or restaurants is not acceptable by Malawians. Arrangements can be made with some hotels for the pets to be kept by the veterinary department.

Translation of pet documents is not required if they are written in English.

Website: www.malawiholiday.com
Website: www.malawitourism.com
Website: www.malawi.net

Canada office
   Malawi Tourist office
   c/o Malawi High Commission
   7 Clemow Avenue
   Ottawa, ON KIS 2A9, Canada
   Telephone: (613) 236-8931/32
   Fax: (613) 326-1054
   E-mail: malawihighcommission@sympatico.ca

Malawi office
   Ministry of Tourism, Parks and Wildlife
   Private Bag 326
   Lilongwe 3, Malawi
   Telephone: 775 499 or 772 702
   Fax: 770 650
   E-mail: tourism@malawi.net

UK office
   Malawi Tourist Office
   c/o Malawi High Commission
   33 Grosvenor Street
   London WIX ODE, UK
   Telephone: 20 7491 4172
   Fax: 20 7491 9916
   E-mail: tourism@malawihighcomm.prestel.co.uk

UK office
   Malawi Tourism
   c/o Geo Group
   4 Christian Fields
   London SW16 3JZ, UK
   Telephone: (0115) 982 1903

Fax: (0115) 981 9418
E-mail: enquiries@malawitourism.com

Embassy of Malawi
2408 Massachusetts Avenue, NW
Washington, DC 20008
Telephone: (202) 797-1007
Fax: (202) 265-0976
E-mail: malawidc@aol.com
Website: none
The embassy will also handle tourist inquiries.

Malaysia

Certain breeds of dogs cannot be imported into the country while there are restrictions on the import of some other breeds of dogs. Dogs and cats shall be at least 3 months of age at the time of import. There is no restriction on the number of pets that can be imported by a person. However, the local authorities in Malaysia may have regulations pertaining to the number of dogs that can be kept within residential premises.

You are required to obtain an import permit from the Department of Veterinary Services. If it is an exotic animal or wildlife, you may also be required to obtain an approval from the wildlife conservation authorities to import exotic pets before applying for the import permit from DVS. For importation into Peninsular Malaysia, import permits shall be obtained from the Directors of State Veterinary Departments. You may obtain the Application Form from the abovementioned offices, download the Microsoft Word Version, or print out the application from the Website listed below. For importation into the States of Sabah and Sarawak, enquiries and application shall be made to the states concerned. You should submit the application together with a copy of current vaccination records and import permit fee of five Ringgit (RM 5.00) per dog/cat. The fee can be paid in cash, bank draft, money order, or postal order, made payable to the Director of the State concerned. You may also request a local representative to apply for the permit on your behalf. The import permit is valid for 30 days from the date of issue.

Pets can only be imported as manifested cargo and shall be declared to the Animal Quarantine Officer at the landing point for entry clearance. It is not compulsory but it will be good to inform the Animal Quarantine Officer at the point of entry with details of estimated arrival time and flight details for faster entry clearance.

Apart from the Customs charges, entry of pets is subject to veterinary inspection charges. The original copies of the import permit, the health certificate from the veterinary authority of the exporting country and CITES approval (where necessary) shall be submitted to the Animal Quarantine Officer for clearance. All documents shall be in Bahasa Malaysia or English. The pet may travel unaccompanied. A local representative may be appointed by the owner to handle clearance at the point of entry and to attend to quarantine matters.

Dogs and cats from the United Kingdom, Republic of Ireland, Sweden, Australia, New Zealand, Japan, Brunei, and Singapore are not subject to quarantine provided the pets are healthy and all documents are in order. Dogs and cats from other countries are subject to a minimum of 7 days quarantine. The quarantine charge for dogs and cats is approximately RM 79.00 and RM 72.00 per week respectively. This charge is exclusive of feed and any treatment costs that may be incurred.

Banned Breeds of Dogs: Akita, American Bulldog, Dogo Argentino, Fila Brasileiro, Japanese Tosa, Neapolitan Mastiff, and Pit Bull Terrier/Pit Bull.

Restricted Breeds of Dogs: Bull Mastiff, Bull Terrier, Doberman, German Shepard/Alsatian including Belgian Shepard and East European Shepard, Perro de Presa Canario (also known as Canary Dog) and Rottweiler. These breeds may be imported if they are a pet. These dogs are not for sale or for breeding. A permit is required to import these breeds from The Director General of Veterinary Services of Malaysia. The dog must also have pedigree papers and a microchip embedded for identification.

Applications for the permit to import a pet may be obtained from:
    Department of Veterinary Services Malaysia,
    Ministry of Agriculture Malaysia,

8 & 9th Floors, Wisma Chase Perdana,
Off Jalan Semantan, Bukit Damansara,
50630 Kuala Lumpur, Malaysia
Telephone: 603 254 0077 / 79 / 82 / 84 / 85 / 90
Fax: 603 253 5804 / 254 0092
E-mail: Webmaster@jph.gov.my

The Website to obtain this information and to download the application is www.mcsl.mampu.gov.my. Then proceed to Government Machinery, Federal Government, Ministry of Agriculture, Veterinary Service and import.

Website: www.tourism.gov.my
Website: www.visitmalaysia.com/

Canada office
    Tourism Malaysia
    830 Burrard Street
    Vancouver, BC V6Z 2K4, Canada
    Telephone: (604) 689-8899
    Fax: (604) 689-8804
    E-mail: mtpb-yvr@email.msn.com

Malaysia office
    Tourism Malaysia
    17th Floor, Menara Dato' Onn
    Putra World Trade Centre
    45 Jalan Tun Ismail
    50480 Kuala Lumpur, Malaysia
    Telephone: (3) 2693 5188
    Fax: (3) 2693 5884 or 2693 0207
    E-mail: tourism@tourism.gov.my

UK office
    Tourism Malaysia
    57 Trafalgar Square
    London WC2N 5DU, UK
    Telephone: 0171-930-7932
    Fax: 0171-930-9015
    E-mail: mtph.london@tourism.gov.my

USA: California office
    Tourism Malaysia
    818 West 7th Street, Suite 804
    Los Angeles, CA 90017
    Telephone: (213) 689-9702
    Fax: (213) 689-1530
    E-mail: mtph.LA@tourism.gov.my

USA: New York office
    Tourism Malaysia
    313 East 43rd Street
    New York, NY 10017
    Telephone: (212) 754-1113/14/15
    Fax: (212) 754-1116
    E-mail: mtpb@aol.com

Embassy of Malaysia
2401 Massachusetts Avenue, NW
Washington, DC 20008
Telephone: (202) 328-2700
Fax: (202) 483-7661
E-mail: mwwashdc@erols.com

Maldives

Pets are required to have and International Health Certificate from an authorized veterinarian, stating that the animal is free from infections or contagious diseases. Pets may enter as passenger's checked baggage, in the cabin or as cargo.

Dogs require an import permit, contact:
    Ministry of Foreign Affairs
    Male, Republic of Maldives
    Telephone: 960-323841
    Telex: 66008 MINEX MF

Website: www.visitmaldives.com

Maldives office
    Maldives Tourism Promotion Board
    4th Floor, Bank of Maldives Building

Malé 20-05
Republic of Maldives
Telephone: +960 32 3228
Fax: +960 32 3229
E-mail: mtpb@visitmaldives.com.mv

Maldives Mission to the United Nations
800 Second Avenue, Suite 400E
New York, NY 10017
Telephone: (212) 599-6195
Fax: (212) 661-6405
E-mail: mdvun@undp.org
Website: none

Mali

An International Health Certificate of country of origin issued not more than 3 days before departure, specifying that the place of origin has been free from any infectious disease for at least 6 weeks; and, for animals of the dog family, that no case of rabies has occurred during same period. A rabies certificate is also required. Both documents must be translated into French. These documents must be legalized by the Mali Embassy at a cost of $10 per page.

Website: www.tourisme.gov.ml
Website: www.culture.ml

Mali office
 Ministry of Culture
 BP 4075
 Bamako, Mali
 Telephone: 215 725 or 225 301/2
 Fax: 215 727
 E-mail: malilink@mAli.net

Embassy of the Republic of Mali
2130 R Street, NW
Washington, DC 20008
Telephone: (202) 332-2249
Telephone: (202) 939-8950
Fax: (202) 332-6603

E-mail: info@maliembassy-usa.org
Website: www.maliembassy-usa.org

Malta

Cats and dogs imported from Australia, Ireland, New Zealand, Norway, Sweden, and the United Kingdom are quarantined at the Small Animal Quarantine Section at Luqa for 21 days. For animals arriving from Austria, Belgium, Canada, Cyprus, France, Germany, Italy, Netherlands, Switzerland, and the United States the quarantine period is 30 days. The quarantine period is six months for domestic pets arriving from other countries.

The animal must have an International Health Certificate issued by a recognized veterinarian, just before traveling to Malta, stating that the cat or dog is healthy and shows no evidence of clinical disease or parasitic infection, and that it has been vaccinated against rabies by an inactivated vaccine not less that 30 days and no more than six months before export.

The Ministry of Agriculture and Fisheries' Veterinary Service (Telephone: 225030/225638 or Fax: 238105) in Malta must be notified of the exact date of the animal's arrival at least one week before and also whether the animal will be accompanied or not.

An import license, from the Department of Trade, and an entry form (#2) from the Customs Department must be completed before the release of the cat or dog from quarantine.

Website: www.visitmalta.com/

Malta office
 Malta Tourism Authority
 280 Republic Street
 Valletta CMR 02, Malta
 Telephone: 224 444/5
 Fax: 220 401
 E-mail: info@visitmalta.com

UK office
    Malta National Tourist Office
    Malta House
    36/38 Piccadilly
    London WIV OPP, UK
    Telephone: (0171) 2 92-49 00
    Fax: (0171) 7 34-18 30
    E-mail: office.uk@tourism.org.mt
    Website: www.tourism.org.mt

USA office
    Malta Tourist Office
    65 Broadway, Suite 823
    New York, NY 10006
    Telephone: (212) 430-3799
    Fax: (425) 795-3425
    E-mail: office.us@visitmalta.com

Embassy of Malta
2017 Connecticut Avenue, NW
Washington, DC 20008
Telephone: (202) 462-3611
Fax: (202) 387-5470
E-mail: Malta_Embassy@compuserve.com
Website: www.magnet.mt

Marshall Islands

Anyone importing pets into the Marshall Islands will have to go through the Customs and Quarantine department. People traveling to the Marshall Islands will have to obtain a Quarantine permit before entering the Marshall Islands.

To ensure that you are not breaking the law, please contact the Agriculture Department, and ask to speak with the Quarantine Section before you import any plants, plant material, or pets.

When you bring fruits, vegetables, plants, and plant material, animals, or animal products from overseas into the RMI, you must declare them on the Quarantine and Customs Declaration Form handed to you while in flight. Remember honesty is the best policy when filling in the form!!

Contact Information:
   Department of Agriculture, Quarantine Section
   P.O. Box 1727
   Majuro, Marshall Islands 96960
   Telephone: (692) 625-3206
   Fax: (692) 625-3821
   E-mail: agridiv@ntamar.com

The following specific information was obtained from:
   Banner Bwijtak
   Quarantine Officer
   Ministry of Resources and Development
   Majuro, MH. 96960
   E-mail: agridiv@ntamar.com

Animal quarantine – regulations and quarantines
For the importation of live animals generally, including embryos and ova, the following minimum conditions and requirements must be met:
1. The first port of entry into the RMI shall be specified in the import permit and shall be a designated, official point of entry;
2. The time and date of embarking, the estimated time and date of arrival in the RMI and the airline/flight number or ship/voyage number shall be communicated to the Administrator at the earliest possible time and no later than one weekday working day before embarkation of the animals for the RMI;
3. All animals shall be consigned to the RMI as manifested cargo unless otherwise specified in the import permit;
4. The facilities for the transport of animals shall conform with internationally accepted codes of practice as appropriate;
5. All importation of animals are to be accompanied by:
   - The import permit issued for that importation;
   - A declaration signed by the owner or exporter of the animals providing such information and guarantees as

may be required regarding the identification, history and origin of the animals; and

- An international animal health certificate signed and stamped by an official veterinarian of the exporting country certifying the state of good health of the animals and giving particulars where applicable of the biological tests to which the animal have been subjected and the vaccinations carried out on the animals which are the subject of the certificate and of any measurements taken to prevent the spread of disease;

6. All animals shall be transported directly without trans-shipment, off-loading or contact with animals not the subject of the same import permit or animals not of equivalent certified health status from the port of departure to the port of arrival in the RMI unless other provisions have been made in the import permit;
7. Notice of the death, loss or sickness of any animals during the voyage shall be given to an Inspector immediately on arrival in the RMI by the person in charge of the vessel or aircraft;
8. All foodstuffs, litter, manure, straw or bedding and packing material, crates, containers or any other related articles shall be off-loaded only on the instructions of an Inspector, who may order their cleaning, disinfection, destruction, incineration or other means of disposal;
9. All animals and documents shall be inspected on arrival by an Inspector;
10. No animal shall be released from quarantine unless an authorized veterinarian or his delegate is satisfied, following inspection, that the import is in accordance with the provision of these regulations, that all conditions of the import permit have been met up to the time of arrival in the RMI and that no period of quarantine detention, treatment or tests are required.
11. Unless an imported animal is released from quarantine following its arrival in the RMI it shall be detained under quarantine control unit further notice and may be subjected to any test or treatment required to satisfy the conditions of entry for such animal;
12. Any import permit granted is not transferable;

13. Any import permit may be cancelled or amended at any time after issuance and before arrival of the animal/s in the RMI should the animal health and/or quarantine status of the country or origin change or be reported to have changed before arrival;
14. All costs and expenses of, and attendant upon, any importation, including any documentation, tests, inspections, treatments, detention in quarantine, destruction or re-exportation, or of any other procedure or action taken or brought about under the provisions of these Regulations, shall be borne by the importer or owner, as applicable, and no compensation shall be payable by RMI for any loss or reduction in value caused by such action.

In the case of any O.I.E. List A or List B disease, any communicable disease which is considered to be of socio-economic or public health importance and which is significant in the international trade of livestock and livestock products, or any communicable disease with important socio-economic or sanitary influence at the national level that affects live animals, for which export health certification conditions have not been prescribed in these Regulations, no permit shall be issued unless:
1. The exporting country is free from such disease and no case of such disease was officially reported during the six months immediately preceding the importation of the animals concerned; or
2. If the country of export is not free from any such disease, the Administrator attaches such conditions on the import permit sufficient in his opinion to safeguard against the introduction of such diseases. Such conditions shall not be less than those recommended in the International Animal Health Code of the O. I. E.

Website: www.visitmarshallislands.com

Marshall Islands office
Marshall Islands Visitors Authority
P. O. Box 5
Majuro, Marshall Islands 96960
Telephone: (692) 625-6482

Fax: (692) 625-6771
E-mail: tourism@ntamar.com

Embassy of the Republic of the Marshall Islands
2433 Massachusetts Avenue, NW
Washington, DC 20008
Telephone: (202) 234-5414
Fax: (202) 232-3236
E-mail: info@rmiembassyus.org
Website: www.rmiembassyus.org/usemb.html

Martinique

Cats and dogs over three months old are admitted temporarily with certificates of origin and good health (or anti-rabies inoculation), issued by a licensed veterinarian from the country of shipment. Check with hotels regarding their policy on pets.

Website: www.martinique.org/
Website: www.touristofficemartinique.com
Website: www.franceguide.com
Website: www.nyo.com/martinique

Canada office
    Martinique Tourist Office
    2159 rue Mackay
    Montreal, QC H3G 2J2, Canada
    Telephone: (514) 844-8566
    Telephone: (800) 361-9099 toll-free in Canada
    Fax: (514) 844-8901
    E-mail: tourist-martiniquemontreal@qc.aira.com

Martinique office
    Office du Tourisme de la Martinique
    BP 520, Pavillon du Tourisme
    rue Ernest Desproge
    97206 Fort-de-France Cédex, Martinique
    Telephone: 637 960
    Fax: 736 693
    E-mail: odtm@cgit.com

UK office
 Maison de la France
 (French Government Tourist Office)
 178 Piccadilly
 London W1J 9AL, UK
 Telephone: (09068) 244 123 (information line; calls cost 60p per minute)
 Fax: (020) 7493 6594
 E-mail: info@mdlf.co.uk

USA office
 Martinique Promotion Bureau
 444 Madison Avenue, 16th Floor
 New York, NY 10022
 Telephone: (800) 391-4909 toll-free in USA
 Fax: (212) 838-7855
 E-mail: martinique@nyo.com

Martinique is an Overseas Department of the Republic of France and does not maintain overseas missions/embassies. See also: France.

Mauritania

A rabies vaccination certificate and a current International Health Certificate from the country of origin must accompany all pets. Dogs and cats of less than 3 months are accepted without complying with sanitary regulations.

Mauritania office
 Mauritania Tourist Office
 BP 182
 Nouakchott, Mauritania
 Telephone: 5257 671
 Fax: 5251 057
 E-mail: none

Embassy of the Islamic Republic of Mauritania
2129 Leroy Place, NW
Washington, DC 20008
Telephone: (202) 232-5700
Fax: (202) 319-5701

E-mail: info@mauritaniembassy-usa.org
Website: www.mauritaniembassy-usa.org/

Mauritius

All pets require:
1. Import permit from the Ministry of Agriculture and Natural Resources and the Environment obtained in advance.
2. Sanitary certificate of country of origin.

All animals must be declared to the Customs immediately on arrival. Landing is only allowed if the certificate issued by the Veterinary Authorities of the exporting country is in conformity with the Import Permit.

3. Quarantine: dogs and cats: 6 months, birds: 3 weeks.

PROHIBITED: dogs and cats, coming from areas of 100 km. radius where rabies occurred during the past 12 months and invertebrate animals.

Pet importation on the island is subject to some rules, regulations, and restrictions. For more information, contact the following:

Ministry of Agriculture, Food Technology, and Natural Resources
Division of Veterinary Services
Reduit, Mauritius
Telephone: 00 230 454 1016 - 17
Fax: 00 230 464 2210
E-mail: none

Website: www.mauritius.net

Mauritius office
Mauritius Tourism Promotion Authority
11th Floor, Air Mauritius Centre, John Kennedy Street
Port Louis, Mauritius
Telephone: 210 1545
Fax: 212 5142
E-mail: info@mtpa.mauritius.net

UK office
    Mauritius Tourism Promotion Authority
    32-33 Elvaston Place
    London SW7 5NW, UK
    Telephone: (020) 7584 3666
    Fax: (020) 7225 1135
    E-mail: mtpa@btinternet.com

Embassy of Mauritius
4301 Connecticut Avenue, NW
Suite 441
Washington, DC 20008
Telephone: (202) 244-1491
Fax: (202) 966-0983
E-mail: mauritius.embassy@prodigy.net
Website: www.idsonline.com/usa/embasydc.html

Mexico

Pets may enter Mexico from the USA and Canada with an International Health Certificate issued not more than 72 hours before entering Mexico. A vaccination certificate indicating vaccination against rabies, hepatitis, PIP, and leptospirosis is also required. No translation of documents is required. There is no required permit or quarantine.

An import permit from the Ministry of Agriculture is required for pet birds accompanying passengers, except for birds destined to Merida and Campeche.

Website: www.mexico-travel.com
Website: www.visitmexico.com
Website: www.fonatur.gob.mx

Canada: British Columbia office
    Mexican Tourism Board
    999 West Hastings Street, Suite 1110
    Vancouver, BC V6C 2W2, Canada
    Telephone: (604) 669-2845
    Telephone: (800) 44-MEXICO toll-free in Canada

Fax: (604) 669-3498
E-mail: mgto@bc.sympatico.ca

Canada: Ontario Office
Mexican Tourism Board
2 Bloor Street West, Suite 1502
Toronto, ON M4W 3E2, Canada
Telephone: (416) 925-0704
Telephone: (800) 44-MEXICO toll-free in Canada
Fax: (416) 925-6061
E-mail: toronto@visitmexico.com

Canada: Quebec office
Mexico Tourism Board
One Place Ville Marie, Suite 1526
Montreal, QC H3B 2B5, Canada
Telephone: (514) 871-1052
Telephone: (800) 44-MEXICO toll-free in Canada
Fax: (514) 871-3825
E-mail: montreal@visitmexico.com

Mexico: Acapulco office
Acapulco Convention & Visitors Bureau
Avenue Costera Miguel Aleman No.3111
Fracc. Costa Azul, Suites 204-205
Acapulco, GRO 39850 Mexico
Telephone: 74-84-8554 or 8555
Fax: 74-84-8134
E-mail: cvb@acapulco-cvb.org
Website: www.acapulco-cvb.org/

Mexico: Mexico City office
Fondo Nacional de Fomento al Turismo (FONATUR)
22nd Floor, Insurgentes Sur 800
Colonia del Valle, 03100 México DF, Mexico
Telephone: (5) 687 2697 or (250) 01 23 01 53 (travel hotline)
Fax: (5) 687 5052
E-mail: ibotas@fonatur.gob.mx

UK office
 Mexican Tourism Promotion Board
 Wakefield House
 41 Trinity Square
 London EC3N 4DJ, UK
 Telephone: (020) 7488 9392
 Fax: (020) 7265 0704
 E-mail: info@visitmexico.com

USA: California office
 Mexico Tourism Board
 10100 Santa Monica Boulevard, Suite 224
 Los Angeles, CA 90067
 Telephone: (310) 203-8191
 Telephone: (800) 44-MEXICO toll-free in USA
 Fax: (310) 203-8316
 E-mail: losangeles@visitmexico.com

USA: Illinois office
 Mexico Tourism Board
 300 North Michigan Avenue, 4th floor
 Chicago, IL 60601
 Telephone: (312) 606-9252
 Telephone: (800) 44-MEXICO toll-free in USA
 Fax: (312) 606-9012
 E-mail: chicago@visitmexico.com

USA: New York office
 Mexico Tourism Board
 450 Park Avenue, Suite 1401
 New York, NY 10022
 Telephone: (800) 44-MEXICO toll-free in USA
 Fax: (212) 821-0367
 E-mail: newyork@visitmexico.com

USA: California office
 Mexico Tourism Board
 2401 West 6th Street, 5th Floor
 Los Angeles, CA 90057
 Telephone: (213) 351-2069

Telephone: (800) 44-MEXICO toll-free in USA
Fax: (213) 351-2074
E-mail: 104045.364@compuserve.com

USA: Texas office
Mexico Tourism Board
1010 Fomdren Street
Houston, TX 77096
Telephone: (713) 772-3819
Telephone: (800) 44-MEXICO toll-free in USA
Fax: (713) 772-6058
E-mail: houston@visitmexico.com

Embassy of Mexico
1911 Pennsylvania Avenue, NW
Washington, DC 20006
Telephone: (202) 728-1600
E-mail: info@embassyofmexico.org
E-mail: mexembusa@aol.com
Website: www.embassyofmexico.org

Micronesia
Importation of dogs into the FSM (Federated States of Micronesia)
The importation of dogs into the FSM requires presentation of an international animal health certificate, attesting that the animals:
1. Were examined within 48 hours of shipment, found to be in good health and showed no sigh of any infectious disease;
2. Have been effectively vaccinated against distemper, hepatitis and canine parvovirus at least one month and not more than three months before shipment;
3. Have been effectively treated against echinococcosis-hydatidosis, round, hook, and whip worms within three days of shipment;
4. Have been effectively treated against and found on examination to be visibly free of all ectoparasites within three days of shipment;
5. Showed no clinical sign of rabies on the day of shipment, and were kept from birth or for six months before shipment in the exporting country, or a port of the territory of the exporting

country where no case of rabies was officially reported during the two years immediately preceding the importation of the animals concerned;
6. Have been vaccinated with an inactivated rabies virus more than thirty days before entry into the FSM; and
7. For animal originating from a country or a part of a country where rabies occurs or is reported to occur or where rabies vaccination is routinely practiced such animals must undergo a period of not less than 120 days in an approved quarantine facility in a rabies free area before entry to the FSM, or
8. Meet the entry requirements of the State of Hawaii or the Territory of Guam.

Upon arrival in the FSM, imported dogs shall immediately be taken under the control of an Inspector to the quarantine premises previously approved by the Administrator, whereat the animals shall remain until an Inspector releases them.

Movement of dogs within the FSM
The movement of dogs within the FSM requires presentation of a certificate issued by a veterinarian or authorized official, stating that the animals:
1. Originated in the FSM; and
2. Were apparently free of any signs of infectious or communicable disease; and
3. Have been treated against and found on examination to be free of any ectoparasites or endoparasites within three days of shipment.

Importation of cats into the FSM
The importation of cats into the FSM requires presentation of an international animal health certificate, attesting that the animals:
1. Were examined within 48 hours of shipment, found to be in good health and showed no sign of any infectious disease;
2. Have been effectively vaccinated against Feline Panleukopenia at least one month and not more than twelve months before shipment, and Feline Viral Rhinotracheitis/Calici virus at least one month and not more than three months before shipment;

3. Have been effectively treated against echinococcosis-hydatidosis, round, hook and whipworms within three days of shipment;
4. Have been effectively treated against, and found on examination to be visibly free of all ectoparasites within three days of shipment;
5. Showed no clinical sign of rabies on the day of shipment, and were kept from birth or for six months before shipment in the exporting country, or a part of the territory of the exporting country where no case of rabies was officially reported during the two years immediately preceding the importation of the animals concerned;
6. Have been vaccinated with an inactivated rabies virus more than thirty days before entry into the FSM; and
7. For animals originating form a country or a port of a country where rabies occurs or is reported to occur or where rabies vaccination is routinely practiced such animals must undergo a period of not less than 120 days in an approved quarantine facility in a rabies free area before entry to the FSM; or
8. Must meet the entry requirements of the State of Hawaii or the Territory of Guam.

Upon arrival in the FSM, imported cats shall immediately be taken under the control of an Inspector to the quarantine premises previously approved by the Administrator, whereat the animals shall remain until they are release by an Inspector.

Movement of cats within the FSM
The movement of cats within the FSM requires the presentation of a certificate issued by a veterinarian or authorized official, stating that the animals:
1. Originated in the FSM;
2. Are apparently free of any signs of infectious or communicable disease; and
3. Have been treated against and found on examination to be free of any ectoparasites or endoparasites within three days of shipment.

Website: www.visit-micronesia.com

Micronesia office
   Federated State of Micronesia Visitors Board
   P. O. Box PS-12
   Palikir, Pohnpei FSM 96941
   Telephone: (691) 320-2646
   Fax: (691) 320-5854
   E-mail: fsminfo@visit-fsm.org
   E-mail: Visit_FSM@mail.fm

USA: Guam
   Federated State of Micronesia Consulate General
   P.O. Box 10630
   Tamuning, Guam 96911
   Telephone: (671) 646-9154
   Fax: (671) 646-6320
   E-mail: fsmcongm@kuentos.guam.net

USA: Hawaii
   Federated State of Micronesia Consulate General
   3049 Ualena Street, Suite 904
   Honolulu, HI 96819
   Telephone: (808) 836-4775
   Fax: (808) 836-6896
   E-mail: fsmcghnl@gte.net

Embassy of Micronesia
1725 N Street, NW
Washington, DC 20036
Telephone: (202) 223-4383
Fax: (202) 223-4391
E-mail: fsmemb@aol.com
Website: www.fsmembassy.org

Moldova

Moldova requires an International Pet Passport, International Health Certificate, and a current rabies vaccination certificate. No translation or legalization is necessary. No quarantine is required. There is no official tourism office in the United States.

Website: www.turism.md
Website: www.moldova.org
Website: www.ournet.md

Moldova office
>National Agency for Tourism
>Government House, Office 569
>Piata Marii Adunari Nationale
>Chisinau, MD-2033, Moldova
>Telephone/Fax: (2) 234 264
>E-mail: tourism_ant@moldova.md

Embassy of The Republic of Moldova
2101 S Street, NW
Washington, DC 20008
Telephone: (202) 667-1130 / 31 / 37
Fax: (202) 667-1204
E-mail: moldova@dgs.dgsys.com
E-mail: embassy@moldova.org
Website: www.moldova.org

Monaco

Pets from other European countries may circulate freely if vaccinated against rabies. Pets from non-EU countries will be given an obligatory sanitary inspection by a French Veterinarian upon entering customs. The general rules of France will apply. (See France)

Website: www.monaco-tourism.com
Website: www.monaco-congres.com
Website: www.monaco.mc

UK office
>Monaco Government Tourist Office
>The Chambers
>Chelsea Harbour
>London SW10 OXF, UK
>Telephone: 020 7352 9962
>Fax: 020 7352 2103
>E-mail: monaco@monaco.co.uk

USA: New York office
    Monaco Government Tourist Office
    (Consulate General for the Principality of Monaco)
    565 Fifth Avenue
    New York, NY 10017
    Telephone: (800) 753-9696 toll-free in USA
    Telephone: (212) 286-3330
    Fax: (212) 286-9890
    E-mail: mgto@monaco1.org
    Website: www.monaco.mc/usa

Mongolia

The U.S. Embassy in Ulaanbaatar, Mongolia was helpful in finding this information. A pet needs to have an International Health Certificate. That certificate needs to state that the pet is free of evidence of diseases communicable to people. The record of rabies vaccination is also needed. The rabies vaccination must be more than one month and less than one year before entering Mongolia. At the port of entry, the pet needs to be registered with the Custom's veterinarian.

Website: www.mongoliatourism.gov

Mongolia office
    Mongolia Tourism Board
    Chinggis Avenue- 11
    Ulaanbaatar- 28
    Mongolia, 210628
    Telephone: 976-11 311102
    Fax: 976-11 318492
    E-mail: ntc@mongol.net

Embassy of Mongolia
2833 M Street, NW
Washington, DC 20007
Telephone: (202) 333-7117
Fax: (202) 298-9227
E-mail: monemb@aol.com
E-mail: monconsul@aol.com (Consulate Section)
Website: www.monemb.org

Montserrat

Montserrat requires the owner to obtain a license for the importation of pets. The conditions of the license are:
1. The animals must be accompanied by an International Health Certificate issued within 72 yours before travel by a competent veterinary authority in the country in which the animal last resided for a period of at least three months immediately before transfer to Montserrat. The veterinarian must certify that the animal is free from contagious diseases. For dogs, the diseases are: distemper, hepatitis, leptospirosis, parvovirus, rabies, and heartworm. For cats, the diseases are: distemper, rhinotracheitis, rabies, and parvovirus.
2. The animals shall not be landed without the approval of the Veterinary Officer of Montserrat. The Veterinary Officer must be notified of time of arrival and port of entry at least 48 hours before arrival time.
3. The animal shall be subjected to house quarantine for a period not less than four months or such longer prescribe. (Please note that the quarantine site must be inspected before entry is granted.)
4. The valid certificate of immunization/vaccination for these diseases must accompany the animal at the time of import together with an International Health Certificate.

The form is available from:
Department of Agriculture
P.O. Box 272
Brades, Montserrat
Telephone: (664) 491-2546/2075
E-mail: malhe@candw.ag

Website: www.visitmontserrat.com

Canada office
Caribbean Tourism Organization
Taurus House
512 Duplex Avenue
Toronto, ON M4R 2E3, Canada
Telephone: (416) 485-7827

Fax: (416) 485-8256
E-mail: assoc@thermrgroup.ca

Montserrat office
Montserrat Tourist Board
P.O. Box 7
Olveston, Montserrat, West Indies
Telephone: 491 2230 or 491 8730
Fax: 491 7430
E-mail: mrattouristboard@candw.ag

UK office
Caribbean Tourism Organization
42 Westminster Palace Gardens
Artillery Row
London SW1P 1RR, UK
Telephone: 207 222 4335
Fax: 207 222 4325
E-mail: cto@caribtourism.com

USA office
Caribbean Tourism Organization
80 Broad Street, 32nd Floor
New York, NY 10004
Telephone: (212) 635-9530
Fax: (212) 635-9511
E-mail: get2cto@dorsai.org

Montserrat is a British Overseas Territory and is represented abroad by British Embassies. See also: United Kingdom.

Morocco

Morocco requires a current International Health Certificate and a vaccination certificate dated no more than one year before arrival. There is no imposed quarantine. No permit to import is required. The USDA must stamp the certificate if the pet originates from the U.S.

Website: www.tourism-in-morocco.com/
Website: www.mincom.gov.ma

Canada office
  Moroccan National Tourist Office
  Place Montreal Trust, Suite 2450
  1800, Avenue McGill College
  Montreal, QC H3A 3J6, Canada
  Telephone: (514) 842-8111 or 842-8112
  Fax: (514) 842-5316
  E-mail: none

UK office
  Moroccan National Tourist Office
  Second Floor, 205 Regent Street
  London W1B 4HB, UK
  Telephone: (020) 7437 0073
  Fax: (020) 7734 8172
  E-mail: mnto@btconnect.com

USA: Florida office
  Moroccan National Tourist Office
  P.O Box 22663
  Lake Buena Vista, FL 32830
  Telephone: (407) 827-5337
  Fax: (407) 827-0146
  E-mail: none

USA: New York office
  Moroccan National Tourist Office
  20 East 46th Street, Suite 1201
  New York, NY 10017
  Telephone: (212) 557-2520
  Fax: (212) 949-8148
  E-mail: none

Embassy of the Kingdom of Morocco
1601 21st Street, NW
Washington, DC 20009
Telephone: (202) 462-7979
Fax: (202) 462-7643
E-mail: sifarausa@erols.com
Website: none

Mozambique

The following are the requirements in bringing pets into Mozambique:
1. Certificate of vaccinations;
2. Certificate that the pet/animal does not have any diseases; and,
3. Proof of ownership

Website: none

Mozambique office
    Mozambique National Tourism Company
    6th floor, Avenida 25 de Setembro nr1502
    Maputo, Mozambique
    Telephone: 307 667
    Fax: 421 166
    E-mail: none

Embassy of Mozambique
1990 M Street, NW
Suite 570
Washington, DC 20036
Telephone: (202) 293-7146
E-mail: mozambvisa@aol.com (visa section)
E-mail: embamoc@aol.com
Website: www.embamoc-usa.org/

Myanmar

Travelers are allowed to bring their personal pets on the condition that they are accompanied with a current International Health Certificate.

Website: www.myanmar.com
Website: www.myanmars.net
Website: www.myanmar-tourism.com

Myanmar office
    Myanmar Tourism Promotion Board
    5 Signal Pagoda Road
    Dagon Township

Yangon, Myanmar
Telephone: (1) 2436 3943
Fax: (1) 245 001
E-mail: info@myanmartourismboard.com

UK office
Embassy of the Union of Myanmar
19a Charles Street
London W1J 5DX, UK
Telephone: (020) 7499 8841 or (0906) 550 8924 (recorded visa and tourism information; calls cost £1.00 per minute)
Fax: (020) 7629 4169
E-mail: none

USA office
Myanmar National Tourist Office
2514 University Drive
Durham, NC 27707
Telephone: (919) 493-7500
Fax: none
E-mail: none

Embassy of Myanmar
2300 S Street, NW
Washington, DC 20008
Telephone: (202) 332-9044
Fax: (202) 332-9046
E-mail: mewashdc@cjb.net
Website: www.mewashdc.cjb.net

Namibia

Namibia requires that an application for an import permit be submitted well in advance (not less than 3 days before it is required-30 days in the case of animals or birds requiring quarantine on arrival in Namibia). There is no time limit for the pet as long as the owner has permission to be in Namibia. The Health Certificate on the import permit, which will be issued on payment of N $50, must be completed by an official veterinarian in the country of origin and must accompany the pet to Namibia. Depending on the country of origin, the pet may have to go into quarantine for 30 days. You must indicate

clearly, where the pet is coming from on your application form. This application may be obtained from:
>Director of Veterinary Services
>Private Bag 12022
>Windhoek, Namibia
>Telephone: (61) 2087505
>Fax: (61) 2087779

The Namibia Tourism office in Namibia was very helpful in providing additional information. No pets are allowed into any of the game parks or nature reserves. The Hospitality Association of Namibia sent out a brief questionnaire to its members across Namibia to determine whether Namibian accommodations would allow pets (accompanying visiting guests) into their establishments. In general, NO PETS are allowed at most of the establishments, for various reasons. Most lodges and guest farms have game or domestic animals at or close to the establishments, therefore do not allow outside animals. Health, hygiene, and possible allergies among other guest were given as other reasons why pets would not be allowed. Some establishments have indicated that they would use some discretion, when deciding whether pets would be allowed and when not. Conditions under which pets might be allowed at some few establishments are:

1. If the pets do not disturb other guests;
2. If there is not problem with staff cleaning the rooms;
3. If pets are clean and have the necessary; certificate from the state veterinarian;
4. If they do not "interfere" with pets of the establishment;
5. If they do not pose a threat to guests and staff.

Here is a list of definite NO PETS:
Hotels:
- Swakapmund Hotel and Entertainment Centre
- Kalahari Sands Hotel
- Furstenhof Hotel
- Cresta Lodge, Ondangwa

Groups:
- Discover Africa, (with some 30 lodges/guest farms across Namibia)
- Wilderness Safaris

Lodges/Guest Farms:
- Ozumbanda Guest Farm
- Kavita Lion Lodge
- Airport Lodge
- Huab Lodge
- Namib Naukluft Lodge

Other:
- Swakopmund Municipal Bungalows

Those who indicated that they might accept pets under conditions:
- Langholm Hotel-Garni, Walvis Bay
- Hotel Pension Steiner, Windhoek

Website: www.tourism.com.na
Website: www.namibiatourism.com
Website: www.iwwn.com.na

Namibia office
  Namibia Tourism
  Private Bag 13346
  Windhoek, Namibia
  Telephone: (61) 284 2366/67
  Fax: (61) 221 930 or 284 2364
  E-mail: tourism@mweb.com.na

UK office
  Namibia Tourism
  6 Chandos Street
  London W1M 0LQ, UK
  Telephone: 171 636 2924 or 2928
  Fax: 171 636 2969
  E-mail: namibia@globalnet.co.uk

USA office
  Namibia Tourism
  Kartagener Associates Inc.
  12 West 37th Street
  New York, NY 10018

Telephone: (212) 465-0619
Telephone: (800) 626-4242
Fax: (212) 868-1654
E-mail: none

Embassy of The Republic of Namibia
1605 New Hampshire Avenue, NW
Washington, DC 20009
Telephone: (202) 986-0540
Fax: (202) 986-0443
E-mail: embnamibia@aol.com
Website: www.grnnet.gov.na

Nauru

Cats and dogs can only be imported from Australia. Permit required, issued in Nauru, and obtainable from Director of Health and Medical Services - Nauru.

Website: www.dfat.gov.au/geo/nauru

Australia office
  Consulate General of the Republic of Nauru
  Level 50, Nauru House
  80 Collins Street
  Melbourne, Victoria 3000, Australia
  Telephone: (613) 9653 5709
  Fax: (613) 9654 4738
  E-mail: none

UK office
  Commonwealth Institute
  Kensington High Street
  London W8 6NQ, UK
  Telephone: (020) 7603 4535
  Fax: (020) 7602 7374
  E-mail: information@commonwealth.org.uk
  Website: www.commonwealth.org.uk
  Provides information on Nauru.

United Nations office
  800 2nd Avenue, Suite 400 D
  New York, NY 10017
  Telephone: (212) 937-0074

Nepal

There are no hard and fast rules for bringing pets to Nepal. A tourist can bring in pets to Nepal and the Customs Department has no objections if a tourist wants to bring his pet to Nepal. However, pets (dogs) are usually not allowed in hotels and there are no arrangements for keeping them in hotels. It will be also a problem for transporting pets from one place to another in public transport. An International Health Certificate and a rabies certificate must accompany cats and dogs.

Website: www.welcomenepal.com/

Nepal office
  Nepal Tourism Board
  Bhrikuti Mandap
  P.O. Box 11028
  Katmandu, Nepal
  Telephone: 1-256909/256229
  Fax: 1-256910
  E-mail: bsharma@ntb.wlink.com.np

UK office
  Shangrila Tours & Travels
  41 Nightingale Road
  London NW 104RG, UK
  Telephone: 965 6042
  Fax: 961 6314

USA office
  Anik Travels
  5938 SW Luradei
  Portland, OR 97219
  Telephone: (503) 244-1674
  Fax: (503) 244-1674
  E-mail: info@ntb.wlink.com.np

Embassy of Nepal
2131 Leroy Place, NW
Washington, DC 20008
Telephone: (202) 667-4550
Fax: (202) 667-5534
E-mail: nepali@erols.com
Website: www.nepalembassyusa.org

Netherlands

No quarantine is required if you submit an International Health Certificate and rabies vaccination certificate. The rabies vaccination should be at least 30 days old and not older than 12 months. The International Health Certificate must be issued by a U.S. certified veterinary surgeon, and must be dated not more than 10 days before departure from the U.S.; this information can be added to the rabies vaccination certificate.

The rabies vaccination certificate must be issued by a U.S. certified veterinary surgeon and must contain the following information:
1. A statement in Dutch or English that the animal has been inoculated with a U.S. officially inspected and approved rabies vaccine;
2. Date of vaccination;
3. Type of vaccine used and expiration date, the name of the manufacturer and the manufacturer's batch number;
4. Description of the animal (sex, age, breed, hair color and markings);
5. Name of the owner of the animal.

Please note:
The vaccination of your cat or dog must be given at least 30 days and not more than nine months before entry into the Netherlands. If this is not possible, a veterinary surgeon can inoculate the animal at the airport in Amsterdam. The animal must then be held in quarantine at home for 30 days after the shot.

Please be informed that Pit Bull Terriers, American Staffordshire Terrier, Fila Brasileiro, Dogo Argentino, and Mastino Napolitano are prohibited from entering the Netherlands.

Cats and dogs (when younger than 12 weeks old) entering the Netherlands for the purpose of trade, either temporarily or on a permanent basis, including attending trade shows, have to travel with a health certificate issued by the official State Veterinary Officer of your State Department of Agriculture and a rabies vaccination certificate.

Psittacine Birds (parrots or parrot-like birds) for entry or transit: Always consult the local Ministry of Agriculture or Veterinary Service or nearest Dutch Consulate before travel, because "endangered species", whether alive or stuffed or parts thereof may not be imported and will be returned, even if the health documents are in order. Dispensation to be obtained before arrival from the Department for Nature Conservation, Environmental Protection and Wild Life Management, Bezuidenhoutseweg 73 (P.O. Box 20401), 2500 EK The Hague (phone 31-70-3793390 or 31-70-3792922). Entry or transit limited to 2 birds per family or person traveling alone, provided bird(s) are accompanied by health certificate issued and signed, not more than 2 months before, by the veterinary service of the country where birds have been taken from, stating that animals have been submitted for examination by a member of the family or person traveling alone and upon examination fowl plague, Newcastle disease, fowl cholera, psittacosis and pullorum disease have not been diagnosed.

PROHIBITED: Psittacine birds if coming from Australia, Bolivia, Colombia, Ghana, Hong Kong, Honduras, Indonesia, Nicaragua, or Paraguay (from Ghana between January 01 and September 01).

If you are departing from the Netherlands, please contact:
  Foreign Agricultural Service
  U.S. Embassy in The Hague
  Lange Voorhout 102
  2514 EJ The Hague
  The Netherlands
  Telephone: +31 (0) 70-3109 299
  Fax: +31 (0) 70-3657 681

If you would like to take a ferret, rabbit or a rat as a pet to the Netherlands, please contact our office at the number listed below since you will need a special health certificate. This health certificate must be filled out, signed by your local U.S. certified veterinary doctor, and is valid up to ten days after completion.

For other questions or information, please feel free to contact:
Office of the Agricultural Counselor
The Royal Netherlands Embassy
Telephone: (202) 274-2716/2718
Fax: (202) 244-3325
E-mail: laura.wieling@minbuza.nl

Website: www.holland.com
Website: www.goholland.co.uk
Website: www.goholland.com

Canada office
Netherlands Board of Tourism
25 Adelaide Street East, Suite 710
Toronto, ON M5C 1Y2, Canada
Telephone: (888) GOHOLLAND toll-free in Canada and USA
Telephone: (888) PAYS-BAS appellez sans frais
Fax: (416) 3631470
E-mail: info@goholland.com

UK office
Netherlands Board of Tourism
P.O. Box 30783
London WC2B 6DH, UK
Telephone: 020 7539 7950
Fax: 020 7539 7953
Brochure-line: 0891 717 777
E-mail: Hollandinfo-UK@nbt.org.uk

USA office
Netherlands Board of Tourism
355 Lexington Avenue
New York, NY 10017

Telephone: (888) GOHOLLAND toll-free in Canada and USA
E-mail: info@goholland.com

Embassy of The Netherlands
4200 Linnean Avenue, NW
Washington, DC 20008
Telephone: (202) 244-5300
Fax: (202) 362-3430
E-mail: nlgovwas@netherlands-embassy.org
Website: www.netherlands-embassy.org

New Caledonia
See also: South Pacific Tourism Organization

Pets checked as cargo with an airway bill and carried on the same aircraft, as the accompanying passenger should have a blood test completed more than 3 months before arrival. Contact the Veterinary Service in Nouméa. Contact information below.

Dogs and Cats:
1. Import generally prohibited (also coming from USA);
   - Prohibited: all types of "Pitbull" dogs (e.g. Staffordshire terrier, American Staffordshire terrier) Mastiff, and Tosa will be sent back to country of origin.

   Ask the air carrier if they will transport your breed (e.g. Air France will not transport above breeds). Rottweilers may now be imported loaded in a rigid plastic container conforming to Air France rules.
2. Import allowed from E.U. countries: accompanied by certificate of residency (valid for more than 6 months when travel commences). Rabies vaccination: rabies control measures and quarantine period is 1 month.
3. Import from all other countries: quarantine period is 6 months. Allowed only if coming from a country that has been rabies free for at least 2 years. A 5-day quarantine period is compulsory. The animal must be accompanied by:
   - Import permit: apply at least one month in advance. Indicate the number, breed, age, sex, origin); and

- Zoosanitary certificate issued by an official veterinary surgeon in country of origin within 3 days before departure.

Birds:
1. Generally prohibited: except if coming from a country free of aviary pest and Newcastle disease.
   - Parrots: import maximum of two per person (owner for more than 6 months), and the animal must be free of psittacosis.
   - In all cases: apply for "import permit" at least one month in advance.

Importation of pets is subject to a certificate of importation. Contact the Ministry of Agriculture:
Ministry of Agriculture
Plant and Animal Department
BP 256
98845 Nouméa Cedex
Telephone: (687) 24 37 45
Fax: (687) 25 11 12
E-mail: svpv@gov.nc

Website: www.newcaledoniatourism-south.com
Website: www.franceguide.com

New Caledonia office
New Caledonia Tourism
20 rue Anatole France - Immeuble Nouméa-Centre
Place des Cocotiers
BP 688 - 98845 Nouméa Cedex
New Caledonia
Telephone: (687) 24 20 80
Fax: (687) 24 20 70
E-mail: tourisme@offratel.nc
E-mail: info@nouvellecaledonietourisme-sud.com

USA office
Maison de la France
9454 Wilshire Boulevard, Suite 715

Beverly Hills, CA 90212-2967
Telephone: (310) 271-6665
Fax: (310) 276-2835
E-mail: none

New Caledonia is a French Overseas Territory. Contact information regarding the French Embassy and tourist office is in the France section.

New Zealand

The New Zealand government has two very helpful Websites: www.maf.govt.nz and www.customs.govt.nz. The procedures for importing pets are quite extensive and detailed. To bring pets from countries recognized as countries in which canine rabies is absent or well controlled entails a permit and the pet will be quarantined for a minimum of 30 days in a quarantine facility. Pets arriving from Hawaii will not be quarantined. The permit may be obtained from:
The Director of Animal Biosecurity
Ministry of Agriculture and Forestry
P.O. Box 2526
Wellington, New Zealand

The pet will need to have either a microchip or tattoo for identification. Because the rules are so lengthy and detailed, they are not included in this book. Please refer to the above address or Website for additional information: www.purenz.com

The Tourism New Zealand office recommended travelers visit the New Zealand Immigration Service Website www.immigration.govt.nz. U.S. or Canadian citizens traveling on a passport that expires at least three months after they plan to leave New Zealand can stay up to three months without a visitor visa and UK passport holders up to six months.

UK office
New Zealand Tourism Board
80 Haymarket
London SW1Y 4TQ, UK
Telephone: 171 930 1662
Telephone: 09 063 640 650 information line (60p/minute)

Fax: 171 839 8929
E-mail: enquiries@nztb.govt.nz
E-mail: go to Feedback at: www.purenz.com

USA: California office
New Zealand Tourism Board
501 Santa Monica Boulevard, Suite 300
Santa Monica, CA 90401
Telephone: (310) 395 7480
Telephone: (866) 639-9325 toll-free in Canada and USA
Fax: (310) 395-5453
E-mail: nzinfo@nztb.govt.nz
E-mail: go to Feedback at: www.purenz.com

Embassy of New Zealand
37 Observatory Circle
Washington, DC 20008
Telephone: (202) 328-4800
Fax: (202) 667-5227
E-mail: nz@nzemb.org
Website: www.nzemb.org

Nicaragua

Entry requirements include a vaccination certificate less than one year old and an International Health Certificate dated less than 15 days before travel. There is no quarantine in Nicaragua.

Website: www.intur.gob.ni

Nicaragua office
Nicaraguan Institute of Tourism (INTUR)
Hotel Intercontinental
1 cuadra al Oeste y 1 cuadra al Sur
Managua, Nicaragua
Telephone: 222 2962 or 222 3333
Fax: 222 6610
E-mail: promocion@intur.gob.ni

Embassy of Nicaragua
1627 New Hampshire Avenue, NW
Washington, DC 20009
Telephone: (202) 939-6570
Fax: (202) 939-6542
E-mail: none
Website: www.intur.gov.ni
The embassy also deals with enquiries relating to Canada.

Niger

The Niger Embassy recommended contacting Air France to update the requirements before travel. The current requirements are an International Health Certificate and a certificate of vaccination. The documents do not require translation or certification by the embassy.

Niger office
    National Tourist Office
    Avenue du Président H Luebke
    BP 612
    Niamey, Niger
    Telephone: 732 447
    Fax: 733 940
    E-mail: none

Embassy of the Republic of Niger
2204 R Street, NW
Washington, DC 20008
Telephone: (202) 483-4224
Fax: (202) 483 3169
E-mail: embassyofniger@ioip.com
Website: www.nigerembassyusa.org

Nigeria

For pet owners, they are required to administer adequate vaccination to their pets at least two weeks before entry into Nigeria. They should also carry their pet's International Health Certificate with them for verification.

Nigeria office
>Nigeria Tourism Development Corporation
>P.O. Box 167
>Old Federal Secretariat, Area 1, Garki
>Abuja, Nigeria
>Telephone/Fax: 234 2775
>E-mail: ntdc@metrong.com

Embassy of the Federal Republic of Nigeria
1333 16th Street, NW
Washington, DC 20036
Telephone: (202) 986-8400
Fax: (202) 775-1385
E-mail: infocenter@nigeria-government.com
Website: www.NigeriaembassyUSA.org
Website: www.Nigeria-Government.com

Niue
See also: South Pacific Tourism Organization

Application for the permit to import animals to Niue is compulsory. Prior permission in writing must be obtained from the appropriate Niue Authorities (Quarantine Dept).

Conditions (import permit):
1. Each animal must be accompanied by a signed declaration from the exporter detailed in Zoo Sanitary Certificate on the application permit to import animals.
2. Each animal must be accompanied by the International Animal Health Certificate detailed in Veterinary Certificate on the application permit to import animals signed by an official veterinary officer of the exporting country.
3. Before unloading on arrival, the documents required (Zoo Sanitary Certificate and Veterinary Certificate) must be presented to a quarantine officer of the Niue Department of Agriculture.
4. The animal must be consigned to Niue by air as manifested cargo.
5. The actual date of embarkation and the airline flight number must be advised to the Director of Agriculture, Niue

(Telephone: 683 4032 / Fax: 683 4079 at the earliest opportunity and at least one working day before shipping.
6. The animals must be transported in accordance with the recommendations for the transport of live animals of the Office International des Epizooties (OIE) and the International Air Transport Association (IATA) live animal regulations as appropriate.
7. The animal will be inspected and treated as necessary on arrival in Niue by a quarantine officer and may not leave the quarantine area of the port of entry until a quarantine release is issued.
8. Translation of documents is not required
9. No accommodation properties have facilities for animals. Arrangements would have to be made outside the accommodation property for pets.

Website: www.niueisland.com

Niue office
Niue Tourism Office
P.O. Box 42
Alofi, Niue
Telephone: (683) 4224
Fax: (683) 4225
E-mail: niuetourism@mail.gov.nu
E-mail: admin.tourism@mail.gov.nu

USA office
Niue Island Tourism Office
DCI, 959 Thornhill Road
Lexington, VA 24450
Telephone: (540) 463-7092
Fax: (540) 463-7182
E-mail: dunlapkj@yahoo.com

Niue is a self-governing state in "free association" with New Zealand. (New Zealand retains responsibility for external affairs.)

Northern Ireland
See also: United Kingdom

All animals entering Northern Ireland must meet the criteria for the United Kingdom Pet Travel Scheme. See United Kingdom for specifics.

Website: www.ni-tourism.com

Canada office
    Northern Ireland Tourist Board
    2 Bloor St West, Suite 1501
    Toronto, ON M4W 3E2, Canada
    Telephone: (416) 925-6368
    Fax: (416) 925-6033
    E-mail: infocanada@nitb.com

UK: Glasgow office
    Northern Ireland Tourist Board
    135 Buchanan Street
    Glasgow G1 2JA, UK
    Telephone: 141 204 4454
    Fax: none
    E-mail: none

USA office
    Northern Ireland Tourist Board
    551 Fifth Avenue, Suite 701
    New York, NY 10176
    Telephone: (212) 922-0101
    Telephone: (800) 326-0036 toll-free in USA
    Fax: (212) 922-0099
    E-mail: infousa@nitb.com

Northern Marianas
See also: South Pacific Tourism Organization

Cats and dogs other than those arriving directly from Hawaii, Guam, Australia, New Zealand, or the United Kingdom will be held in agriculture quarantine facilities in Saipan for 120 days unless this has been done in Hawaii or in Guam, which must be stated in the document below.

All dogs and cats need a certificate issued by an authorized or licensed veterinarian showing that the animal originated in the exporting country:
1. Has been vaccinated with a killed (inactivated) rabies virus vaccine or a modified live virus vaccine more than 30 days and less than 90 days before entry;
2. Has been dipped or treated to free that animals of external parasites within 5 days of entry;
3. Is free from any signs of infectious or communicable disease.

PROHIBITED: psittacine birds (parrots, parakeets, macaws etc.), monkeys.

Animals must be given prior approval before entry. Animals must be quarantined. Contact:
Quarantine
Caller Box 10007
Saipan, MP 96950
Telephone: (670) 234-8340
Fax: (670) 322-2633

Pets may enter as passenger's checked baggage, in the cabin or as cargo.

Website: www.visit-marianas.com

North Marianas office
Marianas Visitors Authority
P.O. Box 861
Saipan, MP 96950
Telephone: (670) 664-3200/1
Fax: (670) 664-3237
E-mail: mva@saipan.com

Norway

Importation of dogs and cats from USA (not Hawaii) will require a 4-month quarantine and registration with the Norwegian Animal Health Authority. An import permit is not required, but reservations at the quarantine station and registration of the upcoming import must be made at the District Veterinary Officer for Mysen and Spydeberg 30 days before importation. A full description of the regulation may be obtained from the Norwegian Animal Health Authority.

According to the regulation "Forskrift nr 507 av 2.7.1991 om forbud mot innførsel av dyr og smitteførende gjenstander § 1" it is forbidden to bring small pets (cage birds, rabbits, guinea pigs, hamsters, chinchillas, rats, mice etc.) to Norway. If people want to move permanently to Norway, they may apply to The Norwegian Animal Health Authority - Central Unit for an exception from this regulation on special forms. The Central Unit can, according to § 10, stipulate terms for the import permit. There are special provisions for animals from Denmark, Sweden and Finland (temporary import permits) and cage birds for breeding.

Contact:
    The Norwegian Animal Health Authority-Central Unit
    P.O. Box 8147
    Dept N-0033
    Oslo, Norway
    Telephone: (47) 23 21 65 00
    Fax: (47) 23 21 65 01
    E-mail: post@dyrehelsetilsynet.no
    Website: www.dyrehelsetilsynet.no/english

Website: www.visitnorway.com
Website: www.goscadanavia.com
Website: www.norway.org/
Website: www.tourist.no/

UK office
    Norwegian Tourist Board
    5th Floor, Charles House
    5 Regent Street (Lower)
    London SW1Y 4LR, UK

Telephone: 171 839 6255 information line
Fax: 171 839 6014
E-mail: greatbritain@nortra.no
E-mail: infouk@ntr.no
Website: www.norway.org.uk/travel.htm

USA office
Norwegian Tourist Board
65 Third Avenue, 18th Floor
New York, NY 10017
Telephone: (212) 885-9700
Fax: (212) 885-9710
E-mail: usa@ntr.no

Royal Embassy of Norway
2720 34th Street, NW
Washington, DC 20008
Telephone: (202) 333-6000
Fax: (202) 337-0870
E-mail: info@norway.org
Website: www.norway.org

Oman

Pets entering Oman require an import permit from the Ministry of Agriculture and Fisheries, Department of Animal Health, before shipment. Forms may be obtained from the Ministry by one's sponsor and must be submitted with a copy of the pet's rabies vaccination record and a health certificate. Vaccination against rabies is required no less than one month and no more than six months before the travel date. There are additional vaccination requirements for dogs and cats less than 30 days old. A second health certificate dated 48 hours before the pet travels is also a requirement. Pets may be subjected to six-month quarantine, although this is usually not required when importing the pet from a rabies-free country. Pets must be manifested as cargo on an airway bill when transported by air (carriage as passenger's baggage is prohibited).

Website: www.tourismoman.com
Website: www.oman.org
Website: www.omanet.com

Oman office
    Directorate General of Tourism
    P.O. Box 550
    Postal Code 113
    Muscat, Sultanate of Oman
    Telephone: 771 6527 or 771 4730
    Fax: 771 4436

Embassy of the Sultanate of Oman
2535 Belmont Road, NW
Washington, DC 20008
Telephone: (202) 387-1980
Fax: (202) 745-4933
E-mail: emboman@erols.com
Website: none
The embassy also deals with enquiries from Canada.

Pakistan

Pets (birds, cats, and dogs) are required to have a rabies vaccination certificate, an International Health Certificate, and an import permit. The Office of Imports and Exports Control Organization issues the permit at the point of entry. The International Health Certificate stating that the animal is clear of any disease must accompany the applications for permits. Monkeys must be branded and have an International Health Certificate. The certificate must also state the monkey has never been in a yellow fever region and has not been in such an area within 31 days of arrival in Pakistan.

Website: www.tourism.gov.pk

Pakistan office
    Pakistan Tourism Development Corporation (PTDC)
    P.O. Box 1465
    Markaz F-6, Agha Khan Road
    Islamabad 44000, Pakistan
    Telephone: (51) 921 2760 or 920 2766
    Fax: (51) 920 4027
    E-mail: tourism@isb.comsats.net.pk

Embassy of the Islamic Republic of Pakistan
2315 Massachusetts Avenue, NW
Washington, DC 20008
Telephone: (202) 939-6200
Fax: (202) 387-0484
E-mail: info@pakistan-embassy.com
Website: www.pakistan-embassy.com/

Palau
I was unable to obtain specific requirements to bring pets into Palau despite numerous attempts. The reader is advised to contact:
Division of Agriculture and Marine Resource
E-mail: damr@palaunet.com

Website: www.visit-palau.com

Palau office
Palau Visitors Authority
P.O. Box 256
Koror, Republic of Palau 96940
Telephone: (680) 488-1930/2793
Fax: (680) 488-1453
E-mail: pva@palaunet.com

Embassy of the Republic of Palau
1150 18th Street, NW
Suite 750
Washington, DC 20036
Telephone: (202) 452-6814
Fax: (202) 452-6281
E-mail: none
Website: www.palauembassy.com

Panama
The requirements to enter Panama with pets are:
1. International Health Certificate (original);
2. Certificate of rabies (original).

It must be issued within 10 days before the departure day. These documents need to be sent to the nearest consulate. Washington is the only consulate that authenticates documents from any State (in 24 hours). The fee for each document is $30.00 (money order). If it is sent by mail, a self-addressed stamped envelope is required. Translation of documents is not required. There will be house quarantine once in Panama.

Pet birds (only two birds per passenger) also require an International Health Certificate. Birds are prohibited if arriving from Mexico. Adult birds will be quarantined for 15 days. Birds require an Import Permit from the Ministry of Agriculture in Panama City. For further details, contact the Panamanian Embassy/Consulate.

Website: www.panamatours.com

Panama office
    Instituto Panameño de Turismo (IPAT) (Institute of Tourism)
    Apartado 4421
    Centro de Convenciones ATLAPA
    Vía Israel, Panamá 5, Republic of Panamá
    Telephone: 226-7000 or 226-2544
    Telephone: (800) 231-0568 toll-free
    Fax: 226-5046
    E-mail: none

Embassy of the Republic of Panama
2862 McGill Terrace, NW
Washington, DC 20008
Telephone: (202) 483-1407
Fax: (202) 483-8413
E-mail: infotur@ns.ipat.gov.pa
Website: www.ipat.gov.pa

Papua New Guinea
See also: South Pacific Tourism Organization

Pets arriving from Australia and New Zealand will be quarantined for 48 hours. Pets from all other countries require 9-month quarantine in Australia. Pets may arrive only as cargo.

For additional information to import a pet contact:
Department of Agriculture and Livestock
P O Box 417
Konedobu, NCD
Papua New Guinea
Telephone: 321-3302/ 321-3308
Fax: 321-1387

Website: www.paradiselive.org.pg

Papua New Guinea office
Papua New Guinea Tourism Promotion Authority
P. O. Box 1291
Port Moresby, National Capital District
Papua New Guinea
Telephone: (675) 320 0211
Fax: (675) 320 0223
E-mail: tourismpng@dg.com.pg
E-mail: info@pngtourism.org.pg

Embassy of Papua New Guinea
1779 Massachusetts Avenue, NW
Suite 805
Washington, DC 20036
Telephone: (202) 745-3680
Fax: (202) 745-3679
E-mail: KunduWash@aol.com
Website: www.pngembassy.org

Paraguay

The documentation needed for the entering of pets in Paraguay is a vaccination certificate issued by an authorized veterinarian and legalized by a Paraguayan Consulate. They have four consulates in the U.S.: Miami, Los Angeles, New York, and Washington, DC. The documents do not need translation. Pets are not allowed on most public transportation, taxis, or buses in Paraguay.

Paraguay office
Secretaría Nacional de Turismo
Palma 468

casi 14 de Mayo
Asunción, Paraguay
Telephone: (21) 441 530 or 441 620
Fax: (21) 491 230
E-mail: senatur1@pla.net.py
Website: www.senatur.gov.py

The Website of the Ministry of Foreign Affairs is www.mre.gov.py and there one can access the link to this embassy.

Embassy of Paraguay
2400 Massachusetts Avenue, NW
Washington, DC 20008
Telephone: (202) 483-6960
Fax: (202) 234-4508
E-mail: embapar@erols.com
Website: none

Peru

Pets must have an International Health Certificate that states the pet was examined within 30 days before departure and found to be free of any infectious diseases. The International Health Certificate must be legalized by the Department of Agriculture from each State and then the nearest Peruvian Consulate must legalize the Certificate. The rabies certificate must indicate that the vaccination was no less than 14 days and no more than one year before departure. Dogs require documentation of inoculation against distemper, leptospirosis, hepatitis, parvovirus, and parainfluenza (DHLPP) within the past 12 months before embarkation. There is no entry permit required or quarantine.

This applies only to cats and dogs; if you want to bring any kind of bird, you must contact the offices of the SENASA before flight to Peru in order to get the appropriate documentation. Contact office:
SENASA (Servicio Nacional de Sanidad Agraria)
Psj. Francisco Zela s/n
Piso 10 - Jesús María
Lima, Peru
Telephone: 51 1 575-1599
E-mail: postmaster@senasa.gob.pe

Website: www.peru.org.pe

Peru office
PromPerú (Commission for the Promotion of Peru)
Calle 1 Oeste 50
Edificio Mitinci, 13th Floor
Urbanizacion Córpac, San Isidro
Lima 27, Peru
Telephone: (1) 223-3118 or (1) 224-3395
Fax: (1) 224 3323
E-mail: postmaster@promperu.gob.pe
E-mail: infoperu@promperu.gob.pe
Website: www.peru.org.pe

Embassy of Peru-Tourist Department
1700 Massachusetts Avenue, NW
Washington, DC 20036
Telephone: (202) 833-9860
Fax: (202) 659-8124
E-mail: peru@peruemb.org
E-mail: informacion@consulado.peru.com (Miami consulate)
Website: www.peruemb.org

Philippines
Guidelines for the importation of live pet animals into the Philippines:
1. Apply for an import permit with the Animal Health Division (AHD), Bureau of Animal Industry (BAI) by writing a letter addressed to the BAI Director containing the following information: species and breed of animal, sex, color, and number of pets and the expected date of arrival. The BAI address and contact number is:
   Animal Health Division
   Bureau of Animal Industry
   Visayas Avenue, Diliman,
   Quezon City, Philippines
   Telephone: (632) 926-6883
   Fax: (632) 926-6866
2. If the number of animals to be brought to the Philippines exceeds five, the animals have to be inspected at the quarantine site.

3. Issuance and inspection fees are P50.00 pesos and P165.00 pesos for the first two heads and P220.00 pesos for each succeeding head, respectively. Payment may be made upon arrival at the Veterinary Quarantine Unit, Ninoy Aquino International Airport.
4. A valid certificate from the country of origin must be presented upon arrival.

The permit is good for two (2) months. Extension for another month may be requested before the permit's expiry date.

The vaccination certificate must be between 60 and 180 days old. The International Health Certificate must be dated less than 10 days before entry. There is no quarantine.

Website: www.tourism.gov.ph

Philippine office
Philippine Department of Tourism
Department of Tourism Building
T M Kalaw Street
Rizal Park
Manila 1000, Philippines
Telephone: (2) 523 8411-30
Fax: (2) 521 7374/5 or 522 2194
E-mail: deptour@info.com.ph

UK office
Philippines Cultural and Tourism Office
146 Cromwell Road
London SW7 4EF, UK
Telephone: 20 7835 1100
Fax: 20 7835 1926
E-mail: tourism@pdot.co.uk

USA office
Philippine Tourist Office
3660 Wilshire Boulevard, Suite 285
Los Angeles, CA 90010

Telephone: (213) 487-4527
E-mail: none

Embassy of The Philippines
1600 Massachusetts Avenue, NW
Washington, DC 20036
Telephone: (202) 467-9300
Fax: (202) 467-9417
E-mail: wdce@aol.com
Website: www.embassyonline.com

Poland

Pets (parrots excluded) must have a health and vaccination certificate issued by a licensed veterinarian and translated into Polish (such certificate is valid 10 days from the date of issue).

Website: www.polandtour.org
Website: www.pot.gov.pl

Poland office
   Polish Tourism Organisation
   4-6 Chalubinskiejo Street
   00-928 Warsaw, Poland
   Telephone: (22) 630 1747-8
   Fax: (22) 630 1719
   E-mail: pot@pot.gov.pl

UK office
   Polish National Tourist Office
   First Floor, Remo House
   310-312 Regent Street
   London W1B 3AX, UK
   Telephone: (020) 7580 8811
   Fax: (020) 7580 8866
   E-mail: info@visitpoland.org

USA: New York office
   Polish National Tourist Office
   275 Madison Avenue, Suite 1711
   New York, NY 10016

Telephone: (212) 338-9412
Fax: (212) 338-9283
E-mail: pntonyc@polandtour.org
This office also deals with inquires from Canada.

Embassy of Poland
2640 16th Street, NW
Washington, DC 20009
Telephone: (202) 234 3800
Fax: (202) 328-6271
E-mail: information@ioip.com
Website: www.polandembassy.org

Portugal

It is necessary to present an International Health Certificate issued before embarkation by the Veterinary Health Authority of the country of origin, certifying that the animal shows no clinical signs of disease and that it is from a country or region that is free from any contagious diseases to which the species is susceptible. This certificate must include translation into the Portuguese language. The vaccination certificate must be less than one year old. There is no mandatory quarantine. Parrots are prohibited. Other birds require an International Health Certificate.

Website: www.portugal.org/
Website: www.icep.pt
Website: www.portugalinsite.pt

Canada: Toronto office
   Portuguese Trade and Tourism Commission
   60 Bloor Street West, Suite 1005
   Toronto, ON M4W 3B8, Canada
   Telephone: (416) 921-7376
   Fax: (416) 921-1353
   E-mail: iceptor@idirect.com

Portugal office
   Investimentos, Comércio e Turismo de Portugal (ICEP)
   (Portuguese Trade and Tourism Office)
   Avenida 5 de Outubro 101

1050-051 Lisbon, Portugal
Telephone: 2179 09500
Fax: 2179 35028 or 2179 50961
E-mail: dinf@icep.pt

UK office
ICEP - Portuguese Trade and Tourism Office
2nd Floor
22, Sackville Street
London W1S 3LY, UK
Telephone: 20 7494 1517
Fax: 20 7494 1868
E-mail: tourism@portugaloffice.org.uk
Website: www.portugalinsite.pt

USA: DC office
Portuguese Trade and Tourism Office
1900 L Street, Suite 310
Washington, DC 20036
Telephone: (202) 331-8222
Fax: (202) 331-8236
E-mail: none

USA: New York office
Portuguese National Tourist Office
590 Fifth Avenue, 4th Floor
New York, NY 10036-4704
Telephone: (212) 354-4403
Telephone: (800) 767-8842 toll-free in USA
Fax: (212) 764-6137
E-mail: tourism@portugal.org

Embassy of Portugal
2125 Kalorama Road, NW
Washington, DC 20008
Telephone: (202) 328-8610
Fax: (202) 462-3726
E-mail: portugal@portugalemb.org
Website: www.portugalemb.org/

Puerto Rico

Puerto Rico is a commonwealth state of the United States, it requires that pets be accompanied with a current International Health Certificate, and a vaccination certificate dated between 7 days and 180 days. There is no permit requirement. No quarantine is imposed. The International Health Certificate requires a USDA stamp if the pet originates in the U.S. Birds require an International Health Certificate issued immediately prior to shipment. The certificate must sate that the bird is free of psittacosis or ornithosis.

Website: www.meetpuertorico.com/
Website: www.prtourism.com/

Canada office
    Puerto Rico Tourism Co.
    43 Colborne Street, Suite 200
    Toronto, ON M5E 1E3, Canada
    Telephone: (800) 667-0394 toll-free in Canada
    Telephone: (416) 368-2680
    Fax: (416) 368-5350
    E-mail: 104436.3257@compuserve.com
    E-mail: prcbLA@prcb.org

USA: California office
    Puerto Rico Tourism Co.
    3575 West Cahuenga Boulevard, Suite 405
    Los Angeles, CA 90068
    Telephone: (800) 866-STAR toll-free in USA
    Fax: (213) 874-7257
    E-mail: none

USA: Florida office
    Puerto Rico Tourism Co.
    901 Ponce de Leon Boulevard, Suite 101
    Coral Gables, FL 33134
    Telephone: (800) 866-STAR toll-free in USA
    Telephone: (305) 445-9112
    Fax: (305) 445-9450
    E-mail: none

USA: New York office
    Puerto Rico Tourism Co.
    666 Fifth Avenue, 15th Floor
    New York, NY 10103
    Telephone: (212) 586-6262
    Telephone: (800) 223-6530 toll-free in USA and Canada
    Fax: (212) 586-1212
    E-mail: none

Puerto Rico is a commonwealth state of the USA. Puerto Rico manages its own affairs, but is represented abroad by U.S. Embassies and Consulates.

Qatar

Pets entering Qatar require an import permit from the Ministry of Agriculture. Cats with proper documentation are allowed to enter with no difficulty, but some breeds of dogs, especially large dogs, are not admitted. Application forms for import permits may be obtained from the Ministry of Agriculture through a sponsoring employer. A copy of the pet's health certificate and vaccination record must be submitted with the application. Contact:
    Ministry of Municipal Affairs & Agriculture
    P.O. Box: 44556
    Doha, State of Qatar
    Telephone: (+974) 4337577
    Fax: (+974) 4411464
    E-mail: webmaster@mmaa.gov.qa
    Website: www.mmaa.gov.qa

Website: qatar-info.com

Embassy of The State of Qatar
4200 Wisconsin Avenue, NW
Suite 200
Washington, DC 20016
Telephone: (202) 274-1600
Fax: (202) 237-0061
The embassy also deals with inquires from Canada.

Romania

Documents needed to take your pet into Romania include an International Health Certificate and proof of rabies vaccination, less than six (6) months. There are no time limits to travel with pets. Pets are allowed on trains and buses but big dogs must wear a muzzle. Translation of documents is not needed if they are in English, French, or German. Romanians love pets. It is common for kids or adults to pet a pet they like, without asking permission from the pet owner. There are no specific customs regarding pets. However, each hotel or restaurant has its own pet policy. In general, pets are allowed in hotels and restaurants.

Website: www.romaniatourism.com
Website: www.mtromania.ro
Website: www.rezq.com/ronto

Romanian office
  Ministry of Tourism
  Strada Apolodor 17
  Bucharest 570633, Romania
  Telephone: (1) 410 12 62
  Fax: (1) 410 05 79
  E-mail: turism@kappa.ro

UK office
  Romanian National Tourist Office
  22 New Cavendish Street
  London W1M 7LH, UK
  Telephone: (207) 224 3692
  Fax: (207) 935 6435
  E-mail: uktouroff@romania.freeserve.co.uk

USA office
  Romanian National Tourist Office
  14 East 38th Street, 12th Floor
  New York, NY 10016
  Telephone: (212) 545-8484
  Fax: (212) 251-0429
  E-mail: ronto@erols.com
  Website: www.ramiatourism.com

Embassy of Romania
1607 23rd Street, NW
Washington, DC 20008
Telephone: (202) 332-4848
Fax: (202) 32-4748
E-mail: info@roembus.org
E-mail: office@roembus.org
Website: www.roembus.org

Russia

Russia does not require a vaccination certificate to enter. The International Health Certificate must be dated less than 10 days before arrival. There is no imposed quarantine. No entry permit is required. Pigeons are prohibited entry. Generally, pets are not permitted in hotels.

Website: www.russia-travel.com
Website: www.intourist.co.uk

Russian office
    Ministry of Tourism
    18 ul. Kazakova
    103064 Moscow, Russian Federation
    Telephone: (095) 202 7117 or 202 3891
    Fax: (095) 263 0761
    E-mail: info@russia-travel.com

UK office
    Intourist Ltd.
    7 Wellington Terrace
    Notting Hill
    London W2 4LW, UK
    Telephone: (020) 7727 4100
    Fax: (020) 7727 8090
    E-mail: info@intourist.co.uk or info@intourist2.co.uk

UK office
    Intourist Ltd.
    Duckworth House

Lancastrian Office Centre
32 Talbot Road
Old Trafford
Manchester M32 0FP, UK
Telephone: (0161) 872 4222
Fax: (0161) 872 4888
E-mail: intourist.man@btclick.com

UK office
Intourist Ltd.
29 St Vincent Place
Glasgow G1 2DT, UK
Telephone: (0141) 204 5809
Fax: (0141) 204 5807

USA office
Russian National Group
130 West 42nd Street, Suite 412
New York, NY 10036
Telephone: (212) 575-3431
Telephone: (877) 221-7120 toll-free in USA
Fax: (212) 575-3434
E-mail: info@russia-travel.com

Embassy of The Russian Federation
2650 Wisconsin Avenue, NW
Washington, DC 20007
Telephone: (202) 298-5700
Fax: (202) 298-5735
E-mail: none
Website: www.russianembassy.org

Rwanda

A current International Health Certificate issued at the point of origin must accompany dogs and cats. Dogs: vaccination flury lep (against rabies) and cats: vaccination flury hep. Pets may enter as passenger's checked baggage, in the cabin or as cargo.

Rwanda office
    Office Rwandais du Tourisme et des Parcs Nationaux
    BP 905
    Kigali, Rwanda
    Telephone: 76514
    Fax: 76512
    E-mail: ortpn@rwanda1.com

Embassy of The Republic of Rwanda
1714 New Hampshire Avenue, NW
Washington, DC 20009
Telephone: (202) 232-2882
Fax: (202) 232-4544
E-mail: rwandemb@rwandemb.org
Website: www.rwandemb.org

Saba

At the time of writing, Saba does not have its own representation in North America or Canada. They are however represented by the CTO (Caribbean Tourist Organization) in both the USA and Europe. Inquiries however should be directed to the Tourist Bureau in Saba.

Document necessary for bringing pets into the country:
- A health certificate from a registered veterinary. The health certificate is valid for 2 weeks. The health certificate can be either in Dutch or in English. The local veterinarian must then revalidate it. Contact:
    Mr. Michael Hassell
    Windwardside
    Saba, Dutch Caribbean
    Telephone: (599) 416-2273

Pets are generally welcome throughout the island, unless otherwise stated. Inquiries should be first made to hotels, whether pets are accepted. Airlines have certain regulations on size of pets and how they travel (whether in the aircraft or the luggage compartment). Interested persons should make these inquiries directly with the carriers concerned.

Web Site: www.sabatourism.com

Saba office
    Saba Tourist Bureau
    P.O. Box 527
    Windwardside
    Saba, Dutch Caribbean
    Telephone: (599) 416-2231 or 416-2322
    Fax: (599) 416-2350
    E-mail: iluvsaba@unspoiledqueen.com

USA office
    Telephone: (800) 722-2394

Saba is part of the Netherlands Antilles and is represented abroad by Royal Netherlands Embassies. See also: The Netherlands.

St Barthelemy

Dogs and cats are permitted if older than 3 months and have an International Health Certificate and a rabies certificate issued by a veterinarian from the country of origin.

Website: www.st-barths.com

St Barthelemy office
    Office du Tourisme
    Quai General-de-Gaulle
    Gustavia, St Barthelemy, French West Indies
    Telephone: (590) 27-87-27
    Fax: (590) 27-74-47

USA: California office
    French Government Tourist Office
    9454 Wilshire Boulevard, Suite 715
    Beverly Hills, CA 90212-2967
    Telephone: (310) 271-6665
    Fax: (310) 276-2835
    E-mail: fgto@gte.net

USA: Illinois office
    French Government Tourist Office
    676 North Michigan Avenue, Suite 3360

Chicago, IL 60611-2819
Telephone: (312) 751-7800
Fax: (312) 337-6339
E-mail: fgto@mcs.net

USA: New York office
French Government Tourist Office
444 Madison Avenue
New York, NY 10022-6903
Telephone: (212) 838-7800
Fax: (212) 838-7855
E-mail: info@francetourism.com

St Barthelemy is an Overseas Department of the Republic of France and is represented abroad by French Embassies. See also: France.

St Eustatius

Pets are admitted temporarily with an International Health Certificate dated no more than 10 days before entry and a record of inoculations (including rabies) at least 30 days before entry.

Website: www.turq.com/statia

St Eustatius office
St Eustatius Tourist Office
Oranjestad
St Eustatius
Netherlands Antilles
Telephone: (599) 3-182433
Fax: (599) 3-182433
E-mail: euxtour@goldenrock.net

USA office
St Eustatius Tourist Office
Telephone: (800) 722-2394 toll-free in USA
Fax: (561) 488-4292
E-mail: none

St Eustatius is part of the Netherlands Antilles and is represented abroad by Royal Netherlands Embassies. See also: The Netherlands.

St Kitts and Nevis

Cats and dogs must be accompanied by a veterinarian good health and rabies inoculation certificate, issued at the point of origin, and an import permit from the Ministry of Agriculture. Advance notice to station manager on either St. Kitts or Nevis of the transporting airline is necessary, also in case of transit.

For pets send to The Veterinary Authority - St. Kitts
E-mail: doastk@caribsurf.com

Website: www.stkitts-tourism.com
Website: www.stkittstourism.kn
Website: www.nevisisland.com
Website: www.stkitts-nevis.com

Canada office
 St. Kitts-Nevis Tourism Office
 133 Richmond Street West, Suite 311
 Toronto, ON M5H 2L3, Canada
 Telephone: (416) 368-6707
 Fax: (416) 368-3934
 E-mail: Canada.office@stkittstourism.kn

Nevis office
 Nevis Tourism Authority
 Main Street
 Charlestown, Nevis
 Telephone: 469 7550
 Fax: 469 7551
 E-mail: nta2001@caribsurf.com

St Kitts office
 St Kitts & Nevis Ministry of Tourism, Commerce & Consumer Affairs
 P.O. Box 132
 Bay Road
 Basseterre, St Kitts
 Telephone: 465 2620 or 465 4040
 Fax: 465 8794
 E-mail: hospitality@stkittstourism.kn

UK office
> St Kitts & Nevis Department of Tourism
> 10 Kensington Court
> London W8 5DL, UK
> Telephone: (020) 7376 0881
> Fax: (020) 7937 6742
> E-mail: uk-europe.office@stkittstourism.kn

UK office
> Nevis Tourist Office
> P.O. Box 160
> Edgware HA8 5YB, UK
> Telephone: 208-200-3020
> Fax: 208-931-2472
> E-mail: none

USA office
> St Kitts & Nevis Tourist Office
> 414 East 75th Street, Fifth Floor
> New York, NY 10021
> Telephone: (212) 535-1234
> Telephone: (800) 582-6208 toll-free in USA
> Fax: (212) 734-6511
> E-mail: info@stkitts-nevis.com

Embassy of Saint Kitts and Nevis
3216 New Mexico Avenue, NW
Washington, DC 20016
Telephone: (202) 686-2636
Fax: (202) 686-5740
E-mail: info@stkittsnevis.org
Website: www.stkittsnevis.org

St Lucia

Pets are allowed to enter St Lucia only if quarantined in the United Kingdom for a period of six months. Dogs and cats must have a microchip for identification purposes. The pets must have a Veterinary Import Permit before entering St Lucia. This is obtained from the Ministry of Agriculture's Veterinary Department. Contact:

Mr. Julius Polius
Director of Agricultural Services
Ministry of Agriculture, Forestry and Fisheries
4th Floor Sir Stanislaus Building
Telephone: (758) 452-2526/468-4123
Fax: (758) 453-6314
E-mail: adminag@candw.lc
E-mail: chiefvet@slumaffe.org (Chief Veterinarian)

Website: www.stlucia.org
Website: www.st-lucia.com
Website: www.sluonestop.com

Canada office
St Lucia Tourist Board
8 King Street East, Suite 700
Toronto, ON M5C 1B5, Canada
Telephone: (416) 362 4242
Fax: (416) 362 7832
E-mail: sltbcanada@aol.com

St Lucia office
St Lucia Tourist Board
Point Seraphine Complex
Box 221
Castries, St Lucia
Telephone: (758) 452-4094/5968
Fax: (758) 453-1121
E-mail: slutour@canw.lc

UK office
St Lucia Tourist Board
421A Finchley Road
London NW3 6HJ, UK
Telephone: (020) 7431 3675 or 7431 4045
Fax: (020) 7431 7920
E-mail: stlucia@axissm.com

USA office
    St Lucia Tourist Board
    820 Second Avenue, 4th Floor
    New York, NY 10017
    Telephone: (212) 867-2950
    Telephone: (800) 456-3984 toll-free in USA
    Fax: (212) 867-2795
    E-mail: stlucia@worldnet.att.net

Embassy of Saint Lucia
3216 New Mexico Avenue, NW
Washington, DC 20016
Telephone: (202) 364-6792/93/94/95
Fax: (202) 364-6723
E-mail: none
Website: none

St Maarten

The rabies inoculation document must be at least one month in advance. The International Health Certificate must be dated 7 to 8 days before the travel date. No quarantine is necessary for pets. The hotels on the Dutch side do not allow pets to stay at the property. You will not be able to bring pets into the restaurants.

Website: www.st-Maarten.com

Canada office
    St Maarten Tourist Office
    Suite 3120 Centre Tower
    3300 Bloor Street West
    Toronto, ON M8X 2X3, Canada
    Telephone: (416) 236-1800
    Fax: (416) 233-9367
    E-mail: melaine@inforamp.net

Canada office
    St Maarten Tourist Office
    c/o Melaine Communication Group
    703 Evans Avenue, Suite 106

Toronto, ON M9C 5E9, Canada
Telephone: (416) 622-4300
Fax: (416) 622-3431
E-mail: postmaster@melainecommunications.com

St Maarten office
St Maarten Tourist Board
Vineyard Park Building
WG Boncamper Road 33
Philipsburg, St Maarten
Telephone: 542-2337
Fax: 542-2734
E-mail: none

USA office
St Maarten Tourist Office
675 Third Avenue, Suite 1806
New York, NY 10017
Telephone: (212) 953-2084
Telephone: (800) STMAARTEN toll-free in USA
Fax: (212) 953-2145
E-mail: none

St Maarten is part of the Netherlands Antilles and is represented abroad by Royal Netherlands Embassies. See also: The Netherlands.

St Martin

Cats and dogs above the age of 3 months are admitted temporarily as pets upon presentation of a certificate of origin and good health and or a certificate of anti-rabies inoculation issued by a licensed veterinarian valid for not more than 30 days. No quarantine is necessary for pets.

Website: www.st.martin.org

USA office
French St Martin Tourist Office
675 Third Avenue, Suite 1807
New York NY 10020
Telephone: (877) 956-1234 toll-free in USA
Telephone: (212) 475-8970

Fax: (212) 260- 8481
E-mail: sxmtony@msn.com

St Martin is an Overseas Department of the Republic of France and is represented abroad by French Embassies. See also: France.

St Vincent and the Grenadines

Pets require 6 months quarantine from North and South America, Europe, Africa and Asia. Pets are allowed from the United Kingdom, New Zealand, and Australia with the proper health certificate, rabies certificate, and an import permit. Contact the Government Veterinary Officer. Advance notice to the station manager on St. Vincent and the Grenadines of the transporting airline is necessary, also in case of transit.

Website: www.svgtourism.com

Canada office
    St Vincent and The Grenadines Tourist Office
    333 Wilson Avenue, Suite 601
    Toronto, ON M3H 1T2, Canada
    Telephone: (416) 398-4277
    Fax: (416) 398-4199
    E-mail: none

St Vincent office
    Ministry of Tourism, Information, Telecommunications, Commerce and Consumer Affairs
    P.O. Box 834
    Bay Street
    Kingstown, St Vincent
    Telephone: 457 1502
    Fax: 456 2610
    E-mail: tourism@caribsurf.com

UK office
    St Vincent & the Grenadines Tourist Office
    10 Kensington Court
    London W8 5DL, UK
    Telephone: (020) 7937 6570

Fax: (020) 7937 3611
E-mail: svgtourismeurope@aol.com

USA: *New York office*
St Vincent and The Grenadines Tourist Office
801 Second Avenue, 21st Floor
New York, NY 10017
Telephone: (800) 729-1726
Fax: (212) 949-5946
E-mail: svgtory@aol.com

Embassy of St Vincent and the Grenadines
3216 New Mexico Avenue, NW
Washington, DC 20016
Telephone: (202) 364-6730
Fax: (202) 364-6736
E-mail: none
Website: none

Samoa

See also: South Pacific Tourism Organization

Only pets from Australia and New Zealand are allowed into the country. If it is a dog, the 'Big Bull' breed is not allowed. The owner of the pet must write a letter to the Director of the Agriculture Department, Quarantine Section stating the breed, sex, origin of pet, treatments, and medication undertaken and request entry into the country. The duration of stay must be stated in the letter. The letter should be faxed to 0685 21271 or contact by telephone: 0685 22561.

Hoteliers should be notified of your intention to bring your pet beforehand. Domestic transportation should be no problem provided you inform the bus or taxi owner. Documents can be supplied in English.

Samoa does not have direct tourism representation in the USA, Canada, and UK. However, you could contact the SPTO (South Pacific Tourism Organization) E-mail: info@spto.org or visit their Website: www.spto.org.

Website: www.visitsamoa.ws

Samoa office
    Samoa Visitors Bureau
    P. O. Box 2272
    Apia, Samoa
    Telephone: (685) 20 180/26 557
    Fax: (685) 20 886
    E-mail: info@visitsamoa.ws

Honorary Consulate of Samoa
5150 Wilshire Blvd.
Los Angeles, CA 90036

Permanent Mission of Samoa to the United Nations
800 Second Avenue, Suite 400J
New York, NY 10017
Telephone: (212) 599-6196
Fax: (212) 599-0797
E-mail: samoa@un.int
This office also deals with enquiries from Canada.

San Marino

Please be informed that rules in force in Italy also apply for San Marino. Travelers entering Italy may bring the following pets provided they have a certificate of health issued by a private veterinarian within 30 days of departure:
- Small birds (except parrots*)
- Cats/dogs (required proof of vaccination against rabies and distemper)
- Small fish
- Frogs
- Common lizards
- Rodents (squirrels, hamsters, guinea pigs, marmot, chinchilla but excluding rabbits/hares)
- Small turtles

*Parrots (maximum -2 large or 4 small) can be introduced into Italy accompanied by an original health certificate proving that they were in a state approved zoological or breeding facility within the last 6 months. The certificate must also state that there were no cases of psittacosis or ornithosis within a 15-mile radius of the birds' location.

Website: www.omniway.sm
Website: www.sanmarinosite.com

San Marino office
    Ufficio di Stato per il Turismo (State Tourist Office)
    Palazzo del Turismo
    Contrada Omagnano 20, 47890 Republic of San Marino
    Telephone: (0549) 882 410 or 882 400
    Fax: (0549) 882 575
    E-mail: none
    E-mail: none

Consulate General of The Republic of San Marino
1899 L Street, NW
Suite 500
Washington, DC 20036
Telephone: (202) 223-3517
Fax: none
E-mail: none

São Tomé e Príncipe

Pets may enter São Tomé e Príncipe with an International Health Certificate, vaccination certificate, and a pet registration. Pets need to travel inside an appropriate cage.

São Tomé Embassy to the United Nations
801 Second Avenue, Suite 1604
New York, NY 10017
Telephone: (212) 697-4211
Fax: none
E-mail: stpun@undp.org

Consulate of The Democratic Republic of Sao Tome & Principe
512 Means Street, Suite 305
Atlanta, GA 30318
Telephone: (404) 221-0203

Fax: (404) 221-1006
E-mail: consul@saotome.org

Embassy of the Democratic Republic of São Tomé e Príncipe
400 Park Avenue, 7th Floor
New York, NY 10022
Telephone: (212) 317-0533
Fax: (212) 317-0580
E-mail: stp@un.int
Website: www.saotome.org

Saudi Arabia

Only watchdogs, hunting dogs, seeing-eye dogs for the blind, and hearing dogs for the deaf are permitted entrance into the country. The purpose of the dog should be outlined on the International Health Certificate. Pets must have two copies of the International Health Certificates and rabies certificates. Permission must also be obtained from the Saudi Arabian Consulate and from the Customs Director in Saudi Arabia. All other canines are prohibited, but authorities may grant exemptions from this prohibition.

Cats must also have two International Health Certificates and a rabies inoculation certificate stating that the animal has been inoculated between 1 and 12 months before arrival in Saudi Arabia.

A current International Health Certificate and import permit required are required to import birds. PROHIBITED: live chickens, turkeys, pigeons, ducks, geese, and parrots.

Website: www.sctsaudi.com

UK office
    Saudi Arabian Information Centre
    Cavendish House
    18 Cavendish Square
    London W1G 0AQ, UK
    Telephone: (020) 7629 8803
    Fax: (020) 7629 0374
    E-mail: none
    Website: www.saudinf.com/main/start.htm

Royal Embassy of Saudi Arabia
601 New Hampshire Avenue, NW
Washington, DC 20037
Telephone: (202) 337-4076
E-mail: info@saudiembassy.net
Website: www.saudiembassy.net

Scotland
See also: United Kingdom

Website: www.holiday.scotland.net
Website: visitscotland.com

Scotland office
    Scottish Tourist Board
    23 Ravelston Terrace
    Edinburgh EH4 3EU, UK
    Telephone: 0131-332-2433
    Fax: 0131-315-2906
    E-mail: info@visitscotland.com

Senegal
Pets may come into Senegal with:
1. An International Health Certificate issued 48 hours before departure and;
2. A vaccination certificate indicating the rabies inoculation was more than 15 days and less than 6 months before travel.

Website: www.senegal-tourism.com

Senegal office
    Ministry of Tourism
    23 Rue Calmette
    P.O. Box 4049
    Dakar, Senegal
    Telephone: 822 9226
    Fax: 822 9413
    E-mail: mtta@primature.sn
    Website: www.primature.sn/tour

USA office
    Senegal Tourist Office
    350 Fifth Avenue, Suite 3118
    New York, NY 10118
    Telephone: (212) 279-1953
    Telephone: (800) 443-2527 toll-free in USA
    Fax: (212) 279-1958
    E-mail: information@senegal-tourism.com

Embassy of the Republic of Senegal
2112 Wyoming Avenue, NW
Washington, DC 20008
Telephone: (202) 234-0540
Fax: (202) 332-6316
E-mail: none
Website: none

Seychelles

All pets entering the Seychelles must have the authorization of the Veterinary Services. Pet owners should apply for a Veterinary Import Permit from the Director of Veterinary Services. This must be in writing, by fax or email. The address is below.

All animals entering the Seychelles are subject to quarantine.
1. Two (2) weeks if the pet is from rabies free country.
2. One (1) month for animals originating from countries where rabies is well controlled but the cat/dog must be accompanied by a Rabies Neutralization Antibody Titer Test.
3. Six (6) months for rabies affected countries

Only returning Seychelles citizens are allowed to import birds if it has been a family pet for one (1) year and must be authorized by both the Ministry of Agriculture & Marine Resources and Division of Environment. Rabbits, guinea pigs, and other pets can be considered but reptiles are prohibited. Certain breeds of dogs must be sterilized before entry.

Being a signatory of the Convention on Biodiversity, approval has to be obtained from the Division of Environment before the importation of any exotics into the country.

Any further queries and requests for Veterinary Import Permits can be addressed to:
Director of Veterinary Services
P. O. Box 166
Union Vale, Mahe, Seychelles
Telephone: 32 22 19/32 22 10
Fax: 22 52 45
E-mail: vetmamr@seychelles.net

Website: www.aspureasitgets.com

Seychelles office
Seychelles Tourism Marketing Authority
P.O. Box 1262, Bel Ombre
Mahé, Seychelles
Telephone: +248 620 000
Fax: +248 620 610
E-mail: seychelles@aspureasitgets.com

UK office
48 Glentham Road
Barnes
London SW13 9JJ, UK
Telephone: (+44) (0) 20 8741 6262 or 6086
Fax: (+44) (0) 20 8741 6107
E-mail: sto@seychelles.uk.com

Embassy of the Republic of Seychelles
800 Second Avenue, Suite 400
New York, NY 10017
Telephone: (212) 972-1785
Fax: (212) 972-1786
E-mail: seychelles@un.int

Sierra Leone

This information was obtained from Judy at the International D.O.V.E. organization in Freetown, Sierra Leone. My thanks to her.

The current procedure for bringing pets:
1. Current health/immunization certificate must arrive with the animal.
2. An import certificate must be obtained from the Government Vet office showing size, color, breed, age, etc. must accompany the animal. That means someone has to get it ahead of time and fax it to you. It is valid for a 3-month period. It costs approx. $30 USD – varies.
3. When the animal arrives, it must go through Customs at the airport (beware - duty may be assessed so carry some cash in your pocket - amount to be determined, well, you know, the "B" word (bribe). The amount depends on the Customs officials and what kind of day they are having. The Health Officer also has to clear the animal and it is the same process just mentioned - no set fee.

Unfortunately, Judy in Sierra Leone could not get the Government Veterinarian's telephone number. She suggested having a contact "in-country" do the paperwork for you in Freetown. She also mentioned that the U.S. Government does not want tourists in Sierra Leone.

Website: www.sierra-leone.org
Website: www.sierra-leone.gov.sl

Sierra Leone office
National Tourist Board of Sierra Leone
P.O. Box 1435
Freetown, Sierra Leone
Telephone: (22) 272 520
Fax: (22) 272 197

UK office
Sierra Leone High Commission UK & Ireland
1st & 3rd Floors
Oxford Circus House
Oxford Street
London W1D 2LX, UK
Telephone: (+44) 0207 287 9884
Fax: (+44) 0207 734 3822
E-mail: info@slhc-uk.org.uk

Permanent Mission of Sierra Leone to the United Nations
245 East 49th Street
New York, NY 10017
Telephone: (212) 688-1656

Embassy of Sierra Leone
1701 19th Street, NW
Washington, DC 20009
Telephone: (202) 939-9261
Fax: (202) 483-1793
E-mail: salonemb@starpower.net
Website: none

Singapore

With few exceptions, dogs and cats entering Singapore are required to undergo a 30-day quarantine period. Only animals originating from Australia, New Zealand, UK, and Ireland are exempt.

The following are required for the importation of cats or dogs:
1. Import license from the AVA (Agri-food & Veterinary Authority). The Application for Permit to Import Animals/Birds as Personal Pets form must be completed and delivered to the Regulatory Services Branch at least 2 weeks before import. A fee of S$50 per animal is payable.
2. An Application & Acceptance for Quarantine Space (AA Form) completed & sent to the Regulatory Services Branch (AVA).
3. Health certificate from the country of export dated not more than 7 days from the date of export. Pregnant and "incapacitated" animals will not be permitted entry. The AVA must be notified of arrival at least one working day in advance.
4. ISO-compatible microchip (dogs only).
5. Quarantine for not less than 30 days from countries except those described above. It is vital to reserve quarantine kennels well in advance due to limited accommodation space.

Certain breeds of dogs are prohibited entry into Singapore. These breeds are Pit Bull- including the American Pit Bull Terrier,

American Staffordshire Terrier, Staffordshire Bull Terrier, American Bulldog; Akita; Neapolitan Mastiff; Tosa; Any crosses of any of Pit Bull, Akita, Neapolitan Mastiff, or Tosa.

A separate group must be leashed and muzzled at all times when in public. These breeds are Bull Mastiff; Bull Terrier; Doberman Pinscher; German Shepherd or related Shepherd Dog breeds; Rottweiler; Perro de Presa Canario.

The following are required for the importation of pet birds:
1. Import license from the AVA.
2. CITES import permit from Singapore and CITES export / re-export permit from country of export.
3. International Health Certificate from country of export dated not more than 7 days from date of export (maybe waived for personal pet birds accompanying owners).

Permits and inquiries should be directed to:
Regulatory Services Branch (AVA)
City Veterinary Centre
5 Maxwell Road
#02-00 MND Complex, Tower Block
Singapore 069110
Telephone: (65) 6227 0670
Fax: (65) 6227 6305
E-mail: AVA_E-mail@ava.gov.sg
Website: www.ava.gov.sg

Website: www.visitsingapore.com

Canada office
2 Bloor Street West, Suite 404
Toronto, ON M4W 3E2, Canada
Telephone: (416) 363-8898
Fax: (416) 363-5752
E-mail: AskMich@TourismSingapore.com

Singapore office
Singapore Tourism Board
Tourism Court

1 Orchard Spring Lane
Singapore 247729
Telephone: (65) 6736 6622
Fax: (65) 6736 9423
E-mail: stb_sog@stb.gov.sg

UK office
Singapore Tourism Board
1st floor, Carrington House
126-130 Regent Street
London W1B 5JX, UK
Telephone: (207) 437-0033
Telephone: (08080) 656565 toll-free in UK only
Fax: (207) 734-2191
E-mail: info@stb.org.co.uk

USA: California office
Singapore Tourism Board
4929 Wilshire Boulevard, Suite 510
Los Angeles, CA 90010
Telephone: (323) 677-0808
Fax: (323) 677-0801
E-mail: AskVince@TourismSingapore.com

USA: Chicago office
Singapore Tourism Board
Two Prudential Plaza, Suite 2615
180 North Stetson Avenue
Chicago, IL 60601
Telephone: (312) 938-1888
Fax: (312) 938-0086
E-mail: AskDave@TourismSingapore.com

USA: New York office
Singapore Tourism Board
590 Fifth Avenue, 12th Floor
New York, NY 10036
Telephone: (212) 302-4861
Fax: (212) 302-4801
E-mail: AskRoc@TourismSingapore.com

Embassy of Singapore
3501 International Place, NW
Washington, DC 20008
Telephone: (202) 537-3100
Fax: (202) 537-0876
E-mail: singemb@bellatlantic.net
Website: www.gov.sg/mfa/washington

Slovakia

All small animals, e.g. dogs, cats, rabbits, guinea pigs, hamsters, small carnivorous animals, birds and apes shall be accompanied by a certificate of origin and International Health Certificate, issued within 3 days before shipment and signed by an authorized State veterinary officer or a veterinary surgeon. Reptiles, amphibians, and aquarium fish do not need to be accompanied by a veterinary certificate.

The certificate must state that the animal has been subjected to a veterinary inspection before shipment and found free from any clinical symptoms of diseases which are transmissible to the mentioned kind of animals and that within a period of more than 28 days and less than 1 year before shipment the animal has been vaccinated with rabies vaccine, approved by the veterinary services of the U.S.

An exception is only granted in cases when no vaccination against rabies is carried out or is prohibited. This fact must be mentioned in the International Health Certificate. The vaccination against rabies is not required for puppies, cats, and other carnivorous animals younger than 3 months. For all imports of animals for a period exceeding 3 months, permission issued by the State Veterinary Administration of the Slovak Republic is required.

At the Slovak border entry crossing the animal should be inspected by an authorized veterinary surgeon. If found unfit from the point of view of veterinary protection, it will not be permitted to enter Slovakia. The arrival of the animal to the place of destination in Slovakia should be immediately reported by the importer to a competent veterinary surgeon. At the place of destination, the animal could be quarantined if necessary. Any serious illness or death of imported animals must be reported by the importer to the veterinary surgeon.

If no vaccination against rabies has been performed in the U.S., it will be done during the quarantine period. The animal will be detained in quarantine for a period of 30 days, or depending on a decision of veterinary surgeon and may be discharged from quarantine if at least 14 days have passed after a vaccination with rabies vaccine, no disturbances of health have been observed in the quarantined animals and no clinical symptoms of diseases were found. Quarantine premises for parrots and apes in place of destination must be approved by county's veterinary surgeon before arrival of birds and animals.

Please note: in Slovakia, all documents in foreign text must be accompanied with a certified Slovak translation.

For more information, contact:
    State Veterinary Office of the Slovak Republic
    Statna Veterinarna sprava
    Botanicka 17
    842 13 Bratislava, Slovakia
    Telephone: 421 2/6025-7212, -7216
    Fax: 421 2/6542-2128
    E-mail: cenker@svssr.sk

Slovakia does not have a full-fledged tourist board in the Americas, as of yet; however, tourist information is available from the office of the Commercial Counselor of the Slovak Embassy, which is located at:
    10 East 40th Street
    Suite 3606
    New York, NY 10016
    Telephone: (212) 679-7044
    Fax: (212) 679-7045
    E-mail: obeo.nyc@verizon.net

Website: www.slovakia.org/tourism
Website: www.slovakiatourism.sk

Slovakian office
    Slovak Tourist Board
    Námestie L. Stura 1
    P.O. Box 35
    974 05 Banská Bystrica, Slovak Republic
    Telephone: (48) 413 6146-8
    Fax: (48) 413 6149
    E-mail: sacr@sacr.sk

Embassy of The Slovak Republic
3523 International Court, NW
Washington, DC 20008
Telephone: (202) 237-1054
Fax: (202) 237-6438
E-mail: info@slovakembassy-us.org
Website: www.slovakembassy-us.org

Slovenia

Live animals (dogs, cats, decorative and exotic birds, turtles, hamsters, aquarium fishes, reptiles, etc.) can be imported into Slovenia only at specific border crossings, at which a veterinary inspector can perform the documentation, identification control, and physical examination of the animals.

For dogs and cats, it is necessary to present a certificate of vaccination against rabies which must be at least thirty days old but no older than six months. An International Health Certificate no more than ten days old must accompany all animals. Dogs and cats less than four months old must be accompanied with a document of property. No requirement of rabies vaccination, but it is recommended. Vaccination against distemper, parvovirus, leptospirosis, and hepatitis are recommended for dogs. The Website www.vurs.gov.si/eng has the proper certificates for birds, cats, and dogs that will require completion. The reader may also contact:
    Veterinary Administration of the Republic of Slovenia
    Parmova 53
    SI-1000 Ljubljana, Slovenia
    Telephone: +386 1 300 13 00
    Fax: +386 1 436 32 14 / 33 63 / 11 76
    E-mail: vurs@gov.si

Website: www.slovenia-tourism.si

Slovenia office
Slovenian Tourist Organization
Dunajska 156
1000 Ljubljana, Slovenia
Telephone: +386 (1) 589 1840
Fax: +386 (1) 589 1841
E-mail: info@slovenia-tourism.si

UK office
Slovenian Tourist Office
49 Conduit Street
London W1S 2YS, UK
Telephone: 20 7287 7133
Fax: 20 7287 5476
E-mail: slovenia@cpts.fsbusiness.co.uk

USA office
Slovenian Tourist Office
345 East 12th Street
New York, NY 10003
Telephone: (212) 358-9686
Fax: (212) 358-9025
E-mail: slotouristboard@sloveniatravel.com
Website: www.tourist-board.si

Embassy of The Republic of Slovenia
1525 New Hampshire Avenue, NW
Washington, DC 20036
Telephone: (202) 667-5363
Fax: (202) 667-4563
E-mail: slovenia@embassy.org
Website: www.embassy.org/slovenia

Solomon Islands
See also: South Pacific Tourism Organization

Dogs and cats can only be imported from Australia, New Zealand, and the United Kingdom.

Solomon Islands office
Solomon Islands Department of Commerce, Employment & Tourism
P. O. Box G26
Honiara, Solomon Islands
Telephone: (677) 22 808
Fax: (677) 25 084
E-mail: commerce@commerce.gov.sb
Website: www.commerce.gov.sb

Solomon Islands office
Solomon Islands Visitors Bureau
P.O. Box 321
Honiara, Solomon Islands
Telephone: (677) 22 442
Fax: (677) 23 986
E-mail: visitors@solomon.com.sb

Permanent Mission of the Solomon Islands to the United Nations
800 Second Avenue, Suite 800L
New York, NY 10017
Telephone: (212) 599-6192
Fax: (212) 661-8925
E-mail: simny@solomons.com
Website: www.solomons.com
This office also deals with enquiries from Canada.

Somalia

A veterinarian health certificate issued at the point of origin must accompany cats and dogs.

The U.S. Embassy of the Somali Democratic Republic ceased operations on May 8, 1991. Somalia is considered quite unstable and travel is not encouraged. The United States Embassy in Nairobi, Kenya handles enquiries relating to Somalia.

South Africa

Please complete the form "Application to Import Animals into South Africa" (from: www.southafrica-newyork.net/sacg/animals) in full for

each animal you wish to import and send it with the R60.00 fee or proof of payment of the fee to the following address:
> The Director of Veterinary Services
> Private Bag X138
> Pretoria 0001, South Africa
> Telephone: (012) 319 6000/7514
> Fax: (012) 329-8291
> Telex: 322259 SA
> E-mail: agriinfo@agriinfo.co.za
> Website: www.southafrica-newyork.net/sacg/animals

An amount of R60.00 must be deposited into the bank account of the Department of Agriculture for each animal you wish to import. This may be done in one of the following ways.
1. If you have a South African Bank account a check for R60.00 can be made out to "Director General of Agriculture" and sent with the application to the above address; or
2. R60.00 can be deposited into the Department of Agriculture's bank account by means of a credit transfer from any commercial bank in the USA. The bank particulars are:
   > S A Reserve Bank - Account Number: 8033-212-9
   > Branch Code: 910145
   > Any transfer fees payable to the bank must be paid in addition to the R60.00 fee.

   A copy of the deposit slip (stamped by the bank) should then be sent with the application form to the above address.
3. As members of the public have been experiencing problems when transferring the fee of R60.00 to South Africa arrangements have been made for an amount of $12.00 to be sent to the South African Consulate in New York to pay for the import fee.

PLEASE NOTE: PERSONAL CHECKS WILL NOT BE ACCEPTED. The money can only be paid in cash or by postal money order. All personal checks will immediately be returned.

A receipt for $12.00 will be issued and sent to you by the South African Consulate. You should then send this official receipt and your application form to the Department of Animal Health in Pretoria.

The Veterinary Import permit and International Health Certificate will be sent to you directly from South Africa.

If the International Health Certificate does not comply with the regulations, the animal/animals will be returned to their point of departure or will be placed in quarantine for a period of 60 days, if accommodation is available.
Remember: Import permits are valid for a limited period only.

The following documents are required:
1. The original veterinary import permit issued by the Directorate of Animal Health in South Africa. The original "International Health Certificate in respect of dogs or cats for export to the Republic of South Africa". This document should be completed in English and signed, within 10 days of departure, by a Government veterinarian authorized thereto by the Veterinary Administration of the United States. Please contact the USDA Vet at Kennedy Airport at (718) 553-1727 for more information.
2. A valid rabies certificate obtained at least 30 days before your departure. This certificate should not have been obtained more than 12 months or less than 30 days before exporting. The vaccine used must be a strain of anti-rabies conforming to a potency standard recognized by the World Health Organization.

Please note that it is a condition of the import permit that dogs/cats imported into South Africa should be booked as **"manifested cargo"** and **NOT** as **"excess baggage."**

The following helpful information was received from the South African Airways regarding the transportation of pets:
1. Livestock enters South Africa as manifested cargo in the temperature-controlled hold of the aircraft. Cabin stowage is not permitted. Dogs and cats must be older than 8 weeks.
2. As available space could be a problem, you are advised to book well in advance when transporting pets.
3. Contact the Airline you are using to find out what their specific requirements are.

The Director of Animal Health Sub-directorate Import-Export Control in Pretoria would be able to assist you should there be any further information required.

Website: www.satour.co.za
Website: www.satour.org
Website: www.southafrica.net

Canada office
    South African Tourism Board (SATOUR)
    504 Wellington W
    Toronto, ON M5V 1E3, Canada
    Telephone: (416) 591-1635
    Fax: (416) 591-1231
    E-mail: none

South Africa office
    South African Tourism Board (SATOUR)
    Private Bag X10012
    Sandton 2146, South Africa
    Telephone: (11) 778 8000
    Fax: (11) 778 8001
    E-mail: info@satour.co.za

UK office
    South African Tourism Board
    5-6 Alt Grove
    Wimbledon SW19 4DZ, UK
    Telephone: 906 364 0600
    Fax: 181 944 6705
    E-mail: satour@satbuk.demon.co.uk

USA: New York office
    South African Tourism
    500 Fifth Avenue, Suite 2040
    New York, NY 10110
    Telephone: (800) 822-5368 toll-free in USA
    Telephone: (212) 730-2929
    Fax: (212) 764-1980
    E-mail: satourny@aol.com

Embassy of South Africa
3051 Massachusetts Avenue, NW
Washington, DC 20008
Telephone: (202) 232-4400
Fax: (202) 265-1607
E-mail: safrica@southafrica.net
Website: usaembassy.southafrica.net

South Pacific Tourism Organization
Represents: American Samoa, Cook Islands, Fiji, Tahiti, Kiribati, New Caledonia, Niue, Papua New Guinea, Samoa, Solomon Islands, Tonga, Tuvalu, and Vanuatu.

Website: www.spto.org

Fiji office
    South Pacific Tourism Organization
    PO Box 13-119, Suva, Fiji
    Telephone: (679) 304 177
    Fax: (679) 301 995
    E-mail: info@spto.org

UK office
    South Pacific Tourism Organization
    203 Sheen Lane
    London SW14 8LE, UK
    Telephone: 181-876-1938
    E-mail: none

USA office
    South Pacific Tourism Organization
    Box 7440
    Tahoe City, CA 96145
    Telephone: (530) 583-0152
    Fax: (530) 583-0154
    E-mail: Ppascal@compuserve.com

Spain
Owners wishing to bring their dogs into Spain, as pets must comply with the following requirements:
- Owners must produce a veterinary card or certificate, dated no earlier than 10-15 days preceding entry into the country, certifying that their dog is immunized against rabies (provided that the dog in question is over 3 months old).
- Specifying the respective vaccines administered on the relevant dates.
- The latest rabies vaccine must have been administered to the dog from one to 12 months before entry into Spain.

Once these requirements have been complied with and the Spanish Customs & Excise Authorities have duly verified the data and checked on the animal's health, the dog is then subject to no quarantine period. Kindly note however that the above information applies solely and exclusively to dogs that are brought in as personal pets, since in cases where the animal is to be sold, the formalities are different.

Pet Regulations for Entry into Spain
General Regulations
- Their owners or duly authorized representatives shall accompany pets.
- Owners shall provide proof by written certification that the animal has been in their care for the past three months or since the first days after birth, should this be less than three months.
- Owners shall also agree not to sell their pet(s) and to accept any inspections that the Spanish Veterinary services may deem necessary to perform at the address (es) provided by the interested parties, pursuant to the health regulations in force.
- The certification shall also be accompanied by a translation into Spanish.

Specific Regulations
1. Dogs and Cats
   Dogs and cats are required to have a Certificate of Origin and Good Health issued by a licensed veterinarian from the originating country of travel, which states:
   - Identification and originating country of travel of the animal (s).
   - That they were examined before leaving the country and showed no clinical signs of disease.
   - That they were vaccinated against rabies between 1 and 12 months before entering Spain. The following inoculation information shall be provided: Originating country of travel, date of vaccination, name and type of vaccination and laboratory, which prepared it, including the manufacturing lot, as well as the name and address of the veterinarian who administered it.
   - The validity of the certificate of origin and good health is 10 days while the rabies vaccination certificate is valid for one year after the issue date. Vaccinations shall not be required for cats and dogs under three months old.
   - If no valid anti-rabies inoculation certificate or health record evidencing vaccination is provided, the animal will not be allowed to enter Spain.
2. Pet Birds
   Birds are required to have a Certificate of Origin and Good Health issued by a licensed veterinarian from the originating country of travel in which the following is guaranteed:
   - Identification and originating country of travel of the bird.
   - That in the region of origin there are no diseases of obligatory declaration, which might affect the bird.
   - That the bird has been examined at least five days before initiating the trip and presents no clinical signs of contagious disease.
   - The validity of the certificate shall be ten days from the date of issue and one of the languages in which it must be written shall be Spanish.

The maximum number of birds accompanying travelers at one time if their departure is not certified is two birds of the order *psittaciformes* (psittacine birds), ten in the event they are grain-eating, insect-eating or fruit-eating.

These regulations are strictly of a health nature and do not exempt owners from other formalities, which may be necessary concerning the protection of certain wild species.

3. Monkeys

    Monkeys are required to have a Certificate of Origin and Health issued by a licensed veterinarian from the originating country of travel in which the following is guaranteed:
    - Identification and originating country of travel of the animals.
    - That they have been examined at least five days before initiating travel and present no clinical signs of contagious disease.
    - That for a minimum period of two months in advance they have been subjected to tests to determine whether they have the following diseases: Tuberculosis or Hepatitis.
    - The rabies vaccination was given more than one month and less than six months ago.

4. Other Species

    Other species are required to have a Certificate of Origin and Health issued by a licensed veterinarian from the originating country of travel in which the following is guaranteed:
    - Identification and originating country of travel of the animals
    - That they have been examined at least five days before initiating travel and present no clinical signs of disease.
    - That in the originating region there has been no confirmation in the last 60 days of any diseases of obligatory declaration affecting the species.
    - The rabies vaccination was given between 1 and 12 months before entry into Spain for sensitive species.

For more information, contact the Ministry of Agriculture, Fishing and Food, Department of Veterinary Health (Ministerio de Agricultura, Pesca y Alimentación, Departamento de Sanidad Veterinaria) at the following:
Telephone: (0034) 91-347-8310
Information service E-mail: infomac@mapya.es
Ministry Website: www.mapya.es

Website: www.tourspain.es
Website: www.okspain.org

Canada office
Spanish National Tourist Office
2 Bloor Street West, 34th Floor
Toronto, ON M4W3E2, Canada
Telephone: (416) 961-3131
Fax: (416) 961-1992
E-mail: none
Website: www.DocuWeb.ca/SiSpain

Spain office
Dirección General de Turespaña
Jose Lázaro Galdiano 6
28036 Madrid, Spain
Telephone: (91) 343 3500 or 343 3689
Fax: (91) 343 3446
E-mail: info@tourspain.es

UK office
Spanish National Tourist Office
22-23 Manchester Square
London W1M 5AP, UK
Telephone: 171 486 8077
Telephone: 09001 66 99 20 Brochure Request Line (60p/minute)
Fax: 171 486 8034
E-mail: info.londres@tourspain.es
Website: www.tourspain.co.uk

USA: Illinois office
    Tourist Office of Spain
    Water Tower Place, Suite 915 East
    845 North Michigan Avenue
    Chicago, IL 60611
    Telephone: (312) 642-1992
    Fax: (312) 642-9817
    E-mail:

USA: California office
    Tourist Office of Spain
    8383 Wilshire Boulevard, Suite 960
    Beverly Hills, CA 90211
    Telephone: (323) 658-7188
    Fax: (323) 658-1061
    E-mail: none

USA: Florida office
    Tourist Office of Spain
    1221 Brickell Avenue, Suite 1850
    Miami, FL 33131
    Telephone: (305) 358-1992
    Fax: (305) 358-8223
    E-mail: none

USA: New York office
    Tourist Office of Spain
    666 Fifth Avenue
    New York, NY 10103
    Telephone: (212) 265-8822
    Fax: (212) 265-8864
    E-mail: none

Embassy of Spain
2375 Pennsylvania Avenue, NW
Washington, DC 20037
Telephone: (202) 452-0100
Fax: (202) 833-5670
E-mail: spain@spainemb.org
Website: www.spainemb.org

Sri Lanka

Any individual who wishes to import a live animal should make an application to the Director-General, Animal Production and Health (DG/APH) on the prescribed form in triplicate. The DG will study the dangers involved, which depends on the type of animal and the country of origin and issue a "permit" together with a set of conditions. These conditions include vaccination, testing, and so on, which must be satisfied at the time of import. Copies of the permit are sent to the quarantine unit at the airport. The animal quarantine officers at the point of entry, port, or airport, will inspect the animal, study the documents, and decide on the course of action.

The application for a permit to import your pet may be obtained from the Tourist Board or by writing to:
Dr. A. Hewakopara
Chief Animal Quarantine Officer
41 Morgan Road
Colombo 2, Sri Lanka
Telephone/Fax: 94-01-448683

Website: www.srilankatourism.org
Website: www.lanka.net/ctb
Website: www.lk.com
Website: www.customs.gov.lk

Sri Lanka office
   Sri Lanka Tourist Board
   P.O. Box 1504
   Colombo 3, Sri Lanka
   Telephone: (1) 437 059 or 437 060 or 427 055
   Fax: (1) 437 953
   E-mail: tourinfo@sri.lanka.net

UK office
   Sri Lanka (Ceylon) Tourist Board
   Clareville House
   26-27 Oxendon Street
   London SW1Y 4EL, UK
   Telephone: 020 7930 2627
   Fax: 020 7930 9070

E-mail: srilanka@cerbernet.co.uk
E-mail: srilankatourism@aol.com

USA office
    Sri Lanka Tourism
    Metro Top Plaza
    111 Wood Ave South
    Iselin, NJ 08830
    Telephone: (732) 516-9800
    Fax: (732) 452-0087
    E-mail: ctbUSA@anlusa.com

Embassy of Sri Lanka
2148 Wyoming Avenue, NW
Washington, DC 20008
Telephone: (202) 483-4025 to 28
Fax: (202) 232-7181
E-mail: slembassy@starpower.net
Website: www.slembassy.org

Sudan

A current International Health Certificate and rabies vaccination certificate issued at the point of origin must accompany cats and dogs. A notice should be sent well in advance to arrange for a veterinary to be at the airport on arrival. Pets may enter as passenger's checked baggage, in the cabin or as cargo. Contact the Ministry of Agriculture and Forestry for additional information. E-mail: moafcc@sudanmail.net

Sudan office
    Ministry of Environment and Tourism
    P.O. Box 300
    Khartoum, Sudan
    Telephone: (11) 462 604
    Fax: (11) 471 437
    E-mail: none

Embassy of The Republic of the Sudan
2210 Massachusetts Avenue, NW
Washington, DC 20008

Telephone: (202) 338-8565
Fax: (202) 667-2406
E-mail: info@sudanembassyus.org
Website: www.sudanembassyus.org

Suriname

An International Health Certificate issued at the point of origin and not older than 2 weeks before departure must accompany pets (including birds and monkeys). Dogs and cats may be imported from any country, provided they are in good health and have been vaccinated against rabies not less than 30 days before arrival. Medical examination at Paramaribo: minimum fee SRG 5.00. If accompanying documents do not meet the requirements, the animals will be quarantined or admittance will be refused.

Suriname office
　Suriname Tourism Foundation
　P.O. Box 656
　Paramaribo, Suriname
　Telephone: 410 357
　Fax: 477 786
　E-mail: stsmktg@sr.net (marketing department)
　E-mail: stsur@sr.net (secretary's division)
　Website: www.sr.net/users/stsur

Suriname office
　Ministry of Transport, Communication and Tourism
　Prins Hendrikstraat 26-28
　Paramaribo, Suriname
　Telephone: 420 422
　Fax: 420 100
　E-mail: tctper@sr.net

Embassy of The Republic of Suriname
4301 Connecticut Avenue, NW
Suite 460
Washington, DC 20008
Telephone: (202) 244-7488
Fax: (202) 244-5878
E-mail: embsur@erols.com

Website: none
The embassy also deals with enquiries from Canada.

Swaziland

The following information was obtained from the Embassy regarding pets in Swaziland.
1. Obtain import permit from the Ministry of Agriculture, Veterinary office.
     Director: Robert Thwala
     Telephone: (09268) 404 6361/4
     E-mail: dvlshqs@realnet.co.sz
2. Rabies vaccination–within one year of travel.
3. Health Certificate by veterinary–within two days of travel.
4. Ship the animal via Nairobi, Kenya

Embassy of The Kingdom of Swaziland
1712 New Hampshire Avenue, NW
Washington, DC 20009
Telephone: (202) 234-5002
Fax: (202) 234-8254
E-mail: swaziland@compuserve.com
Website: none
The embassy also deals with enquiries from Canada.

Sweden

Pet cats and dogs are not able to enter Sweden unless they meet certain conditions depending on what country/region they are imported/coming. All pets require either a microchip or permanent tattoo. The ID number must be present in each document.

Pet dogs, cats and tame polecats/ferrets from countries outside the EU/EFTA-region (USA and Canada) that are not free from rabies will be kept in an official Swedish quarantine of at least four months followed by two months of isolation. Transport from the country of export must not commence before confirmation has been received that quarantine is available. The quarantine is to be booked by the importer. Quarantine facilities usually have waiting lists. The application for license should be to the Swedish Board of Agriculture at least 30 days before the time of the estimated date of import. A health certificate will be needed as well. Dogs will require leptospirosis vaccination as well. The license application may be obtained from the Website listed below. To insure proper adherence to the requirements, it is advisable to contact the Swedish Board of Agriculture. Their Website www.sjv.se is quite exhaustive and informative. The application is available on the Website. The Swedish Board of Customs may also be helpful. The Website is www.tullverket.se

The Swedish Board of Agriculture:
    Statens Jordruksverk
    SE-551 82 Jonkoping, Sweden
    Telephone: +46 36 15 55 33
    Fax: +46 36 15 08 18
    E-mail: jordruksverket@sjv.se

Website: www.visit-sweden.com
Website: www.gosweden.org
Website: www.swedeninfo.com

Sweden office
    Swedish Travel & Tourism Council
    PO Box 90
    SE-881 22, Sollefteå, Sweden
    Telephone: 0046-620 150 10
    Telephone: 00800-3080-3080 toll-free
    Fax: 0046-620 150 11
    E-mail: info@swetourism.org.uk

UK office
    Swedish Travel & Tourism Council
    11 Montagu Place
    London W1H 2AL, UK
    Telephone: 171 870 56 00
    Fax: 171 724 58 72
    E-mail: info@swetourism.org.uk

USA office
    Swedish Travel and Tourism Council
    P.O. Box 4649, Grand Central Station

New York, NY 10163-4649
Telephone: (212) 885-9700
Fax: (212) 885-9710
E-mail: info@gosweden.org

Embassy of Sweden
1501 M Street, NW
Washington, DC 20005
Telephone: (202) 467-2600
Fax: (202) 467-2656
E-mail: ambassaden.washington@foreign.ministry.se
Website: www.swedish-embassy.org

Switzerland

To bring dogs or cats into Switzerland you need to bring an International Health Certificate and rabies vaccination certificate. The vaccination should be done no longer than one year and no less than 30 days before departure. Accepted languages for the certificate are English, French, German, or Italian. If you bring a puppy or kitten up to five months old, a health certificate stating its age is sufficient. Those rules apply for dogs and cats brought into Switzerland from European countries, USA, Canada, Australia, and New Zealand. There is no mandatory quarantine in Switzerland. No import permit is required.

For further information on Swiss Customs and entry regulations for products or animals other than cats and dogs, please contact the Swiss Consulate General near you.

Prohibited animals:
1. Parrots and parakeets from Bolivia, Columbia, Paraguay, and other South and Central American countries according to current disease situation;
2. All primates (prosimians, monkeys and apes) regardless of origin;
3. Import of dogs with clipped ears and cropped tails even if the animal is under the age of 5 months. Young dogs belonging to persons with residence abroad may be temporarily imported for up to three months.

Website: www.myswitzerland.com
Website: www.zoll.admin.ch

Canada office
Switzerland Tourism
Telephone: (416) 695-2090
Fax: (416) 695-2774
E-mail: info.caen@switzerland.com

UK office
Switzerland Tourism
Swiss Centre
Swiss Court
10, Wardour Street
London W1V 6QF, UK
Telephone: 171 734 1921
Fax: 171 437 4577
E-mail: stlondon@switzerland.com

USA: New York office
Swiss National Tourist Office
608 5th Avenue
New York, NY 10020
Telephone: (212) 757-5944
Fax: (212) 262-6116
E-mail: none

USA: Chicago office
Swiss National Tourist Office
150 North Michigan Avenue, Suite 2930
Chicago, IL 60601
Telephone: (312) 630-5840
Fax: (312) 630-5848
E-mail: none

Embassy of Switzerland
2900 Cathedral Avenue, NW
Washington, DC 20008
Telephone: (202) 745-7900
Fax: (202) 387-2564

E-mail: vertretung@was.rep.admin.ch
Website: www.swissemb.org

Syria

Syria requires documents to indicate the owner of the pet, breed, age, and the health status of the pet. The International Health Certificate has this information and should suffice. The health documents are required to be translated. Pets are prohibited to enter hotels or restaurants.

For more information, please contact the Ministry of Agriculture: 963-11-2213613/2213614.

Website: www.syriatourism.org
Website: www.moi-syria.com
Website: www.visit-syria.com

Syria office
    Ministry of Tourism
    Barada Street 14
    Damascus, Syria
    Telephone: (11) 221 0122 or 224 6096
    Fax: (11) 224 2636
    E-mail: min-tourism@mail.sy

Embassy of the Syrian Arab Republic
2215 Wyoming Avenue, NW
Washington, DC 20008
Telephone: (202) 232-6313
Fax: (202) 234-9548
E-mail: none
Website: none

Tahiti
See: French Polynesia

Taiwan

Taiwan is a rabies-free country. To preserve the state of the environment, dogs/cats importation quarantine is enforced. Animal owners are urged to have their animals vaccinated to prevent rabies epidemics. Only inactivated rabies virus vaccines are authorized for international movements of dogs and cats.

In accordance with the publication made by the Council of Agriculture, Executive Yuan, rabies-free countries include R.O.C., Japan, United Kingdom, Sweden, Iceland, Australia, and New Zealand.

An animal owner or the authorized representative (hereinafter referred to as Applicant) who intends to import dogs/cats (pets) via CKS airport should present the following documents to the office for **an import permit two (2) weeks before the date of transport**:
1. An application form (identifying the scheduled date of import, the applicant and local contact person's name, address, telephone number, etc.).
2. A copy of veterinary (quarantine/health) certificate issued by an official veterinarian of the exporting country with the following information:
    a. The pet's breed, sex, age (or date of birth), fur color, physical characteristics and the signature of an official veterinarian of the exporting country.
    b. Date of rabies vaccination and the type of vaccine administered. (Effective period of rabies vaccination pertains to thirty (30) days from the date of the vaccination to one (1) year).
3. A copy of the applicant's passport or ID.

Notice:
1. Where an applicant fails to meet with the document requirements above or if the vaccination exceeds the said effective period, the application should be rejected.
2. The vaccination against rabies should have been carried out when the animal was at least 3 months old.

After acquiring an "import permit," the original veterinary (quarantine/health) certificate issued by an official veterinary quarantine authorities of the exporting country and import permit should be presented by applicant for animal quarantine while arriving in Taiwan.

If the original veterinary (quarantine/health) certificate(s) issued by an official veterinary quarantine organization of the exporting country is not presented, the pet should be returned in shipment or else be destroyed.

Notice:
If the original veterinary (quarantine/health) certificate(s) issued by an official veterinary quarantine organization of the exporting country is not presented, the pet should be returned in shipment or else be destroyed.

The pet imported from rabies epidemic area should be deemed as susceptible animal. After verification of the animal with its veterinary (quarantine/health) certificate(s) issued by an official veterinary quarantine organization of the exporting country, it should be sent to National Taiwan University Veterinary Hospital (for applicant resident in Northern Taiwan and entering via CKS airport)or the Veterinary Teaching Hospital of the National Chung Hsing University (for applicant resident in Middle Taiwan and entering via CKS airport) or the Animal Medical Teaching Hospital of the National Pingtung University (entering via Kaohsiung airport) for 21 days of quarantine. When necessary, the period above should be extended.

Notice:
If the said "import permit document" is not presented or contains incomplete information, the said quarantine period may be extended.

The pet imported from rabies-free area should be accompanied by an original veterinary (quarantine/health) certificate issued by official veterinary quarantine authorities of the exporting country, upon which the following is clearly documented:
1. The country of exportation has had no rabies occurrence in the past 6 months.
2. The dog/cat was born or bred in the country of exportation for more than 6 months.
3. The microchip number of the dog.

Notice:
If the contents of the veterinary (quarantine/health) certificate(s) do not meet the terms above, the pet should be subject to the regulations on the importation of the pet as from rabies epidemic area.
The pet imported from rabies-free area, after
1. Verification of the veterinary (quarantine/health) certificate(s) issued by an official veterinary quarantine authorities of the exporting country,
2. Confirmation of the effectiveness of its vaccination, and
3. Diagnosed at the site as healthy, shall be issued a veterinary certificate, and released.

Notice:
1. The pet imported from rabies-free area that is clinically diagnosed to be questionable or has quarantine certificates with incomplete information, should be detained for inspection or else be subject to the regulations on the importation of the pet as from rabies epidemic area.
2. The pet imported from rabies-free areas, if transshipped via airport or harbor of rabies epidemic area, should be deemed as imported from rabies epidemic area and subject to quarantine.

How to apply an import permit for dogs/cats
Send the applicant's form, copy of owner's passport, and pet certificates by fax or E-mail to one of the following offices.

Via CKS airport:
   Hsin-Chu Office, Bureau of Animal and Plant Health Inspection and Quarantine
   Telephone: 886-3-3982431
   Fax: 886-3-3982310
   E-mail: hc04@mail.hcbaphiq.gov.tw

Via Kaohsiung airport:
   Kaohsiung Office, Bureau of Animal and Plant Health Inspection and Quarantine
   Telephone: 886-7-8057790
   Fax: 886-7-8068427
   E-mail: kh0701@mail.khbaphiq.gov.tw

Notice:
1. The pets imported from Australia must be subject to Hendra virus serum neutralization test and with a negative result.
2. The pets must not be imported from Malaysia, Singapore and China.
3. The pets must not be transshipped through Malaysia, Singapore, and Australia.

INQUIRY
For further information concerning the regulations on animal and plant health inspection and quarantine, contact the following sections of the office:
Animal Quarantine Section:
  Hsin-Chu Office, Bureau of Animal and Plant Health Inspection and Quarantine
  Telephone: 886-3-3982431
  Fax: 886-3-3982310
  E-mail: hc04@mail.hcbaqhiq.gov.tw

  Kaohsiung Office, Bureau of Animal and Plant Health Inspection and Quarantine
  Telephone: 886-7-8057790
  Fax: 886-7-8068427
  E-mail: kh0701@mail.khbaqhiq.gov.tw

National Taiwan University Veterinary Hospital
  Address: No.153, Section 3, Keelung Road, Taipei, Taiwan, R.O.C.
  Telephone: 886-2-27335891

Veterinary Medical Teaching Hospital of the National Chung Hsing University
  Address: No.250-1, Kaokwang Road, Taichung City, Taiwan, R.O.C.
  Telephone: 886-4-2870180 #301
  Website: www.vmth.nchu.edu.tw

Animal Medical Teaching Hospital of the National Pingtung University
   Address: 1, Hseuh Fu Road, Neipu Hsiang, Pingtung Taiwan, R.O.C
   Telephone: 886-8-7740270

This application form must be sent to obtain an import permit.

Application Form

Owner's
Name: _____
Address: _____
Telephone: _____

Taiwan contact person's
Name: _____
Address: _____
Telephone: _____
Scheduled Date of import:

☐ Dog ____Heads   ☐ Cat ____Heads

☐ Microchip number of the dog_____

Enclosed are following documents:

☐ A copy of the applicant's passport or ID.
☐ A copy of veterinary (quarantine/health) certificate by an official veterinarian of the exporting country (or vaccination certificate by animal hospital).

Signature: _____

Website: www.roc-taiwan.org
Website: www.taipei.org
Website: www.gio.gov.tw
Website: www.tbroc.gov.tw
Website: www.tva.org.tw

Taiwan office
   Taiwan Visitors Association
   9th Floor, 290 Jungshiau E. Road
   Section 4

Taipei, Taiwan 106, R.O.C.
Telephone: (2) 2594 3261
Fax: (2) 2594 3265
E-mail: none

USA: San Francisco office
Taiwan Visitors Association
555 Montgomery, Suite 505
San Francisco, CA 94108
Telephone: (415) 989-8677
Fax: (415) 989-7242
E-mail: info@taiwantourismsf.org

USA: New York office
Taiwan Visitors Association
405 Lexington Avenue, 37th Floor
New York, NY 10174
Telephone: (212) 867-1632 or 1634
Fax: (212) 867-1635
E-mail: tvanyc@aol.com

USA: Los Angeles office
Taiwan Visitors Association
3731 Wilshire Boulevard, Suite 504
Los Angeles, CA 90010
Telephone: (213) 389-1158
Fax: (213) 389-1094
E-mail: latva@pacbell.net

Embassy of The Republic of China on Taiwan
4201 Wisconsin Avenue, NW
Washington, DC 20016
Telephone: (202) 895-1800
Fax: (202) 966-0825
E-mail: none
Website: none

Tajikistan

I am grateful to Fiona S. Evans, Public Affairs and Consular Officer, U.S. Embassy Dushanbe, Tajikistan for this information. If additional information is needed, contact +992 372 21 03 52 or Website: www.usembassy.state.gov/dushanbe.

According to the Tajik Customs Department, a pet's owner should:
1. Have a proof from the appropriate sanitation department that the pet is healthy and received the necessary vaccination (a translation of this into Russian or Tajik may be helpful)
2. Fill out a customs declaration upon arrival in a Tajik airport and indicate there that she/he is bringing a pet dog, cat, etc. with her/him and have this declaration certified/stamped by the Tajik customs officials at the airport,
3. Have these documents available (the certified customs declaration and proof of vaccination) upon her/his departure from Tajikistan to submit them to the Tajik customs officials upon departure. It is forbidden to take animals entered into the Red Book of Tajikistan (the list of endangered species) out of the country.

Website: www.traveltajikistan.com/
Website: www.tajiktour.tajnet.com/

Tajikistan Office
    State National Tourism Company
    Telephone: (992) 23-42-33 or 23-23-85
    Telephone/Fax: (992) 23-14-01
    E-mail: gafarov@cada.tajik.net
    E-mail: shig@cada.tajik.net

Tajikistan office
    Intourist Tajikistan
    Hotel Tajikistan
    ul. Shotemur 22
    Dushanbe 734001, Tajikistan
    Telephone: (372) 216 946
    Fax: (372) 215 236 or 215 237
    E-mail: none

Permanent Mission of Tajikistan to the United Nations
136 East 67th Street
New York, NY 10021
Telephone: (212) 744-2196
Fax: (212) 472-7645
E-mail: none
Website: none

Tanzania

Tanzania requires a certificate of ownership as well as the customary International Health Certificate and certificates of vaccination.

Website: www.tanzania-web.com
Website: www.tanzania.go.tz

Tanzania office
    Tanzania Tourist Board
    P.O. Box 2485
    Dar es Salaam, Tanzania
    Telephone: (22) 211 1244 or 213 6105
    Fax: (22) 211 6420
    E-mail: 100711.3161@compuserve.com
    E-mail: ttb@tanza.net
    E-mail: ttb-info@habari.co.tz
    E-mail: md@ttb.ud.or.tz

UK office
    Tanzania High Commission
    43 Hertford Street
    London W1Y 8DB, UK
    Telephone: 207 499 8951
    Fax: 207 491 9321
    E-mail: Balozi@tanzania-online.gov.uk
    Website: www.tanzania-online.gov.uk

Embassy of The United Republic of Tanzania
2139 R Street, NW
Washington, DC 20008
Telephone: (202) 939-6125
Fax: (202) 797-7408

E-mail: balozi@tanzaniaembassy-us.org
Website: www.tanzaniaembassy-us.org

Thailand

Permission of entry for animals coming in by air can be obtained at the airport. If by sea, application must be made at the Department of Livestock Development, Bangkok. Contact them by telephone: 2515136, 2526944. Vaccination certificates are required. An International Health Certificate is also required. Thailand has banned Rottweilers, Pit Bull Terriers, and American Staffordshire Terriers.

Website: www.tat.or.th
Website: www.experiencethailand.com

Thailand office
    Tourism Authority of Thailand
    Le Concorde Building, Huai Khwang
    202 Ratchadapisek Road
    Bangkok 10310, Thailand
    Telephone: (2) 694 1222
    Fax: (2) 694 1220/1
    E-mail: center@tat.or.th

UK office
    Tourism Authority of Thailand
    49 Albemarle Street
    London WIS 4JR, UK
    Telephone: 171 499 7679
    Fax: 171 629 5519
    E-mail: info@tat-uk.demon.co.uk

USA: California office
    Tourism Authority of Thailand
    611 North Larchmont Boulevard, 1st Floor
    Los Angeles, CA 90004
    Telephone: (800) THAILAND toll-free in USA
    Fax: (323) 461-9834
    E-mail: tatla@ix.netcom.com

USA: New York office (temporary offices)
Tourism Authority of Thailand
c/o World Productions
304 Park Avenue, South
8th Floor
New York, NY 10010
Telephone: (212) 219-4627 and 219-7454
Fax: (212) 219-4697
E-mail: tatny@aol.com

Royal Thai Consulate-General
351 East 52nd Street
New York, NY 10022
Telephone: (212) 754-1770
Fax: (212) 754-1907
E-mail: thainycg@aol.com

Royal Thai Embassy
1024 Wisconsin Avenue, NW
Suite 401
Washington, DC 20007
Telephone: (202) 944-3600
Fax: (202) 944-3611
E-mail: thai.wsn@thaiembdc.org
Website: www.thaiembdc.org

Tibet

See also: China

Website: www.tibet-tour.com
Website: www.tibet.com
Website: www.tibettour.net.cn

China: Beijing office
  Tibet Tourism Office
  Room M021 Poly Plaza
  14 Dongzhimennanjie
  Beijing 100027, People's Republic of China
  Telephone: (10) 6500 1188 (ext 3423) or 6593 6538

Fax: (10) 6593 6538
E-mail: none

China: Shanghai office
Tibet Tourism Office
6/F Laojiefu Commercial Building
No.233 East Nanjing Rd
Shanghai 2000002, People's Republic of China
Telephone: (21) 3313 0524 or (21) 6321 1729
Fax: (21) 6323 1016
E-mail: ttbsw@hotmail.com
E-mail: ttbsw@online.sh.cn

Togo

Dogs and other domestic animals need an International Health Certificate issued not later than 3 days before shipment stating that the animals originate from an area free from contagious diseases of the species for the preceding 6 weeks, and in the case of dogs and cats, that no cases of rabies have been noticed for the same period. Pets may enter as passenger's checked baggage, in the cabin or as cargo. An import license is required for such animals originating from countries other than Benin, Burkina Faso, Cameroon, Central African Republic, Chad, Republic of Congo, Democratic Republic of Congo, Cote d'Ivoire, France, French overseas departments, French overseas territories, Gabon, Madagascar, Mali, Mauritania, Niger, and Senegal.

Togo office
Office National Togolais du Tourisme
BP 1289, Route d'Aného
Lomé, Togo
Telephone: 215 662 or 214 313
Fax: 218 927
E-mail: none

USA office
Togo Information Service
1625 K Street, NW
Washington, DC 20006
Telephone: (202) 569-4330

Embassy of The Republic of Togo
2208 Massachusetts Avenue, NW
Washington, DC 20008
Telephone: (202) 234-4212
Fax: (202) 232-3190
E-mail: none
Website: www.togoinformation.com
This is also the tourist information office for the USA.

Tonga

A current International Health Certificate and rabies inoculation certificates issued at the point of origin must accompany cats and dogs. An import permit is also required and must accompany any animal to be imported. The import permit must be obtained in advance from:

>Government Veterinarian
>P.O. Box 14
>Nuku'alofa, Tonga
>E-mail: tongavet@kalianet.to

Restaurants do not allow pets. Most accommodations do not allow pets. It is always best to check before bringing your pet to Tonga.

Website: www.tongaholiday.com
Website: www.tongaonline.com
Website: www.vacations.tvb.gov.to

Tonga office
>Tonga Visitors' Bureau
>P.O. Box 37
>Nuku'alofa, Tonga
>Telephone: (676) 25 334
>Fax: (676) 23 507
>E-mail: tvb@kalianet.to
>E-mail: tourism@kalianet.to

UK office
>Tonga High Commission
>36 Molyneux Street
>London W1H 6AB, UK

Telephone: (020) 7724 5828
Fax: (020) 7723 9074
E-mail: vielak@btinternet.com

USA office
Tonga Visitors Bureau
360 Post Street, Suite 604
San Francisco, CA 94108
Telephone: (415) 758-9666
Fax: (415) 758-6217
E-mail: tvb@value.net
Website: www.sfconsulate.gov.to/

Permanent Mission of Tonga to the United Nations
250 East 51st Street
New York, NY 10022
Telephone: (212) 369-1025
Fax: (212) 369-1024
E-mail: none

Trinidad and Tobago

Dogs and cats brought into Trinidad and Tobago must be quarantined for a period of up to 6 months. The purpose of the law is to ensure that the country remains free from rabies. There are, however, certain exceptions. Trinidad and Tobago releases from quarantine, dogs, and cats coming from rabies free countries. These are Anguilla, Australia, Antigua, Barbados, Great Britain, Jamaica, New Zealand, Northern Ireland, Republic of Ireland, St Kitts/Nevis, and St Lucia.

In order to bring pets from any country, the law requires that the dog or cat be accompanied by a health certificate stating that the animal is in good health, and free from infectious diseases and that there has been no rabies in that country over the last 6 months before exportation. A government veterinarian of the country from which the dog or cat will arrive must issue the health certificate.

An import permit is also required from the Animal Production and Health Division of the Ministry of Agriculture, Land and Marine Resources in Trinidad and Tobago, before the arrival of the pet in Trinidad and Tobago. This is necessary to ensure accommodation in the quarantine compound. The application for a permit may be obtained from the Embassy of Trinidad and Tobago. The application should be made at least three months in advance of the animal being landed in Trinidad and Tobago. In addition to the above, there are inspection fees and quarantine fees to be paid.

Pregnant dogs or cats are not permitted into quarantine. No dog or cat shall be bred while in quarantine.

Website: www.visittnt.com
Website: www.tidco.co.tt

Canada: Ontario office
Consulate General of the Republic of Trinidad & Tobago
2005 Sheppard Avenue East
Suite 303
Willowdale, ON M2J 5B4, Canada
Telephone: (416) 495-9442/3/7342/7847
Fax: (416) 495-6934
E-mail: ttcontor@idirect.com

Canada: Ottawa office
High Commission of the Republic of Trinidad & Tobago
200 First Avenue
Ottawa, ON K1S 2G6, Canada
Telephone: (613) 232-2418/9
Fax: (613) 232-4349
E-mail: Ottawa@ttmissions.com

Canada: Toronto office
Trinidad & Tobago Tourism Office
The RMR Group Inc.
512 Duplex Avenue
Toronto, ON M4R 2E3, Canada
Telephone: (416) 485-7827 or 485-3490
Telephone: (888) 535-5617 toll-free in Canada
Fax: (416) 485-8256
E-mail: assoc@thermrgroup.ca

Trinidad office
   Tourism and Industrial Development Company Ltd (TIDCO)
   10-14 Philipps Street
   Port of Spain, Trinidad
   Telephone: (868) 623-1932-4
   Fax: (868) 623-3848
   E-mail: tourism-info@tidco.co.tt

UK office
   Trinidad & Tobago Tourism Office
   c/o MKI, Mitre House
   66 Abbey Road
   Bush Hill Park
   Enfield, Middlesex EN1 2QE, UK
   Telephone: (020) 8350 1009
   Fax: (020) 8350 1011
   E-mail: mki@ttg.co.uk

USA: Miami office
   Consulate General of the Republic of Trinidad & Tobago
   1000 Brickell Avenue
   Suite 800
   Miami, FL 33131-3047
   Telephone: (305) 374-2199
   Telephone: (888) 595-4TNT toll-free in USA
   Fax: (305) 374-3199
   E-mail: ttmiami@worldnet.att.net

USA: New York office
   Consulate General of the Republic of Trinidad & Tobago
   733 Third Avenue
   Suite 1716
   New York, NY 10017-3204
   Telephone: (212) 682-7272
   Telephone: (888) 595-4TNT toll-free in USA
   E-mail: ttconsulateny@npl.net

Embassy of Trinidad and Tobago
1708 Massachusetts Avenue, NW
Washington, DC 20036

Telephone: (202) 467-6490
Fax: (202) 785-3130
E-mail: info@ttembwash.com or embttgo@erols.com
Website: www.ttembassy.cjb.net

Tunisia

Pets are admitted only upon presentation of a certificate showing that the animal was vaccinated for rabies at least one month before and less than six months before date of entry. An International Health Certificate stating that no contagious diseases of animals occurred at the place of origin for 6 weeks before shipment.

Website: www.tourismtunisia.com
Website: www.tunisiaguide.com

Canada office
    Tunisian National Tourist Office
    1253 McGill College Avenue, Suite 655
    Montreal, QC H3B 2Y5, Canada
    Telephone: (514) 397-1182
    Fax: (514) 397-1647
    E-mail: tunisinfo@qc.aira.com

Tunisia office
    Office National du Tourisme Tunisien (ONTT)
    1 avenue Mohamed V
    1001 Tunis, Tunisia
    Telephone: (1) 341 077
    Fax: (1) 350 997
    E-mail:

UK office
    Tunisian National Tourist Office
    77a Wigmore Street
    London W1U 1QF, UK
    Telephone: (020) 7224 5561
    Fax: (020) 7224 4053
    E-mail: tntolondon@aol.com

USA office
    Tunisian Tourism Office
    1515 Massachusetts Avenue, NW
    Washington, DC 20005
    Telephone: (202) 466-2546
    Fax: (202) 466-2553
    E-mail: none

Embassy of Tunisia
1515 Massachusetts Avenue, NW
Washington, DC 20005
Telephone: (202) 862-1850
Fax: (202) 862-1858
E-mail: none
Website: www.tunisiaonline.com

Turkey

To bring domestic animals into the country the following are required:
1. Pets have to be 3 months and older,
2. An International Certificate of Health issued within 15 days before the travel,
3. The identification card,
4. Vaccination card

The Turkish Consulate must stamp the International Certificate of Health and if the pet is from the U.S., it must bear a USDA stamp.

Note: If you have an official certificate, you can bring one cat, one bird, one dog, and 10 aquarium fish into the country.

Website: www.tourism.gov.tr
Website: www.tourism.gov.tr

Canada office
    Turkish Tourist Office
    360 Albert Street, Suite 801
    Ottawa, ON K1R 7X7, Canada
    Telephone: (613) 230-8654
    Fax: (613) 230-3683

E-mail: info@turkishtourism.ca
Website: www.turkishtourism.ca

Turkey office
Ministry of Tourism
Ismet Inönü Bulvar 5
Bahçelievler
Ankara, Turkey
Telephone: (312) 212 8300
Fax: (312) 212 8595
E-mail: none

UK office
Turkish Tourist Office
First Floor, 170-173 Piccadilly
London W1J 9EJ, UK
Telephone: (020) 7629 7771
Fax: (020) 7491 0773
E-mail: tto@turkishtourism.demon.co.uk
Website: www.tourist-offices.org.uk/turkey

USA: New York office
Turkish Tourist Office
821 United Nations Plaza
New York, NY 10017
Telephone: (212) 687-2194
Fax: (212) 599-7568
E-mail: ny@tourismturkey.org

USA: Washington, DC office
Turkish Tourism Office
1717 Massachusetts Avenue, NW
Suite 306
Washington, DC 20036
Telephone: (202) 429-9844 or (202) 429-9409
Fax: (202) 429-5649
E-mail: dc@tourismturkey.org
Website: www.tourismturkey.org

Embassy of The Republic of Turkey
2525 Massachusetts Avenue, NW
Washington, DC 20036
Telephone: (202) 612-6700
Fax: (202) 612-6744
E-mail: info@turkey.org
E-mail: Turkish@erols.com
Website: www.turkey.org/turkey

Turkish Republic of Northern Cyprus

Cat and dog entries to the country are subject to prior approval. These approvals can be obtained from the Veterinary Office, which is part of the Ministry of Agriculture and Forestry. Before the process of importation, the disease status of the country of origin is monitored via Office International des Epizootique (O.I.E.), and then the decision is made to import the animal. Importation of dogs and cats younger than three months is not allowed. Otherwise, the animals are subject to one-month quarantine and a legitimate health certificate from the relevant government authorities is required. The animals should be vaccinated against rabies at least 15 days before or at the latest six months before their entry into the country and should have a legal health certificate from the relevant government authorities.

Office of the Representative, Turkish Republic of Northern Cyprus
1667 K Street, NW
Suite 690
Washington, D.C. 20006
Telephone: (202) 887-6198
Fax: (202) 467-0685
E-mail: info@trncwashdc.org
E-mail: kktc@erols.com
Website: www.trncwashdc.org

Turkmenistan

Dogs and cats need a veterinarian certificate of good health issued at the point of origin no longer than 10 days before arrival in Turkmenistan. In case these regulations are not complied with, the animal will be kept in quarantine. Pets may enter as passenger's checked baggage, in the cabin or as cargo.

Turkmenistan office
    Turkmensiyakhat (State Tourist Corporation of Turkmenistan)
    17 Pushkin Street
    744000 Ashgabat, Turkmenistan
    Telephone: (12) 354 777 or 397 777
    Fax: (12) 396 740 or 357 934
    E-mail: travel@online.tm

Embassy of Turkmenistan
2207 Massachusetts Avenue, NW
Washington, DC 20008
Telephone: (202) 588-1500
Fax: (202) 588-0697
E-mail: none
Website: www.turkmenistanembassy.org

Turks and Caicos

There is no lengthy quarantine for incoming and visiting pets. A recent International Health Certificate stating that the animal is in good health and a current rabies vaccination certificate is required. The Public Health Inspector will examine the animal on arrival. No translation of documents is required. Most hotels and restaurants do not allow pets.

Website: www.turksandcaicostourism.com

Grand Turk office
    Turks & Caicos Islands Tourist Board
    P.O. Box 128
    Front Street
    Grand Turk, Turks & Caicos Islands, British West Indies
    Telephone: 946 2321
    Fax: 946 2733
    E-mail: tci.tourism@tciway.tc

UK office
    Turks & Caicos Tourist Information Office
    Mitre House
    66 Abbey Road
    Bush Hill Park

Enfield, Middlesex EN1 2QE, UK
Telephone: 181 350 1017
E-mail: mki@ttg.co.uk
Website: www.ttg.co.uk/t&c/index.htm

USA office
    Turks & Caicos Islands Tourist Office
    11645 Biscayne Boulevard, Suite 302
    North Miami, FL 33181
    Telephone: (305) 891-4117
    Telephone: (800) 241-0824 toll-free in North America
    Fax: (305) 891-7096
    E-mail: tcitrsm@bellsouth.net

The Turks & Caicos Islands are a British Overseas Territory and are formally represented abroad by British diplomatic missions.

Tuvalu
See also: South Pacific Tourism Organization

A current International Health Certificate and rabies inoculation certificate issued at the point of origin must accompany cats and dogs. Moreover, an import license is required (obtainable from the Officer in charge of Agriculture-Vaitupu, Tuvalu) except for pets arriving from the Australian states of New South Wales, Victoria, South Australia, and Tasmania or from Fiji, New Zealand, or the United Kingdom.

Website: www.tuvalu.tv

Tuvalu office
    Ministry of Tourism, Trade and Commerce
    Private Mail Bag
    Vaiaku, Funafuti
    Tuvalu
    Telephone: (688) 20 184
    Fax: (688) 20 829
    E-mail: mmtc@tuvalu.tv

Uganda

Regulations governing importation of dogs and cats to Uganda:
1. Permit
   The importation of dogs and cats into Uganda is subject to the availability of an official and authentic permit, which must be obtained and signed from the authoritative Veterinary Surgeon of the area in the country of origin.
2. Certificates
   The following certificates are normally required:
   - A health and origin certificate issued by a local veterinary authorized surgeon or official, properly signed and stamped within ten days of shipment certifying freedom from disease.
   - A certificate issued by an authorized and official department giving country or area freedom from rabies. This certificate is referred to as a "Movement Permit."
   - A valid certificate of all relevant vaccinations.
3. Vaccinations
   - Dogs require vaccination against distemper, hepatitis, leptospirosis, parvovirus, and rabies not less than 30 days before arrival at any entry point to Uganda.
   - Cats require vaccinations against feline enteritis and rabies not less than 30 days before arrival at any entry point to Uganda.
4. Transport
   - Dogs and cats must not be exposed to any dog or cat whilst in transit. To ensure this, each animal should be crated.

Website: www.visituganda.com

Uganda office
   Uganda Tourist Board
   P.O. Box 7211
   Impala House, Ground Floor
   Kimathe Avenue
   Kampala, Uganda
   Telephone: (41) 342 197

Fax: (41) 342 188
E-mail: utb@starcom.co.ug

Embassy of The Republic of Uganda
5911 16th Street, NW
Washington, DC 20011
Telephone: (202) 726-7100
Fax: (202) 726-1727
E-mail: ugembassy@aol.com
Website: www.ugandaweb.com/ugaembassy

Ukraine

Pets entering the Ukraine must have an International Health Certificate attesting to the animal's good health and current vaccination certificates. Pigeons are prohibited entry. Cats and dogs less than 3 months of age are also prohibited entry. Additional information is available from:

    State Customs Service of Ukraine
    11-g, Dehtiarivska St,
    04119, Kyiv, Ukraine
    Telephone: (044) 247-26-06, 247-27-06
    Fax: (044) 247-28-51
    E-mail: dmsu@rada.kiev.ua
    Website: www.customs.gov.ua

Website: www.mfa.gov.ua

Ukraine office
    Ministry of Foreign Affairs
    Mykhailovska Square 1
    01018 Kyiv, Ukraine
    Telephone: (44) 226 3379
    Fax: (44) 226 3169
    E-mail: zsmfa@mfa.gov.ua

Embassy of Ukraine
3350 M Street, NW
Washington, DC 20007
Telephone: (202) 333-0606
Fax: (202) 333-0817

E-mail: infolook@aol.com
Website: www.ukremb.com

United Arab Emirates

UAE includes Dubai, Abu Dhabi, Ajman, Fujairah, Ras Al Khaimah, Sharjah, and Umm Al Quwain.

A current International Health Certificate must accompany cats, dogs, and birds. An import permit issued at the point of origin is required if pets are shipped as cargo. If pets are taken as baggage and cleared in the passenger terminal an import permit is not required. In all cases, prior permission must be obtained from Ministry of Agriculture and Fisheries.

Obtain import permits and permission for pets from:
Ministry of Agriculture & Fisheries
P.O. Box 1509
Dubai, UAE
Telephone: 971 4 2958161
Fax: 971 4 2957766
E-mail: archieves.maf@uae.gov.ae
Website: www.uae.gov.ae/maf

There are various regulations for pet owners issued by the Dubai Municipality relating to treatment, health care, and safety regulations for pets. As mentioned in the guidelines, when dogs are in public places, they must be on a leash. The Dubai Veterinary Services may be contacted for more information at Fax: 971 4 852977 or Telephone: 971 4 857335.

UAE Sharjah Government Customs Department
E-mail: shjcustm@emirates.net.ae

Website: www.dubaitourism.com
Website: www.dubaitourism.co.ae
Website: www.emirates.org.ae
Website: www.uaeforever.com

UAE office
    Dubai Department of Tourism & Commerce Marketing
    National Bank of Dubai Building, 10th-12th Floors
    Baniyas Road, Deira
    P.O. Box 594
    Dubai, UAE
    Telephone: 4 223 0000
    Fax: 4 223 0022
    E-mail: info@dubaitourism.co.ae

UK office
    Department of Tourism and Commerce Marketing
    1st floor, 125 Pall Mall
    London SW1Y 5EA, UK
    Telephone: +44 207 839 0580
    Telephone: +44 207 839 0581 24-hour brochure order line
    Fax: +44 207 839 0582
    E-mail: dtcm_uk@dubaitourism.co.ae

USA: California office
    Department of Tourism and Commerce Marketing
    901 Wilshire Boulevard
    Santa Monica, CA 90401
    Telephone: (310) 752-4488
    Fax: (310) 752-4444
    E-mail: dubaiusa@aol.com

USA: Pennsylvania office
    Dubai Commerce & Tourism Promotion Board
    8 Penn Center
    Philadelphia, PA 19103
    Telephone: (215) 751-9750
    Fax: (215) 751-9551
    E-mail: dtcm_usa@dubaitourism.co.ae

Embassy of The United Arab Emirates
1255 22nd Street, NW
Suite 700
Washington, DC 20037
Telephone: (202) 243-2400

Fax: (202) 243-2432
E-mail: none
Website: none

United Kingdom

Countries in the United Kingdom are England, Scotland, Wales, Northern Ireland, Isle of Man and the Channel Islands with consist of Alderney, Guernsey, Jersey, Sark and Hern.

On 28 February 2000, the British Government launched the Pet Travel Scheme (PETS), which allows certain dogs and cats to enter the United Kingdom without quarantine, provided they meet the necessary conditions. PETS currently applies to 24 countries in Western Europe (Andorra, Austria, Belgium, Cyprus, Denmark, Finland, France, Germany, Gibraltar, Greece, Iceland, Italy, Liechtenstein, Luxembourg, Malta, Monaco, Netherlands, Norway, Portugal, San Marino, Spain, Sweden, Switzerland and the Vatican). *Exceptions to the above are Norway excludes Svalbard, Portugal includes the Azores and Madeira; and Spain includes the Canary Islands but excludes Ceuta and Melilla.*

Note: Cyprus and Malta have additional requirements. Please go to www.defra.gov.uk/animalh/quarantine for the specifics.

The Pet Travel Scheme also extends to certain Long Haul (non-European) countries and Territories. These are Antigua and Barbuda, Ascension Island, Australia, Bahrain, Barbados, Bermuda, Canada, Cayman Islands, Falkland Islands, Fiji, French Polynesia, Guadeloupe, Hawaii, Jamaica, Japan, Martinique, Mauritius, Mayotte, Montserrat, New Caledonia, New Zealand, Reunion, St Helena, St Kitts & Nevis, St Vincent, Singapore, United States, Vanuatu and Wallis, and Futuna. The procedure for bringing pets into the UK from these countries or territories is slightly different.

Pets normally resident in the Channel Islands, the Isle of Man, and the Republic of Ireland can enter England under the Scheme from qualifying countries as long as they have the appropriate official certification. They can then travel freely between these countries without the need for official documentation. Jersey, Guernsey, the

Isle of Man, and the Republic of Ireland have each produced their own official PETS certificate.

To bring your pet cat or dog into the UK under the Pet Travel Scheme from one of the qualifying countries you must carry out the following procedures in the order shown. If your pet is a resident in France, these procedures may be done in a different order. Your pet may be microchipped in any country. The rabies vaccination (including boosters), blood sampling, issuing the PETS certificate, the tick and tapeworm treatment, and issuing the official certificate of treatment must all be carried out in either the British Isles, the Republic of Ireland or a qualifying country.

Your pet may not enter the UK under PETS until six months have passed from the date of a successful blood test result. If the veterinarian signs the PETS certificate after that six-month period has passed, your pet may enter the UK immediately.

Entrance procedures (in order):
1. Have your pet microchipped before any of the other procedures for PETS. Your pet must be fitted with a microchip for proper identification.
   - The microchip must meet ISO standards. Have the correct chip fitted or bring your own scanner.
   - Bring the microchip documentation with you that you received at the time of microchipping.
2. Have your pet vaccinated after the microchip has been fitted-against rabies. It must be at least three months old before being vaccinated.
3. Arrange a blood test after your pet has been vaccinated, it must be blood tested to make sure that the vaccine has given it a satisfactory level of protection against rabies. The blood test must be carried out at a laboratory recognized by DEFRA. A list is available from DEFRA.
4. Get a PETS certificate.
   - The valid period for the certificate is 6 months from the time of the satisfactory blood test. Be sure to obtain a new certificate each time your pet is revaccinated (booster shot). This will give your pet continuous entry options.

5. Before your pet enters the UK, have it treated against ticks and tapeworm. This must occur between 24-48 hours before it is checked in for the journey to the UK. A veterinarian must carry out the treatment and issue an official certificate of treatment.
6. Sign a declaration of residency stating that the pet has not been outside any of the PETS qualifying countries in the previous six months.

Pets from the United States and Canada became eligible for entry on December 11, 2002. In the initial stages of PETS, your pet may require a few days of quarantine while the paperwork is scrutinized. Dogs and cats traveling from the USA or Canada are required to travel to the UK on an air route approved for PETS by the UK Government. These routes will take you only to an airport in England, not one in Scotland, Wales, the Channel Islands, the Isle of Man, Northern Ireland or the Republic of Ireland. Animals travelling from the USA or Canada may not enter the UK on a route departing from any other country. Pets must travel in a container approved by the IATA and sealed by a government official (Customs or Immigration officer). Have your airline provide you with the proper proceedure to obtain the seal.

Dogs and cats will be checked at the airport when they land in England. Your animal's microchip and both the official PETS certificates will be checked. You will also have to provide the top copy of the completed PETS 3. The seal on your animal's container should also be intact.

Dogs and cats that have first entered England under PETS can travel freely within the United Kingdom (England, Scotland, Wales, Northern Ireland, the Channel Islands and the Isle of Man) and between these countries and the Republic of Ireland without the need for any additional documentation. However, take your PETS documents with you in case you need to show them.

If you take your dog or cat from the UK to a European PETS country and want to return later, you will need to get a UK PETS 1 certificate from a government-authorised vet in the UK before you go. Make sure you bring your animal's vaccination record and a copy of its blood test result with you. If your travels will include non-UK countries in Europe, have a separate International Health Certificate prepared and ready to produce to authorities.

It is illegal to possess certain types of dogs in the UK. For a list of prohibited breeds visit the Defra Website at www.defra.gov.uk/animalh/welfare(click on 'policy on general animal welfare' and scroll down to 'The Control of Dogs').

These rules also apply to "Service" dogs. Certain PETS countries have additional requirements from those above.

Additional information on PETS and quarantine is available by contacting:
   Pet Travel Scheme
   Department for Environment, Food and Rural Affairs (DEFRA)
   Area 201
   1a Page Street, London SW1P 4PQ, UK
   Telephone: 870 241 1710
   Fax: 207 904 6834
   E-mail: pets.helpline@defra.gsi.gov.uk
   Website: www.defra.gov.uk/animalh/quarantine

Website: www.travelbritain.org
Website: www.visitbritain.com

Canada office
   British Tourist Authority
   5915 Airport Road, Suite 120
   Mississauga, ON L4V 1T1, Canada
   Telephone: (888) VISITUK toll-free in Canada
   Fax: (905) 405-1835
   E-mail: travelinfo@bta.org.uk
   Website: www.visitbritain.com/ca

UK office
   British Tourist Authority
   Thames Tower
   Black's Road

Hammersmith, London W6 9EL, UK
Telephone: (020) 8846 9000
Fax: (020) 8563 0302
E-mail: none

USA: New York office
British Tourist Authority
551 Fifth Avenue, Suite 701
New York, NY 10176-0799
Telephone: (800) 462-2748 toll-free in USA
Telephone: (212) 986-2266
E-mail: travelinfo@bta.org.uk
Website: www.travelbritain.org

USA: New York office
British Information Service
845 Third Avenue
New York, NY 10022
Telephone: (212) 745-0277

Embassy of The United Kingdom of Great Britain
3100 Massachusetts Avenue, NW
Washington, DC 20008
Telephone: (202) 588-6500
Fax: (202) 588-7870
E-mail: none
Website: www.britianusa.com

U.S. Virgin Islands

Pets are welcome, as long as visitors bring an International Health Certificate and inoculation certificates for their animals.

Website: www.usvi.net
Website: www.usvi.org/tourism

Canada office
U.S. Virgin Islands Department of Tourism
3300 Bloor Street West, Suite 3120 Centre Tower
Toronto, ON M8X 2X3, Canada
Telephone: (416) 233-1414

Fax: (416) 233-9367
E-mail: melaine@inforamp.net

UK office
Virgin Islands Division of Tourism
Molasses House
Clove Hitch Quay
Plantation Wharf
London SW11 3TN, UK
Telephone: 171 978-5262
Fax: 171 924-3171
E-mail: usvi@destination-marketing.co.uk

USA: California office
Virgin Islands Division of Tourism
3460 Wilshire Boulevard, Suite 412
Los Angeles, CA 90010
Telephone: (213) 739-0138
Telephone: (800) 372-USVI toll-free in USA
Fax: (213) 739-2005
E-mail: none

USA: DC office
Virgin Islands Division of Tourism
444 North Capital Street, NW
Suite 298
Washington, DC 20001
Telephone: (202) 624-3590
Telephone: (800) 372-USVI toll-free in USA
Fax: (202) 624-3594

USA: Florida office
Virgin Islands Division of Tourism
2655 LaJeune Road, Suite 907
Coral Gables, FL 33134
Telephone: (305) 442-7200
Telephone: (800) 372-USVI toll-free in USA
Fax: (305) 445-9044

USA: Georgia office
   Virgin Islands Division of Tourism
   225 Peachtree Center Avenue
   Marquis One Tower, Suite MB-05
   Atlanta, GA 30303
   Telephone: (404) 688-0906
   Telephone: (800) 372-USVI toll-free in USA
   Fax: (404) 525-1102

USA: Illinois office
   Virgin Islands Division of Tourism
   500 North Michigan Avenue, Suite 2030
   Chicago, IL 60611
   Telephone: (312) 670-8784
   Telephone: (800) 372-USVI toll-free in USA
   Fax: (312) 670-8788

USA: New York office
   Virgin Islands Division of Tourism
   1270 Avenue of the Americas, Suite 2108
   New York, NY 10020
   Telephone: (212) 332-2222
   Telephone: (800) 372-USVI toll-free in USA
   Fax: (212) 332-2223
   E-mail: grusviny@aol.com

USA: Puerto Rico office
   Virgin Islands Division of Tourism
   60 Washington Street, Suite 1102
   San Juan, Puerto Rico 00907
   Telephone: (787) 722-8023
   Fax: (787) 724-6659

USA: U.S. Virgin Islands office
   U.S. Virgin Islands Department of Tourism
   P.O. Box 6400
   St Thomas, USVI 00804
   Telephone: (340) 774-8784
   Telephone: (800) 372-USVI toll-free in USA
   Fax: (340) 774-4390

The U.S. Virgin Islands are a United States External Territory and are represented abroad by U.S. Embassies.

United States

Pets brought into the U.S. are governed by three separate agencies. These are U.S. Customs, the Center for Disease Control (CDC) and the United States Department of Agriculture Animal and Plant Health Inspection Service (USDA-APHIS). All pets will be examined at the time of arrival at the port of entry. They must be accompanied by a valid rabies vaccination with the identification of the pet and the dates of vaccination and the expiration. This certificate should be in English so pets from other countries may need to have translations prepared before entry. Puppies younger than three months will require a period of confinement and vaccination.

Travelers frequently inquire about taking their pets with them to the United States. All such importations are subject to health, quarantine, agriculture, wildlife, and customs requirements and prohibitions. Pets, except for pet birds, taken out of the United States and returned are subject to the same requirements as those entering for the first time. Returning U.S. origin pet birds are subject to different import restrictions than pet birds of non-U.S. origin entering the United States for the first time. For more information on importing pet birds into the United States, see the Website: www.aphis.usda.gov/NCIE.

Unfortunately, pets excluded from entry into the United States must either be exported or destroyed. While awaiting disposition, pets will be detained at the owner's expense at the port of arrival.

The U.S. Public Health Service requires that pet dogs and cats brought into this country be examined at the first port of entry for evidence of diseases that can be transmitted to humans. A valid rabies vaccination certificate must accompany dogs coming from areas not free of rabies. Turtles are subject to certain restrictions, and monkeys may not be imported as pets under any circumstances.

The U.S. Fish and Wildlife Service is concerned with the importation, trade, sale, and taking of wildlife and with protecting endangered plant and animal species. Some wildlife species of dogs, cats, turtles, reptiles and birds, although imported as pets, may be listed as endangered.

Endangered and threatened animal and plant wildlife, migratory birds, marine mammals, and certain injurious wildlife may not be imported without special federal permits. Sportsmen will find the section on wildlife of particular interest, since game birds and animals are subject to special entry requirements.

Dogs must be vaccinated against rabies at least 30 days before entering the United States. This requirement does not apply, however, to puppies less than three months of age or to dogs originating or located for at least six months in areas designated by the U.S. Public Health Service as being rabies-free.

The following procedures pertain to dogs arriving from areas that are not free of rabies:
1. A valid rabies vaccination certificate should accompany the animal. This certificate should be in English or be accompanied by a translation. It should identify the animal, the dates of vaccination and expiration, and be signed by a licensed veterinarian. If no expiration date is specified, the certificate is acceptable if the date of vaccination is no more than 12 months before the date of arrival.
2. If a vaccination has not been performed, or if the certificate is not valid, the animal may be admitted if it is confined immediately upon arrival at a place of the owner's choosing. The dog must be vaccinated within four days after arrival at the final destination, but no more than 10 days after arrival at the port of entry. The animal must remain in confinement for at least 30 days after being vaccinated.
3. If the vaccination was performed less than 30 days before arrival, the animal may be admitted but must be confined at a place of the owner's choosing until at least 30 days have passed since the vaccination.
4. Young puppies must be confined at a place of the owner's choosing until they are three months old, then they must be vaccinated. They must remain in confinement for 30 days.

Dogs that arrive in Hawaii or Guam, both of which are free of rabies, are subject to the state or territory's quarantine requirements, in addition to whatever other Public Health Service requirements, above, apply. The usual quarantine is for 120 days. If the pet has a microchip, it may qualify for 30-day quarantine. For complete information, go to www.hawaiiag.org/hdoa/ai_aqs_info.htm.

All domestic cats must be free of evidence of disease communicable to humans when examined at the port of entry. If the animal is not in apparent good health, further examination by a licensed veterinarian may be required at the owner's expense. Cats arriving in Hawaii or Guam, both of which are free of rabies, are subject to that state or territory's quarantine requirements.

The following animals are prohibited from entry or possession by private individuals in Hawaii.

Alligators	Land snails
Bulbuls	Lion fishes
Coconut crabs	Lories
Electric catfishes	Monk parakeets
Ferrets	Piranhas
Gerbils	Snakes
Hamsters	Snapping turtles
Hermit crabs	Toucans

An important Website is www.aphis.usda.gov/travel/pets

Uruguay

Pets entering Uruguay require a vaccination between 30 days and one year and an International Health Certificate dated less than 30 days before arrival. There is no mandatory quarantine or permit to import. The health certificate must state that the animal is free of external parasites. Birds from anywhere in the world are prohibited.

Website: www.turismo.gub.uy

USA: Florida office
    Tourist Information Office of Uruguay
    P.O. Box 144531
    Coral Gables, FL 33114

Telephone: (305) 443-7431
Fax: none
E-mail: none

Uruguay office
Ministerio de Turismo
Piso 2, Avenida Libertado
1409, Montevideo, Uruguay
Telephone: (2) 900 4148
Fax: (2) 903 1601
E-mail: real@mintur.gub.uy

Embassy of Uruguay
2715 M Street, NW
3rd Floor
Washington, DC 20007
Telephone: (202) 331-1313
Fax: (202) 331-8142
E-mail: uruguay@erols.com
Website: www.embassy.org/uruguay

Uzbekistan

For traveling to Uzbekistan with pets, one should have an International Health Certificate, issued not more than 10 days from departure, which confirms that the pet has been properly immunized and does not have any contagious diseases. Pigeons are prohibited entry. The translation of documents is preferred.

Uzbekistan office
National Company Uzbektourism
47 Khorezm Street
Tashkent 700047, Uzbekistan
Telephone: (71) 133 5414
Fax: (71) 136 7948
E-mail: none

Embassy of The Republic of Uzbekistan
1746 Massachusetts Avenue, NW
Washington, DC 20036

Telephone: (202) 887-5300
Fax: (202) 293-6804
E-mail: emb@uzbekistan.org
Website: www.uzbekistan.org

Vanuatu
See also: South Pacific Tourism Organization

The Vanuatu Quarantine and Inspection Service officials would prefer that those traveling to Vanuatu contact them directly regarding any queries that they may have.
Vanuatu Quarantine and Inspection Service
PMB 095
Port Vila, Vanuatu
Telephone: (678) 23130
Fax: (678) 24653
E-mail: vqisvila@vanuatu.com.vu

Documentation required for entry of pets varies between countries of origin. All animals require a provisional import permit and must meet the conditions specified in the relevant import protocol. Details of these import protocols can be provided on request by fax. However, travelers need to be aware that since there is a lack of resources to maintain physical quarantine facilities only animals from a small number of countries whose disease status we consider acceptable can be admitted directly. These countries include New Zealand, Australia, United Kingdom, and New Caledonia. Pets intended for importation from other countries, such as the USA, normally require quarantine clearance in either New Zealand or Australia before entry in Vanuatu. This quarantine period may be anywhere from 30-180 days. Essentially each case is dealt with on a case-by-case basis depending on the country of origin as to what conditions may apply. All animals are required to be examined on entry and documentation verified. No cat or dog can be under 16 weeks of age or pregnant before travel to Vanuatu. All documentation should be presented in English although French versions of the import protocols for New Caledonia are provided.

Website: www.vanuatutourism.com

UK office
    National Tourism Office of Vanuatu
    203 Sheen Lane
    East Sheen
    London SW 14 8LE, UK
    Telephone: (20) 8876 1938
    Fax: (20) 8878 9876
    E-mail: tcsp.uk@interface-tourism.com
    E-mail: ajbalfour@aol.com

USA office
    National Tourism Office of Vanuatu
    475 Lake Boulevard
    P.O. Box 7440
    Tahoe City, CA 96145
    Telephone: (530) 583-0152
    Fax: (530) 583-0154
    E-mail: sopactour@cs.com

Vanuatu office
    The National Tourism Office of Vanuatu
    P.O. Box 209
    Port Vila, Vanuatu
    Telephone: (678) 22515, 22685, or 22813
    Fax: (678) 23889
    E-mail: tourism@vanuatu.com.vu

Permanent Mission of the Republic of Vanuatu to the United Nations
42 Broadway, 12th Floor
Suite 1200-18
New York, NY 10004
Telephone: (212) 425-9600
Fax: (212) 422-3427 or 425-9652
E-mail: vanunmis@aol.com
Website: none

Venezuela

Venezuela requires an International Health Certificate that has been "stamped" by the USDA. The Miami consulate must legalize this document. The fee is $70 fee. This should include a prepaid, self-addressed envelope to return the document. **Author's note:** although, there is no mention of a vaccination certificate, I would recommend having it available, just in case.

Website: www.venezuela1.com/

USA office
Venezuelan Tourism Association
P.O. Box 3010
Sausalito, CA 94966
Telephone: (415) 331-0100
Fax: none
E-mail: none

Venezuela office
Corporación de Turismo de Venezuela
Avenida v. Lecuna, Parque Central
Torre Oeste, Piso 37
Caracas, Venezuela
Telephone: (212) 574 1968
Fax: (212) 574 2220
E-mail: corpoturismo@platino.gov.ve

Embassy of Venezuela
1099 30th Street, NW
Washington, DC 20007
Telephone: (202) 342-2214
Fax: (202) 342-6820
E-mail: consular@embavenez-us.org
E-mail: conmiami@gate.net (consulate in Miami)
E-mail: prensa@embavenez-us.org
Website: www.embavenez-us.org

Vietnam

Phan Huong at the U.S. Embassy in Hanoi very graciously supplied this information.

IMPORT:
Cats & dogs must have an animal health certificate and vaccination certificate for each pet. After the owners go through immigration,

they will be welcomed at the luggage lounge by the Customs Clerk of the U.S. Embassy (make prior arrangements) who will guide you to get the animal health certificate at Noibai Animal Quarantine Station. The animal health certificates will be issued. The fee for non-diplomatic travelers is $20.00 and for diplomatic travelers is $5.00.

EXPORT:
1. The cats and dogs must be vaccinated against rabies. One international stamp will be issued to your cats or dogs (that is rabies vaccination certificate). Contact:
    Veterinary Ms.Thanh Hai,
    95 Nguyen Thai Hoc Street
    Hanoi, Vietnam
    Telephone: 7732467 or 8349557.
   You can call directly to her and you can request her to come to your residence for service. She speaks English very well. The fee is 50.00 VND.
2. After the immunization against rabies, the cats or dogs must be checked by Hanoi Regional Health Center and a health certificate will be issued. Contact:
    Vice Director Mr. Le Minh Son
    102 Truong Chinh Street
    Hanoi, Vietnam
    Telephone: 8621858 or cell phone 0913514069.
The fee is $20.00.

There is another way for a free Health certificate: you must bring your cats or dogs to the Noibai airport one hour before you check-in. The Customs Clerk at the embassy will go with you. The certificate will be issued at the airport.

NOTE: Customs & Shipping at the GSO section at the embassy will help individuals who have cats and dogs by informing them of the regulations of the government regarding pet import & export and in the "clearing" of pets through local customs. Please feel free to contact Mr. Hieu or Mr. Toan if you have any problems.
   Le Xuan Toan
   Customs & Shipping
   U.S. Embassy
   Hanoi, Vietnam

Telephone: 84-4-7721500
Fax: 84-4-7723351
E-mail: LeTX@state.gov

Website: www.vietnamtourism.gov.vn
Website: www.vietnamtourism.com

USA office
   Vietnam Tourism Office
   P.O. Box 53316
   Indianapolis, IN 46253-0316
   Telephone: (371) 388-0788
   Fax: (371) 488-5510

Vietnam office
   Vietnam Tourism
   30A Ly Thuong Kiet
   Hanoi, Vietnam
   Telephone: (4) 826 4154
   Fax: (4) 825 7583
   E-mail: vntourism2@hn.vnn.vn
   Website: www.vn-tourism.com

Embassy of The Socialist Republic of Vietnam
1233 20th Street, NW
Suite 400
Washington, DC 20037
Telephone: (202) 861-0737
Fax: (202) 861-0917
E-mail: info@vietnamconsulate-sf.org (Consulate in San Francisco)
E-mail: info@vietnamembassy-usa.org
Website: www.vietnamembassy-usa.org

Wales
See also: United Kingdom

Website: www.visitwales.com
Website: www.ceredigion.gov.uk
Website: www.travelbritain.org

Wales office
>Wales Tourist Board
>Brunel House
>2, Fitzalan Road
>Cardiff, Wales, CF24 OUY, UK
>Telephone: 029 20 499909
>Fax: 029 20 485031
>E-mail: info@tourism.wales.gov.uk

Yemen

The Yemen Embassy states that traveling with pets to Yemen is handled case by case and through the respective embassies. An International Health Certificate and an import permit must accompany cats and dogs. The U.S. Embassy in Sanaa suggested contacting the General Department of Livestock, Yemeni Ministry of Agriculture and Irrigation. The contact person is:
>Dr. Ghalib Al-Iryani
>General Manager of the Livestock Department
>P.O. Box 836
>Sanaa, Republic of Yemen
>Telephone: 967-1-250-872
>Fax: 967-1-251-589

Website: www.al-hab.com
Website: www.y.net.ye

Embassy of The Republic of Yemen
2600 Virginia Avenue, NW
Suite 705
Washington, DC 20037
Telephone: (202) 965-4760
Fax: (202) 337-2017
E-mail: info@yemenembassy.org
Website: www.yemenembassy.org

Yugoslavia
Officially the Federal Republic of Yugoslavia

Serbia and Montenegro formed the independent state (the Federal Republic of Yugoslavia) as the successor to the Socialist Federal Republic of Yugoslavia. Diplomatic relations with the United States were re-established on November 17, 2000.

A veterinarian Good Health Certificate legalized by the Veterinary Authorities at the point of origin or departure must accompany cats and dogs.

Website: www.belgradetourism.org.yu
Website: www.visit-montenegro.com
Website: www/serbia-info.com/ntos
Website: www.serbia-tourism.org

Montenegro office
    National Tourism Organization of Montenegro
    Stanka Dragojevica 26
    81 000 Podgorica
    Telephone: +381 81 241 591, 245 959, 243 553
    Fax: +381 81 247 087, 241 591, 245 959, 243 553
    E-mail: tourism@cg.yu
    E-mail: gorankal@mn.yu

Serbia office
    National Tourism Organization of Serbia
    Dobrinjska 11/II
    11000 Belgrade, Yugoslavia
    Telephone: 11 3612 754, 3612 385
    Telephone: 11 686 804
    Fax: 11 686 804
    E-mail: NTOS@EUnet.yu

Yugoslavia office
    Tourism Organization of Belgrade
    Decanska 1
    11000 Belgrade, Yugoslavia
    Telephone: (11) 322 6154 or 324 8404 or 322 7834 or 324 8310
    Fax: (11) 324 8770
    E-mail: tob@yubc.net
    E-mail: office@belgradetourism.org.yu

Embassy of The Federal Republic of Yugoslavia
2134 Kalorama Road, NW
Washington, DC 20008
Telephone: (202) 332-0333
Fax: (202) 332-3933
E-mail: yuembusa@aol.com
Website: www.yuembusa.org/

Zambia

For the importation of any livestock or livestock product and pets into Zambia from another country, it is always obligatory to obtain a veterinary permit from the Department of Research and Specialist Services (formally the Department of Veterinary and Tsetse Control Services). The permit so obtained stipulates the conditions under which the importation will be carried out and which conditions the veterinary authorities of the exporting country must follow in preparing a health certificate.

The importer must first obtain an import permit from the headquarters of the department in Mulungushi House, Lusaka. This could be done through a contact person in Lusaka. The conditions contained on the permit are dependant on the type of livestock, pet or product, the country of origin and its disease status and the purpose for importing them. The import permit so obtained must then be sent to the Veterinary authorities of the exporting country, which will use it as a guide to prepare a health certificate, which must accompany the animals or products on entry into Zambia. The permit issued in Zambia must also accompany the animals or products. On arrival at the destination, the importer MUST inform the nearest veterinary officer of the arrival of the products or animal, for inspection.

Contact Information:
    Department of Research and Specialist Services
    Attention: Senior Veterinary Officer
    Mulungushi House
    P.O. Box 50060
    Lusaka, Zambia
    Telephone: (2601) 253933/45
    Fax: (2601) 260505 or 253520

Website: www.zambiatourism.com
Website: www.zamnet.zm
Website: www.zambia.co.zm
Website: www.africa-insites.com/zambia/zntbhome.htm

UK office
Zambia National Tourist Board
2 Palace Gate
Kensington
London W85NG, UK
Telephone: 171 589-6343/6344
Fax: 171 581 1353
Website: www.zhcl.org.uk

Zambia office
Zambia National Tourist Board
Century House, Cairo Road
Box 30017
Lusaka, Zambia
Telephone: (2602) 229087/90
Fax: (2602) 225174
E-mail: zntb@zamnet.zm

Embassy of The Republic of Zambia
2419 Massachusetts Avenue, NW
Washington, DC 20008
Telephone: (202) 265-9717
Fax: (202) 332-0826
E-mail: embzambia@aol.com
Website: none
The embassy also deals with enquiries from Canada.

Zimbabwe

Regional tourists (except Mozambicans) who wish to bring pets into Zimbabwe should apply for an international import and export permit, together with a health certificate from the nearest Veterinary Office.

Tourists should apply well ahead for a permit to:
   The Director of Veterinary Services
   P. O. Box CY 52, Causeway
   Harare, Zimbabwe

A health certificate can be obtained from their nearest Government Veterinary Office. This certificate must be presented at the border post. Pets are not allowed in any National Parks accommodation, caravan or camping under National Parks jurisdiction. Please check with hotels in advance.

Website: www.tourismzimbabwe.co.zw

UK Office
   Zimbabwe Tourist Office
   428 Strand
   London WC2, UK
   Telephone: 071 836 7755
   Fax: 071 240 5465
   E-mail: none

USA Office
   Zimbabwe Tourist Office
   128 East 56th Street
   New York, NY 10022
   Telephone: (212) 488-3444
   Fax: (212) 486-3888
   E-mail: none

Embassy of The Republic of Zimbabwe
1608 New Hampshire Avenue, NW
Washington, DC 20009
Telephone: (202) 332-7100
Fax: (202) 483-9326
E-mail: zimemb@erols.com
Website: www.zimweb.com/Embassy/Zimbabwe
Website: www.zimembassy-usa.org

Appendix
International Telephone Codes

Country	Code	Country	Code
Afghanistan	93	Chile	56
Albania	355	China	86
Algeria	213	Columbia	57
American Samoa	684	Comoros	269
Andorra	376	Congo	242
Angola	244	Cook Islands	682
Antarctica	672	Costa Rica	506
Argentina	54	Croatia	385
Armenia	374	Cuba (Guantanamo Bay)	53
Ascension Island	247	Cyprus	357
Aruba	297	Czech Republic	420
Australia	61	Diego Garcia	246
Austria	43	Denmark	45
Azerbaijan	994	Dem. Rep. of Congo	243
Bahrain	973	Djibouti	253
Bangladesh	880	East Timor	390
Belarus	375	Ecuador	593
Belgium	32	Egypt	20
Belize	501	El Salvador	503
Benin	229	Equatorial Guinea	240
Bhutan	975	Eritrea	291
Bolivia	591	Estonia	372
Bosnia	387	Ethiopia	251
Botswana	267	Faeroe Islands	298
Brazil	55	Falkland Islands	500
Brunei	673	Fiji	679
Bulgaria	359	Finland	358
Burkina Faso	226	France	33
Burundi	257	French Antilles	596
Cambodia	855	French Guiana	594
Cameroon	237	French Polynesia	689
Cape Verde	238	Gabon	241
Central African Repub.	236	Gambia	220
Chad	235	Georgia	995

Germany	49		Liberia	231
Ghana	233		Libya	218
Gibraltar	350		Liechtenstein	41
Greece	30		Lithuania	370
Greenland	299		Luxembourg	352
Guadeloupe	590		Macao	853
Guam	671		Macedonia	389
Guatemala	502		Madagascar	261
Guinea-Bissau	245		Malawi	265
Guinea	224		Malaysia	60
Guyana	592		Maldives	960
Haiti	509		Malta	356
Herzegovina	387		Marshall Islands	692
Honduras	504		Martinique	596
Hong Kong	852		Mauritania	222
Hungary	36		Mauritius	230
Iceland	354		Mayotte Islands	265
India	91		Moldova	373
Indonesia	62		Mexico	52
Iran	98		Micronesia	691
Iraq	964		Monaco	377
Ireland	353		Mongolia	976
Israel	972		Morocco	212
Italy	39		Mozambique	258
Ivory Coast	225		Myanmar	95
Japan	81		Namibia	264
Jordan	962		Nepal	977
Kazakhstan	7		Netherlands	31
Kenya	254		Netherlands Antilles	599
Kiribati	686		New Caledonia	687
Korea (North)	850		New Zealand	64
Korea (South)	82		Nicaragua	505
Kuwait	965		Niger	227
Kyrgyz Republic	996		Nigeria	234
Laos	856		Niue	683
Latvia	371		Norfolk Island	672
Lebanon	961		Northern Marianas	670
Lesotho	266		Norway	47

Appendix-International Telephone Codes

Oman	968	Togo	228
Pakistan	92	Tonga	676
Panama	507	Tunisia	216
Papua New Guinea	675	Turkey	90
Paraguay	595	Turkmenistan	993
Peru	51	Tuvalu	688
Philippines	63	Uganda	256
Poland	48	Ukraine	380
Portugal	351	United Arab Emirates	971
Qatar	974	United Kingdom	44
Reunion Island	262	Uruguay	598
Romania	40	Uzbekistan	998
Russia	7	Vanuatu	678
Rwanda	250	Vatican City	379
Saipan	670	Venezuela	58
Samoa	685	Vietnam	84
San Marino	378	Yemen	967
São Tomé e Príncipe	239	Yugoslavia	381
Saudi Arabia	966	Zambia	260
Senegal	221	Zimbabwe	263
Seychelles	248		
Singapore	65		
Slovakia	421		
Slovenia	386		
Solomon Islands	277		
Somalia	252		
South Africa	27		
Spain	34		
Sri Lanka	94		
Sudan	249		
Suriname	597		
Sweden	46		
Swaziland	268		
Switzerland	41		
Syria	963		
Taiwan	886		
Tanzania	255		
Thailand	66		

Airlines of the World

This entry is not exhaustive. There are many regional airlines not listed.

AB Airlines (www.abairlines.com)
AOM French Airlines is now part of Air Liberte 1 (800) 892-9136
ASA Aerospace (www.concorde.ch)
Adria Airways (www.adria.si)
Aegean Airlines (www.aegeanairlines.gr)
Aer Lingus (www.aerlingus.ie) 1 (800) 223-6537
Aerocaribe (www.aerocaribe.com
Aero Costa Rica (www.centralamerica.com/cr/tran/aero.htm) (800) 237-6274
Aeroflot (www.aeroflot.com) (800) 995-5555
Aerolineas Argentinas (www.aerolineas.com.ar) (800) 333-0276
Aeromexico (www.aeromexico.com) (800) 237-6639
Aerosur (www.aerosur.com)
Aerosweet (www.aerosweet.com)
Air 2000 (www.air2000.ltd.uk)
Air Afrique (www.airafrique.com) (800) 882-7822
Air Alfa Hava Yollari (www.airalfa.com.tr)
Air Algerie (www.aaco.org/midfrm/algeriedown.asp)
Air Atlanta (www.atlanta.is)
Air Aruba (www.interknowledge.com/air-aruba) (800) 882-7822
Air Baltic (www.airbaltic.lv)
Air Berlin (www.airberlin.de)
Air Caladonie International (www.aircalin.nc) (800) 677-4277
Air Canada (www.aircanada.ca) (800) 776-3000
Air China (www.airchina.com.cn) (800) 986-1985
Air Dolomiti (www.airdolomiti.it)
Air Engiadina (www.airengiadina.ch)
Air Europa (www.air-europa.com)
Air Fiji (www.airfiji.net) (800) 677-4277
Air France (www.airfrance.fr) or (www.airjet.fr) (800) 237-2747
Air Georgia (www.air-georgia.com)
Air India (www.airindia.com) (800) 223-7776
Air Jamaica (www.airjamaica.com) (800) 523-5585
Air Lanka (www.airlanka.com) (800) 421-9898
Air Liberte (www.air-liberte.fr)
Air Littoral (www.air-littoral.fr)

Appendix-Airlines of the World

Air Macau (www.airmacau.com)
Air Maldives (www.airmaldives.com)
Air Malta (www.airmalta.com)
Air Mandalay (www.air-mandalay.com)
Air Mauritius (www.airmauritius.com) (800) 537-1182
Air Namibia (www.airmanibia.com.na) (800) 361-6210
Air Nauru (www.airnauru.com.au) (800) 998-6287
Air Niugini (www.air.niugini.com.pg)
Air Nippon (www.ananet.or.jp/ank)
Air New Zealand (www.airnz.co.nz) (800) 262-1234
Air One (www.air-one.it)
Air Ostrava (www.airastrava.cz)
Air Pacific (www.airpacific.com) (800) 227-4446
Air Rarotonga (www.ck.edairaco.htm)
Air Seychelles (www.airseychelles.net) (800) 677-4277
Air Slovakia (www.airslovakia.sk)
Air Vanuatu (www.pacificislands.com/airlines/vanuatu) (800) 677-4277
Air Zimbabwe (www.airzimbabwe.com) (800) 228-9485
AirFoyle (www.airfoyle.co.uk)
AirTran Airways (www.airtran.com) 1-80-247-8726
AirUK (www.iruk.co.uk)
Aloha Airlines (www.alohaairlines.com) (800) 367-5250
Alaska Airlines (www.alaska-air.com) (800) 426-0333
Alitalia (www.alitalia.it) (800) 223-5730
All Nippon Airways (www.svc.ana.co.jp) (800) 235-7880
Alliance Air (www.saallianceair.com)
ALM Antillean Airlines (www.alm-airlines.com) (800) 327-7197
America West Airlines (www.americawest.com) (800) 247-5692
American Airlines (www.aa.com) (800) 433-7300
American Trans Air (www.ata.com) (800) 433-2995
Angel Air (www.angelairlines.com)
Ansett Australia (www.ansett.com.au) 1-888-442-9626
Ariana Afghan Airlines (www.flyariana.com)
Armenian Airlines (www.armenianairlines.com)
Arctic Air (www.arcticnet.no/artic.air)
Asiana Airlines (www.us.flyasiana.com) (800) 227-4262
Aurigny Air Services (www.aurigny.com)
Aus-Air Regional Airlines (www.vicnet.net.au/~ausair)
Austrian Airlines (www.aua.co.at) (800) 843-0002

Avensa (www.avensa.com.va) (800) 428-3672
Avianca (www.avianca.com) (800) 284-2622
Aviateca (www.grupotaca.com)
Azerbaijan Airlines (www.azal.az)

B
Bahamasair (www.bahamasair.com) (800) 222-4262
Balkan Bulgarian Airlines (www.balkan.com)
Baltia (www.blf.com/baltia.htm)
Bangkok Airways (www.bkkair.co.th)
Bhoja Airlines (www.bhojaair.com.pk)
Biman Bangladesh (www.bimanair.com)
Braathens (www.braathens.no)
Britannia Airways (www.BritaniaAirways.com)
British Airways (www.british-airways.com) (800) 247-9297
British European Airlines (www.jea.co.uk)
British Mediterranean (www.britishmediterranean.com)
British Midland Airways (www.iflybritishmidland.com) 1 (866) 716-3790
Buzz (www.buzzaway.com)
BWIA International (www.bwee.com) (800) 327-7401

C
Cameroon Airlines (www.camairsa.co.za)
Canadian Airlines Int'l Integrated with Air Canada (800) 426-7000
Cathay Pacific Airways (www.cathaypacific.com) (800) 233-2742
China Airlines (www.china-airlines.com) (800) 227-5118
China Eastern Airlines (www.chinaeasternair.com) (800) 227-5118
China Northern Airlines (www.cna.ln.cninfo.net/)
China Southern Airlines (www.cs-air.com)
Cimber Air (www.cimber.com)
City Jet (www.cityjet.com)
CityBird (www.citybird.com)
Coast Air (www.coastair.no)
Color Air (www.colorair.no
Copa (www.copaair.com)
Condor (www.condor.de) (800) 524-6975
Continental Airlines (www.continental.com) (800) 525-0280
Continental Micronesia (www.continental.com)

Appendix-Airlines of the World

COPA Panama (www.copaair.com) (800) 892-2672
Corsair (www.corsair-int.com) (800) 677-4277
Croatia Airlines (www.croatiaairlines.com) (800) 247-5353
Cronus Airlines (www.cronus.gr)
Crossair (www.crossair.ch)
Cubana Airlines (www.cubana.cu)
Cyprus Airways (www.cyprusair.com.cy) (800) 333-2977
Cyprus Turkish Airways (wwww.cypnet.com/cta)
Czech Airlines (www.csa.cz) (800) 223-2365

D

Delta Air Lines (www.delta-air.com) (800) 221-1212
Dragonair (www.dragonair.com)

E

EasyJet Airlines (www.easyjet.com)
Edelweiss Air (www.edelweiss.ch)
Egyptair (www.egyptair.com) (800) 334-6787
El Al Israel Airlines (www.elal.co.il) (800) 223-6700
Emirates (www.emirates.com) (800) 777-3999
Estonian Air (www.estonian-air.ee)
Ethiopian Airlines (www.ethiopianairlines.com) (800) 445-2733 or (800) 443-9677
Euram (www.flyeuram.com) (800) 555-3872
Euroscot Express (www.euroscot.com)
Eurowings (www.eurowing.de)
Eva Airways (www.evaair.com.tw) (800) 695-1188
Excel Airways (www.exelairways.com)

F

Fast Air (www.fastair.cl
Finnair (www.finnair.fi) (800) 950-5000
Falcon Air (www.falconair.se)
Freedom Air International (www.freedom.co.nz)
Frontier Airlines (www.flyfrontier.com)

G

Garuda Indonesia (www.garuda.co.id) (800) 342-7832
Ghana Airways (www.ghana-airways.com) (800) 404-4262

Greenlandair, Inc. (www.greenland-guide.dk
Gulf Air (www.gulfairco.com) (800) 553-2824
Guyana Airways (www.turq.com/guyana/guyanair)

H
Hainan Airlines (www.hnair.com/default.asp)
Hawaiian Airlines (www.hawaiianair.com) (800) 367-5320
Highland Air (www.highlandair.se)

I
Iberia (www.iberia.com) (800) 772-4642
Icelandair (www.icelandair.is) (800) 223-5500
Indian Airlines (www.nic.in/indian-airlines)
Iran Air (www.iranair.co.ir)
Island Air (www.ambergriscaye.com/islandair)
Istanbul Airlines (www.ihy.com.tr)

J
Japan Airlines (www.jal.co.jp) (800) 525-3663
Japan Air System (www.jas.co.jp/e_jashom.ht)
Jersey European Airways (www.jea.co.uk)
Jet Airways (www.jetairways.com)
JetBlue (www.jetblue.com)

K
K L M (www.klm.com) (800) 777-5553
Kazakhstan Airlines (www.airkaz.com)
Kenya Airways (www.kenyaairways.com) (800) 343-2506
Korean Air (www.koreanair.com) (800) 438-5000
Kuwait Airways (www.kuwait-airways.com) (800) 458-9248

L
LanChile (www.lanchile.com) (800) 488-0070
LAPA (www.lapa.com.ar)
Lasca (www.grupataca.com) (800) 225-2272
Lauda Air (www.laudaair.com) (800) 843-0002
Liat (www.flylait.com)
Lithuanian Airlines (www.infosistema.lt/lal)

Appendix-Airlines of the World

LOT Polish Airlines (www.lot.com) (800) 223-0593
LTU Int'l Airways (www.lltu.de) (800) 888-0200
Lufthansa (www.luftansa.com) (800) 645-3880
Luxair (www.luxair.com)

M

Macedonian Airways (www.macedonian-airlines.gr/)
Maersk Air (www.maersk-air.com)
Malaysia Airlines (www.malaysiaairlines.com) (800) 645-3880
Malev Hungarian Airlines (www.malev.hu) (800) 223-6884
Manx Airlines (www.manx-airlines.com) (800) 627-8462
Martinair Holland (www.martinair.com)
Maxair (www.maxairl.com)
Maya Air (www.mayaairways.com)
Meridiana (www.meridiana.lt)
Mexicana Airlines (www.mexicana.com) (800) 531-7921
Midway Airlines (www.midwayair.com) (800) 446-4392
Midwest Express Airlines (www.midwestexpress.com) (800) 452-2022
Middle East Airlines (www.mea.com.lb) (800) 664-7310

N

Northwest Airlines (www.nwa.com) 1-80-225-2525

O

Olympic Airways (www.olympic-airways.gr) (800) 223-1226
Oman Air

P

Pakistan International (www.piac.com) (800) 221-2552
Philippine Airlines (www.philippineair.com) (800) 435-9725
Polynesian Airlines (www.polynesianairlines.co.nz) (800) 677-4277, (800) 644-7659
Portugalia Airlines (www.pga.pt)

Q

Qantas Airways (www.quantas.com.au) (800) 227-4500
Qatar Airways (www.qatarairways.com)

R

Rio-Sul (www.rio-sul.com
Royal Air Cambodge (www.royal-air-combodge.net)
Royal Air Maroc (www.royalairmaroc.co.ma) (800) 344-6726
Royal Brunei Airlines (www.brunieair.com)
Royal Jordanian Airlines (www.rja.com.jo) (800) 223-0470
Royal Nepal Airlines (www.royalnepal.com) (800) 266-3725
Ryanair (www.ryanair.com)

S

Sabena (www.sabena.com) (800) 873-3900
SAS Scandinavian Airlines (www.sas.se) (800) 221-2350
SATA Air Azores (www.sata.pt)
Saudi Arabian Airlines (www.saudiairlines.com) (800) 472-8342
Scandinavian Airlines (www.sas.se) (800) 221-2350
Silk Air (www.silkair.com) (800) 745-5247
Singapore Airlines (www.singaporeair.com) (800) 742-3333
Solomon Airlines (www.solomonairlines.com.au) (800) 677-4277
South African Airways (www.flysaa.com) (800) 722-9675
Southwest Airlines (www.iflyswa.com) (800) 531-5601
Spanair (www.spanair.com)
Spirit Airlines (www.spiritairlines.com) (800) 246-6678
SriLankan Airlines (www.airlanka.com)
Sudan Airways (www.sudanair.com)
Sunflower Airlines (www.fiji.to)
Suriname Airways (www.slm.firm.sr/)
Swiftair (www.swiftair.com)
Swissair (www.swissair.com) (800) 221-4750
Syrian Arab Airlines (www.syrian-airlines.com)

T

T W A (www.twa.com) (800) 221-2000
TACA International Airlines (www.grupotaca.com) (800) 535-8780
Tajikistan Int'l Airlines (www.tajikistanairlines.com)
TAP Air Portugal (www.tap.pt) (800) 221-7370
Tamair (www.tamair.com.au)
Tarom (www.tarom.digiro.net)
Thai Airways (www.thaiair.com) (800) 426-5204
Tower Air (www.towerair.com) (800) 348-6937

Appendix-Airlines of the World

Transaero Airlines (www.transaero.ru) (800) 957-2658
Transavia Airlines (www.transavia.nl)
Transbrasil (www.transbrasil.com.br) (800) 872-3153
Transwede Airlines (www.transwede.se)
Travelair (www.centralamerica.com/cr/tran/travelair.htm)
Tunisair (www.tunisair.com)
Turkish Airlines (www.turkishairlines.com) (800) 874-8875
Turkmenistan Airlines (www.icctm.org/t_tair.html)
Tyrolean Airways (www.tryolean.at) (800) 843-0002

U

Ukraine Int'l Airlines (www.ukraine-international.com)
United Airlines (www.ual.com) (800) 241-6522
U.S. Airways (www.usairways.com) (800) 943-5436
Uzbekistan Airways (www.uzbekistan-airways.com)

V

Varig (www.varig.com.br) (800) 468-2744
Vasp Brazilian (www.vasp.com.br) (800) 468-2744
Vietnam Airlines (www.vietnamair.com.vn) (800) 565-2742
Virgin Atlantic Airways (www.fly.virgin.com) (800) 862-8621
Virgin Blue (www.virginblue.com.au)
Virgin Express (www.virgin-exp.com)
Volare Airlines (www.volare-airlines.com)
VLM (www.vlm-air.com)

W

Westjet (www.westjet.com) (800) 538-5696

Y

Yemenia (www.yemenia.com.ye) (800) 936-3642
Yugoslav Airlines (www.jat.com) (800) 752-6528

Z

Zambia Airways (www.zamsaf.com/zambia/Zambia-Airlines.htm) (800) 223-1136

GLOSSARY

APHIS- Animal and Plant Health Inspection Service
AQIS- Australian Quarantine and Inspection Service
AVA- Agri-Food and Veterinary Authority (See Singapore)
AWA-Animal Welfare Act
CDC-Center for Disease Control and Prevention
CITES- Convention on International Trade in Endangered Species
DHLPP- distemper, hepatitis, leptospirosis, parvovirus, parainfluenza
EEC- European Economic Community
EFTA-European Free Trade Association
EU- European Union
FWS-Fish and Wildlife Service
IATA- International Air Transport Association
NCIE-National Center for Import and Export
OIE- Office International des Epizooties
PPQ- Plant Protection Quarantine
PETS- Pet Travel Scheme
USDA-United States Department of Agriculture
WHO- World Health Organization

Quick Order Form

Printed and e-Books Available

Fax orders: (419) 281-6883 Send this form.

Telephone orders: (800) 247-6553
Have your credit card ready.

Website orders: www.GlobetrottingPets.com
Click on "Order Book"

Please send following:

Qty.	Book	Price each	Total
	Globetrotting Pets-An International Travel Guide	$21.95	
Mail this form and check to: BookMasters, Inc. P.O. Box 388 Ashland, OH 44805		Shipping:	
		Tax:	
		Total:	

Name:_____

Address:_____

City:_____ **State:**_____ **Zip:**_____

Telephone:_____

E-Mail address:_____

Sales Tax: Please add 6.25% for books shipped to Ohio.
Shipping:
U.S.: $4.95 for the first book and $2.00 for each additional book.
International: $10.00 for the first book and $5.00 each additional book.

Payment: ☐ Check ☐ Credit Card
☐ Visa ☐ MasterCard ☐ AMEX ☐ Discover

Card number: _____

Name on Card: _____ Exp. date: _____

NOV 0 7 2003

WITHDRAWN
DAUPHIN COUNTY LIBRARY SYSTEM

EAST SHORE AREA LIBRARY
DAUPHIN COUNTY LIBRARY SYSTEM